Trading Pairs

Founded in 1807, John Wiley & Sons is the oldest independent publishing company in the United States. With offices in North America, Europe, Australia, and Asia, Wiley is globally committed to developing and marketing print and electronic products and services for our customers' professional and personal knowledge and understanding.

The Wiley Trading series features books by traders who have survived the market's ever-changing temperament and have prospered—some by reinventing systems, others by getting back to basics. Whether a novice trader, professional, or somewhere in between, these books will provide the advice and strategies needed to prosper today and well into the future.

For a list of available titles, please visit our Web site at *www.WileyFinance.com.*

Trading Pairs

Capturing Profits and
Hedging Risk with Statistical
Arbitrage Strategies

MARK WHISTLER

WILEY

John Wiley & Sons, Inc.

Published by John Wiley & Sons, Inc., Hoboken, New Jersey
Published simultaneously in Canada

For general information on our other products and services, or technical support, please contact our Customer Care Department within the United States at 800-762-2974, outside the United States at 317-572-3993, or fax 317-572-4002.

Wiley also publishes its books in a variety of electronic formats. Some content that appears in print may not be available in electronic books.

For more information about Wiley products, visit our Web site at www.wiley.com.

Library of Congress Cataloging-in-Publication Data:
Whistler, Mark.
   Trading pairs : capturing profits and hedging risk with statistical
arbitrage strategies / Mark Whistler.
       p.   cm. — (Wiley trading)
   Includes bibliographical references and index.
   ISBN 0-471-58428-2 (cloth/cd-rom)
   1. Pairs trading.   2. Stocks.   I. Title.   II. Series.
   HG4661.W46 2004
   332.64'5—dc22

                                                    2004002263

Printed in the United States of America

10 9 8 7 6 5 4 3 2 1

Contents

Acknowledgments

I would like to dedicate this book to you, Mary; I am so proud of you for all of your accomplishments. Sandy and Ed—your love and support has made me the man I am today. Words cannot express my love for you. Karen and Mike Eck and Sue and Neil Ray—thank you for being who you are; I love you, and you are the most wonderful people in the world. I would like to thank Leigh Stevens, Pamela Van Giessen, Lara Murphy and Michael Lisk for making this book a reality, without you this book would have never made it to print. Thank you so much Scot Darr, Steven Price, Scott P. Evans, Jonathan Crowell, Andrew Long, and Aaron Long for your amazing help and contributions. Francois Safeddine, our trading cemented my knowledge—thank you. Kevin Cuddie, Eric Perlstein, and all of the guys at ETG Securities in Denver—you truly are super traders. Also, thank you Noel Smith and Mike Palumbo (Third Millenium Securities—Chicago) for your time—which helped to greatly further my options knowledge. To all of my loving family on the East Coast, you are amazing and magnificent. Hugh McCulloh, though you may not know this, your guidance two years ago helped make this book, the Web site, and the software possible. I would also like to thank some wonderful people for being who you are, and helping make me who I am: Paul, Lauren, and Alexis Whistler; John Crowley (the man who first opened my eyes to pairs); Randy and Maddie Nichols (I owe much of my impressionable years to you); and Sally Schultz (thanks for helping me pass the fourth grade). Diane Hall, you are the most brilliant godmother anyone could ever ask for, I love you. And last, but certainly not least—Sara Jacobson, Raifford Patton, and Mark Kuniholm—thank you so much for being there when I needed you most.

Introduction

This book is intended for the average investor who would like to gain a new perspective on the market. Traditionally, when we invest, we either buy or sell a stock, and then hope that it moves in our chosen direction. However, at times this strategy leaves us with a "naked" position that is simply at the mercy of the market. Thus, pairs trading offers a unique alternative, and allows the individual investor a way to "hedge" positions. Think about it for a moment. If you have a long and a short position, then you are technically market neutral. And if the broader indices fall 200 points—in theory—your position should still be "flat." The goal is to protect our portfolios from dramatic market swings up or down, while finding stock relationship inequalities, in an effort to make money.

As a result, this book attempts to present the information of pairs in an easy-to-read format that allows the reader a new way of approaching investing. In addition, the book is geared for "at home" investors who do not have expensive trading software. In fact, if you have access to the Internet and Microsoft Excel, you can do everything in this book. A little patience and drive will help you to reshape your current paradigm of the market.

Trading Pairs

CHAPTER 1

The Nuts and Bolts

What Are Pairs?
How Do Pairs Work?
Who Uses Pairs?
Mindset of Reading This Book

WHAT ARE PAIRS?

Where there is a relationship, there is opportunity, and where there is opportunity, there is money. In the ever-elusive world of the stock market, investors often think that the only way to make money is to do it the "old-fashioned" way. By this I mean either investing fundamentally in buy-and-hold companies or seeking more conservative and diversified financial vehicles. However, the computer age has opened a Pandora's Box of trading styles, where many individual investors are now finding new ways to make money previously available only to industry insiders and professionals.

If our cycles of light were tradable, what would you do if you could buy darkness at noon and short the remainder of daylight? In essence, what if you could trade the rotation of daylight, while hedging risk in case of the random eclipse? Amazingly, if we look closely enough, we begin to observe that the stock market is illuminated with the same principles of cyclical relationships. In our markets, there is a rotary motion of money continually occurring in stocks, sectors, indices, options, currencies, and even emotions.

Our job as a pairs trader is to try and understand the fundamental, technical, and emotional cycles of these rotational relationships, while attempting to capitalize on discrepancies when disharmony appears. You may better know this process as *arbitrage*. "Rrrrrrrrrr . . . arbitrage." It sounds sexy, doesn't it? Be careful not to fall in love with this savvy beast, for it can cause you to lose your hair with the stress it presents! The actual definition of arbitrage is: "The simultaneous purchase and selling of a security in order to profit from a differential in the price. This usually takes place on different

1

exchanges or marketplaces." (EN 1.1) For the pairs trader, though, we will utilize another form of arbitrage called "statistical arbitrage," which means: "A profit situation arising from pricing inefficiencies between securities. Investors identify the arbitrage situation through mathematical modeling techniques." (EN 1.2) For the purposes of this book, we will focus mainly on using statistics to (1) identify relationships, (2) assist in determining the direction of the relationship, and (3) ascertain how to execute our trades based on the data presented.

Also, in this text, we will use the term *pairs trading* interchangeably with statistical arbitrage, thus eliminating any possible conflict of semantics. So what exactly is pairs trading and/or statistical arbitrage? Pairs trading is a style of investing/trading that attempts to institute *at least* one long and one short position for every trade, while statistically analyzing the relationship presented. (EN 1.1) What's more, the pairs trader attempts to capitalize on market imbalances between two or more stocks (or other financial instruments) in anticipation of making money when the inequality is corrected. In short, the pairs trader believes two or more stocks have enough of a correlated relationship that statistical analysis will unveil tradable opportunities when the stocks move away from one another. When the two begin to secede from one another, the pairs trader will try to figure out "why" they are separating and then institute a trade in an attempt to capitalize on either additional divergence or possible reconvergence.

To measure these relationships, the pairs trader uses statistics, fundamentals, technical analysis, and even probabilities. One of the main keys to pairs trading is finding strong correlations between financial instruments, thus building a foundation for further analysis. We then hope to dissect the empirical data in an effort to unearth information that allows us an efficient and methodical way of attempting to make money in the stock market. The key word here is *methodical*. I would like to distinguish this word from *system*, as it is important to recognize that we are trying to approach the market with an orderly (backed by statistics in the case of pairs) but not automated trading strategy. What's more, in the first few chapters of this book I hope to relay a few commonsense nuggets of fundamental and technical information that will help assist in making accurate decisions when our math fails. The overall goal of this book is to empower the individual investor with an entirely distinctive paradigm of trading than the typical buy-and-hold strategy. Pairs trading is by no means the "holy grail" of trading and *will* have its ups and downs, like any other trading style. However, with the proper base of applicable knowledge and impeccable money management skills, we may find ourselves with an effective trading strategy with which to work from.

HOW DO PAIRS WORK?

Take a moment and imagine a highway and the service road that parallels it. Generally, the service road will follow the highway very closely, except where terrain or development prevents such. The resulting situation is a divergence of the service road from the highway, while the obstacle is overcome. In the end, the service road will almost always come back together with the highway, as the two have a very highly correlated relationship. Now, imagine the area in between the service road and highway. This area is known as the *spread*. The spread is the measured distance between the two objects traveling together. The pairs trader attempts to measure the spread with statistics in an effort to find a tradable relationship of inequality opportunities, otherwise known as the previously mentioned arbitrage.

The key is the correlation between two (or more) stocks, sectors, indices, or other financial instruments to be studied. Because a highway and service road parallel one another more closely than a highway and Town Boulevard, the highway and service road will likely have a higher correlation than the latter two. I don't want to leave you with the impression that there isn't opportunity to make money between the highway/boulevard relationship. However, one must simply understand the risks presented when using a lower correlation or, in this case, a lesser correlated group of roads.

In fact, think of all the wonderful opportunities with a lower-correlated group of roads. If the highway is the benchmark road that passes a town, it is likely that several roads within the town parallel the interstate. As a trading analogy, this simple observation may allow the trader to buy and sell many smaller streets, avenues, or boulevards using the interstate as a larger guide of general direction. This would be the same as using an index like the Dow Jones Industrial Average as a benchmark for trend, while buying and selling (shorting) many components within that particular index.

Thus, in a nutshell, pairs trading works by betting that two or more securities will diverge or converge in price. You are betting that a $50 stock and a $55 stock will either have a larger or smaller spread ($5 in this case) when the trade is closed. Divergence traders would like to see the spread increase, while convergence traders would prefer to see the spread decrease.

WHO USES PAIRS?

Anyone and everyone! Historically, pairs trading has been more of an "institutional" trading style (coveted by hedge funds) for wealthy investors or those with trading savvy who invest for a living. (As a brief side note, while hedge funds seem mysterious, they are simply mutual finds that can go short. That is not to say that all mutual funds cannot go short, though for the most part, many are able to purchase only long positions.) As computers help to unlock much of the mystery of the financial markets for the average investor, many individuals use the strategy to either "hedge" portfolios or in an effort to make money by intraday or swing trading. (*Swing trading* refers to holding a position anywhere from two days to several weeks.)

It is generally true that institutional investors require more complicated analysis and statistics, though at the heart of the issue, the fundamental concept is the same.

In fact, by the end of this book, my goal is to teach you, the individual investor (or institutional trader), how to create live spreadsheets and track pairs like a pro! The bottom line is anyone can use pairs, so don't fear the concept. As Franklin D. Roosevelt said in 1933, "The only thing we have to fear is fear itself."

MINDSET OF READING THIS BOOK

First, grab a cold beer . . . just kidding—maybe wait until Chapter 3!!! If you smiled or chuckled just now, great! If not, put this book down and seriously go get some air; it's time to relax. While trading is a *very* serious business, and should be approached with complete dedication, it is also important to remember to take life in strides. This book was written with a pinch of humor, while attempting to uncover the very dry (but incredibly interesting) subject of pairs.

My only point here is that you shouldn't take trading so seriously that you forget to kiss your loved ones goodnight or forsake spending time with friends on weekends to work.

This book is written in plain simple English, to make it an easy and fun read. Pairs trading can be a complicated enough subject; thus, it is my goal to make this book NOT! That being said, please read this book with an open mind and remember that pairs trading is not only a foreign concept to many, but can also pull the "old switcheroo" on you at times. At some points you may say, "That doesn't make sense." If a concept, number, or strategy eludes you, please simply read on, and you may find yourself having an epiphany shortly after.

In short, read this book while intoxicated and question nothing. Kidding.

CHAPTER 2

Why Fundamental Analysis?

Common Sense
China.com
How Fundamental Analysis
Relates to Pairs

COMMON SENSE

Before I begin to get into pairs, it is important that I build a small foundation for which to lay our new pairs knowledge on. I will first cover fundamental analysis and then briefly tackle technical analysis. Fundamentally, it is important to understand *at least* a little bit about why stocks move as they do. In other words, it is incredibly valuable to try to understand how and why a stock is currently priced. It is not my goal to make you a superstar analyst, nor am I claiming to have a "fundamental" formula that will miraculously decipher stock valuation. Rather, I am merely attempting to try and make sure that we all have fundamental common sense built on a few easily identifiable numbers.

Fundamental common sense is a necessity, not only to the pairs trader, but to the directional investor as well. Analysts generally study long and hard to truly understand all of the internal workings of a company. However, as a common investor, you may not have 12 hours a day to commit to such analysis. Or perhaps you do not have time to study for the Chartered Financial Analyst (CFA) designation or the Certified Financial Planner (CFP) title. If not, it is extremely important to at least know where a company stands—if only scratching the surface of fundamental analysis.

The information in the next few chapters is designed to assist investors in attempting to understand where a company is headed during the near term. On a commonsense level, if you are directional trading or pairs trading, and a stock is moving away from you (you are losing money), please *at least* take a look at the internal health of a company and consider the practical valuation of the situation. While you may be reading this and possibly saying to yourself "Yeah bub, tell me something I don't know," I encourage you to take a brief moment to remember recent history. How many investors overlooked the reality of the late 1990s Internet bubble and the numerous overextended price-to-earnings (PE) ratios before the bear market ravaged countless portfolios? If you lost money by denying fundamentals during the bubble, then perhaps the next chapter is for you.

CHINA.COM

No matter how much we would like to believe otherwise, even when the market may seem most exuberant, company-specific fundamentals cannot be denied. Spot on; retail investors are usually too quick to overbuy some stocks that seem too good to be true! We have definitely witnessed this through the trading action of many Internet stocks over the last few years. Amazingly, even though you would think we might have learned our lesson, there are still many crazy bulls out there looking for any opportunity to jump on the Internet bandwagon. For example, a newsletter that I recently wrote for (briefly) profiled the Internet stock China.com in July 2003.

On Thursday, July 31, 2003, we received a question from one subscriber inquiring whether China.com was "worth its salt at the present time?" The subscriber was trying to decide whether he should buy China.com even though the stock had run from $5 per share to $12 per share in just under two months. China.com had gained almost 140 percent in just 45 days fueled by rebounding bear market exuberance.

Our reply to the question was:

> *The daily chart of CHINA appears to be forming a lateral wedge as the stock consolidates after running up almost 500% since October 2002. In essence, exuberant bulls have sobered up and are now trying to make sense of their new position. Typically, when a stock has a major rally and then consolidates on lower volume, bulls are trying to set themselves up for another leg up. Once the weaker hands are shaken out of the stock, bulls will likely make an attempt at breaching descending resistance of the current wedge.*
>
> *HOWEVER, in the case of CHINA (see Figure 2.1), one main problem exists . . . and that dilemma is valuation. Tom Jacobs from* The

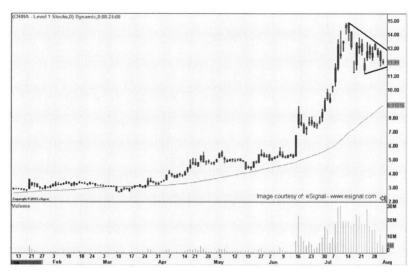

FIGURE 2.1 China.com

Motley Fool *has made this apparent in his recent article "30-Baggers, Anyone?"* (EN 2.1)

Specifically, CHINA does not have earnings and thus, does not have a PE ratio. The book value of the stock is $3.63, while CHINA has negative EBITDA, profit margins, operating margins, ROA, and ROE. Can you say "bubble"? Moreover, sales for the last 12 months clock in at $58.3 million versus the industry average of $122.90 million, while income growth was −$8.9 million versus the industry average of −$21.2 million. Sales growth equals −6.10%, with the broader industry expanding roughly +30%.

So then, what the heck is bullish about this stock?

As an analogy, even if you know your ship has a break in the hull, you can't refute a deck full of mutineers determined to take it out to sea. Thus, I would look at the chart and keep a close eye on wedge consolidation (explained later in the book) during the CURRENT ASCENDING TREND. If the stock breaks out, we may find ourselves on board. However, unlike the rest of our compatriot sailors, we will remember that there is a split in the hull, and thus, we will secretly wear our life vest underneath our swashbuckling suits.

Stocks like CHINA are a good example of the RISKIEST investments in the market. Overall, a good rule of thumb for China.com's current valuation is "when in doubt, stay out."

FIGURE 2.2   China.com thru August 15

We were simply taking the commonsense approach of "how is this company trading at $12.00 per share?" Then, only four days later, the stock dumped $3 to roughly $9 (see Figure 2.2).

Common sense kept us from making a HUGE mistake! We made ourselves aware of fundamental analysis—valuation and investor overexuberance—even though technical analysis told us to possibly board the ship. The resulting commonsense conclusion was "when in doubt, stay out!" and we were very happy that we did. This is why we must have at least *some* tools of fundamental analysis in our trading toolbox.

HOW FUNDAMENTAL ANALYSIS RELATES TO PAIRS

After all of this, you may be asking yourself how and why fundamental analysis relates to pairs. First, I would like to briefly point out that this book will be mostly covering statistical arbitrage as used with convergence trading. However, it is important to understand that underneath the statistics, there must be some sort of fundamental gravity that pulls the pair back together. If you begin to find yourself looking at the statistics of a pair, while also dissecting both companies on a fundamental basis, you are on the right track. Understanding a few fundamental concepts may possibly save many, many mistakes when the statistical math fails. Thus, if you can double-check your statistics with fundamental valuation, you simply become a more effective pairs trader.

CHAPTER 3

Market Basics

Growth and Growth Ratios
Growth, PE, and the PEG Ratio
Tying It All Together

First, there are a few concepts of elementary analysis that should be examined in order to understand why companies "fundamentally" diverge. While much of this chapter is most likely review for some— and definitely arguable by a few analysts—it is simply a commonsense approach to quickly gaining some idea of stock specific valuation, within five minutes or less. This chapter will not make you a professional analyst. Rather, it attempts to uncover a few easily accessible ways that the individual investor can quickly glance at a company's present and future financial health.

The following section will cover:

- Trading liquidity and shares outstanding
- Understanding growth and growth ratios
- Cash and the current ratio
- Earnings and guidance

First, we must evaluate our personal risk preference to individual equity liquidity. Stocks that have less volume tend to be more erratic and volatile, while stocks that trade more shares *each day* generally have slower price movements. The greater a stock's liquidity, the better chance you, the individual, have of getting filled at the price you specify to buy or sell. A good example of this is Microsoft (NASDAQ: MSFT) versus the regional bank Cass Commercial Corporation (NASDAQ: CASS). While both stocks are equally difficult to predict, Microsoft will likely have less volatile short-term swings than a regional bank, due to greater liquidity. By this I mean that because Microsoft has much more demand by investors to buy and sell stock at every penny, it will move up or down slower than a stock with less trading activity. When you want to sell your shares of Microsoft, you can be fairly sure that if you put in a market order, you will receive the current bid price or just slightly below. Conversely, in a thin regional bank stock, one can quickly lose 50 cents to $1 when filled, even on small orders. The problem is that thin stocks (regional bank stocks in this example) quickly move in one direction or another as market makers or specialists only display the minimum shares required on either the bid or the ask. Even though market makers are required to make fair markets, they are not required to go out of business buying or selling all the stock you want to sell at one price. As a general rule of thumb, many investors will not trade stocks that do not have an average daily volume of at least 200,000 shares. Most market tracking programs will display the average daily volume, or you can find the information on sites such as CBSmarketwatch.com or Yahoo.com. The image in Figure 3.1 displays the erratic volatility of CASS versus the more liquid MSFT.

Second in our conversation about liquidity is float. Float is the total amount of authorized and issued outstanding stock that is available to trade on a daily basis. Some of the stock that has been issued may not be available to trade, as corporate insiders cannot always sell when they are in the custody of a "holding period." Thus, the float is simply all stock that

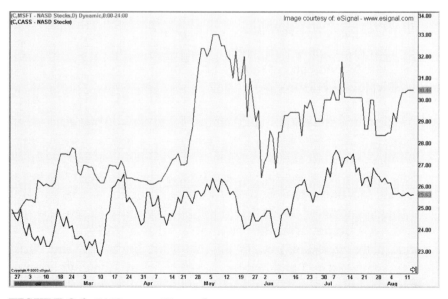

FIGURE 3.1 CASS versus Microsoft

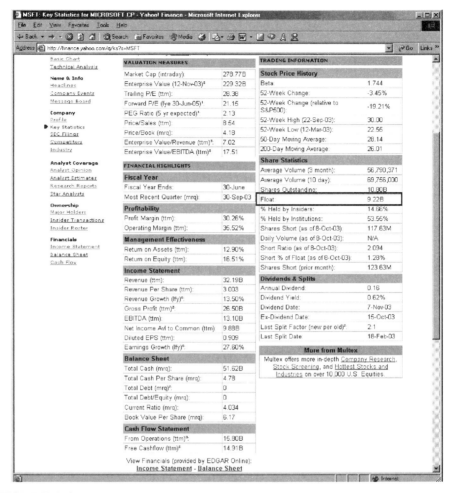

FIGURE 3.2 Yahoo.com—Float

is available in the current market to trade. Stocks with lower floats are more dangerous, as they can move more quickly once a large order is placed.

Where to find float? Check *www.yahoo.com* as displayed in Figure 3.2.

In regard to pairs trading, double-check both of the stocks to make sure that they have similar floats and average daily volumes. Even though two stocks can be highly correlated based on total price, they may still be very dangerous if one has substantially more volatility risk than the other.

GROWTH AND GROWTH RATIOS

In making you an efficient five-minute equity analyst, it is very important that we cover growth ratios. Growth numbers are *very* important in understanding where the stock is going, not where it currently is. After all, we already know that!

There are two types of growth that we will first examine—sales growth and income growth; both are fairly straightforward. We simply want to know how much a company is growing and how the individual company stacks up in its respective sector. If a company had incredible sales growth of 80 percent, but a negative income growth rate of 10 percent, clearly there is a red flag. If this scenario were true for a real stock, we could put an "x" in the "bad income growth" box of our fundamental checklist.

Bottom line: If you are going to buy a stock, we want to see strong income *and* sales growth numbers.

Where to find this information? The crux of fundamental analysis is learning how to be able to do it yourself, which seems much more complicated than it actually is. When looking for earnings growth, you can do a couple of different things. First, it is important to remember that using any Web site is very dangerous. The numbers are sporadically updated and can be hardly reliable at best. Even sites like Yahoo.com can take several days to get updated after earnings reports. You can't blame them; you just have to remember to question every number you come across if you are going to make sure the figures you are examining are accurate. So let's figure out how to find these numbers for yourself. First, the numbers aren't half as hard to find as you think they are, it just takes a little research to unearth them. To find earnings growth, I would like to use the following chart invented by Todd Shaver of BullMarket.com.

Wal-Mart

Quarter	3Q02	3Q03	% Chg
Revenue	$56B	$63B	+13
Net Income	$1.8B	$2.0B	+11
Earnings per Share	$0.40	$0.46	+15

This chart is an excerpt from BullMarket.com. The amazing part is that the numbers are right in front of you in any earnings announcement. Look at the following Wal-Mart press release that the numbers came from. This is the actual press release that the company put forth and can be found on any news service, including Yahoo.com.

Press Release   Source: Wal-Mart Stores, Inc.
Wal-Mart Reports Record Sales and Earnings
Thursday November 13, 6:43 am ET

BENTONVILLE, Ark., Nov. 13/PRNewswire-FirstCall/—Wal-Mart Stores, Inc. (NYSE: WMT - News) reported record earnings and sales for the quarter ended October 31, 2003. Net sales were $62.5 billion, an increase of 13.1 percent over the similar prior year quarter. Net income from continuing operations for the quarter was $2.0 billion, a 13.9 percent increase from the $1.8 billion in the similar prior year quarter. Earnings per share from continuing operations were $0.46 up from $0.40 per share in the same prior year quarter.

Net sales for the nine months ended October 31, 2003, were $181.8 billion, an increase of 11.4 percent over net sales of the similar prior year period. Net income from continuing operations for the nine months increased 14.4 percent to a record $6.1 billion or $1.40 earnings per share, up from $5.4 billion or $1.21 earnings per share in the same prior year period.

On May 23, 2003, Wal-Mart Stores, Inc. completed the sale of McLane Company, Inc. ("McLane"), then a wholly-owned subsidiary, to Berkshire Hathaway Inc. McLane has been accounted for as a discontinued operation in this release.

Lee Scott, President and CEO said, "The excellent results for the quarter reflect the continued efforts by our associates to serve our customers. Of particular note is the performance of our international and SAM'S CLUB teams."

You can see that all we did was take the net income, earnings per share (EPS), and revenue numbers; round them off; and stick them in the chart. Thus, we know immediately what the company is predicting without having to wonder if one of the Web sites that we covet updated their numbers or not.

The issue is that looking at items like the price-to-earnings (PE) ratio divided by the annual EPS growth (PEG ratio), there is always a discrepancy of what numbers an analyst Web site is looking at. We can solve this problem by gathering the numbers ourselves. When looking for forward numbers like one-year earnings growth, use a Web site like Yahoo.com to get an idea of the projected analyst estimates. The only question is whether the estimates are correct. However, using a site like Yahoo—and remembering that there can be errors from time to time—you at least have a reasonable base to work from.

Figure 3.3 shows the Analyst Estimates page on Yahoo.com.

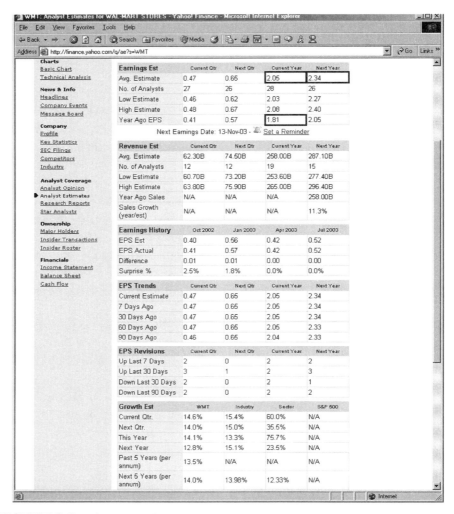

FIGURE 3.3 Yahoo.com—Earnings

Notice that there are three boxes highlighted: the average estimate for the Current Year and Next Year, followed by Year Ago EPS. If we are looking for the previous year's growth—and we trust the Web site's updates—then we would simply subtract 1.81 from 2.05 and then divide the difference by 1.81, which is 13 percent. Referencing the earnings numbers in Figure 3.3, so far so good. For a forward-looking number, subtract 2.05 from 2.34 and then divide the difference from 2.05, which is 14 percent. Thus, our conclusion is that (based on Yahoo's numbers) the company—estimate-wise—is expecting earnings growth of 14 percent. See how easy this is?

The neat thing about growth numbers is that they can really give investors a good snapshot of institutional thinking. Thus, if we look at two stocks and find considerably different growth numbers, we may infer that the two stocks will likely diverge from one another. In essence, what we are doing is uncovering a fundamental reason behind our statistics before we ever even begin to look at statistics. As an analogy, if you learn about sea currents and wind patterns before you ever step foot on a sailboat, when you finally do, you will be that much better of a sailor. Growth ratios are very similar to sea currents. Low income and sales growth compared to a stock's broader industry can drag the stock price out to sea. In other words, your pair may have a hidden riptide that is pulling one side beneath water. If you understand how to read the tides, you will have a better chance of being able to know when and where the currents begin to calm.

GROWTH, PE, AND THE PEG RATIO

Many investors like to look at the PE ratio, though many analysts feel that this ratio is irrelevant, as it does not reflect the future earnings of the stock. And the *future* of the stock is what the market is "pricing in" or anticipating with each individual day's trading action.

The PE ratio is the current price of the stock divided by the current EPS. There are two conflicting schools of thought about where the ratio should be. One school of thought feels that the ratio should be very close to 1, thus assuming that the current stock price is accurately trading near the present earnings valuation. The second school believes that PE ratios should be above 20 but below 40, to indicate that the stock is trading at a premium to the current earnings valuation. Such is said to indicate that investors have confidence that the company will continue to grow in the future—which brings us back to that word again: *growth.*

A newer version of the PE ratio is the PEG ratio, which equates to the PE ratio divided by annual EPS growth. The PEG ratio is said to be a more accurate indication of a stock's perceived future value, unlike the simpler PE ratio. However, because the growth figures used in PEG ratios are forecasts, they can be less accurate than the more current empirical accounting/earnings data used in PE.

PE Ratio

Generally, a PE ratio is calculated by using the last four quarters of earnings data. Thus, similar to the previous example, we could calculate the PE ratio

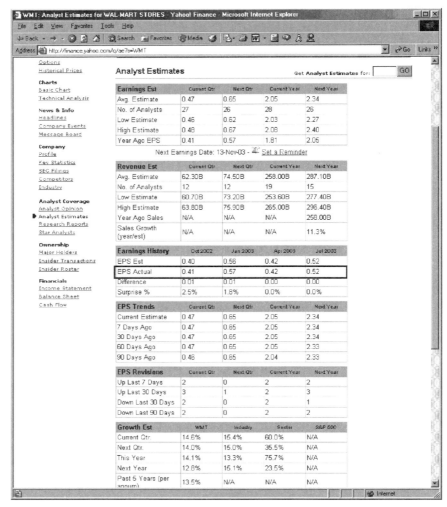

FIGURE 3.4 Yahoo—PE

by taking the full-year earnings numbers and dividing by the price of the stock. Let's actually do one ourselves, just to make sure that we know exactly what we are doing.

In Figure 3.4 the most recent four quarters of earnings data are highlighted in a black box. Simply take all four numbers, add them up, and then divide by the price of the stock, which is $55.52. The result is 29.91, or rounded it would equal 30. This number is known as the trailing PE, since it uses the most recent historical PE data.

If we take a look at the Yahoo.com Key Statistics page (to obtain PE and PEG, please reference Microsoft example in Figure 3.2) where the PE and PEG ratios are, we will see that our PE is very close to what Yahoo is calculating.

However, our PE is a little off. The reason for this is that (in this case) Yahoo.com was not using the most current quarter. In the Yahoo.com earnings data in Figure 3.4, the most recent quarter was July, and the company just reported new numbers that have not been updated. Thus, to get a more accurate number, we can drop the October 2002 earnings number and add in the most recent figure, which was 46 cents. So if we add the three numbers from Yahoo—0.57 + 0.42 + 0.52—and the most recent number (when this was written), 0.46, we get 1.97. Our price of $55.52 divided by 1.97 equals 28.18. In this case, Yahoo did a very good job of making sure the earnings number was updated for the trailing PE. However, in the Earnings History portion of the site, the number was not updated at the same time.

PEG Ratio

To calculate the PEG ratio, we would simply take the PE number and divide it by the annual earnings growth number. This is where the PEG can get a little shady. The problem is that for just about every PEG calculated, different growth projection figures are used. While you may use annual EPS growth of one year, someone else may use five years. Or while you are using full-year EPS number, someone else may be doing the next four quarters that overlap into a new year. Remember that anytime you are using projected numbers, the data becomes less empirical and should be used as a guiding tool but not a grail of stock direction.

Earlier in this chapter we calculated the annual EPS growth number for Wal-Mart by using this year's earnings number and the projected number for the following year. We deduced that the company's forward earnings growth was expected to be 14 percent. Again, keep in mind that this is assuming Yahoo's numbers are correct. If we really wanted to be diligent, we could read the company's earnings report, find a statement of guidance, or listen to the company conference call to get the actual EPS projection for next year. However, for the sake of example, we will just use the number on Yahoo. To calculate the PEG, we would divide the PE ratio by the annual growth projection, which would be (rounded) 28 divided by 14, thus equaling 2. Our PEG is a little above the PEG of 1.8 listed on Yahoo; meaning there is a discrepancy in growth numbers used. However, we are in the same ballpark, so we won't worry too much about it.

In general, a PEG ratio above 3.0 may indicate that a stock is overbought and could cause investors to seek a pullback. Elevated PEG ratios might be indicating that a stock may pull back in order to return to a price relative to current earnings projections. PEG ratios, like many other ratios, can vary widely from sector to sector, so it is very important to cross-reference other

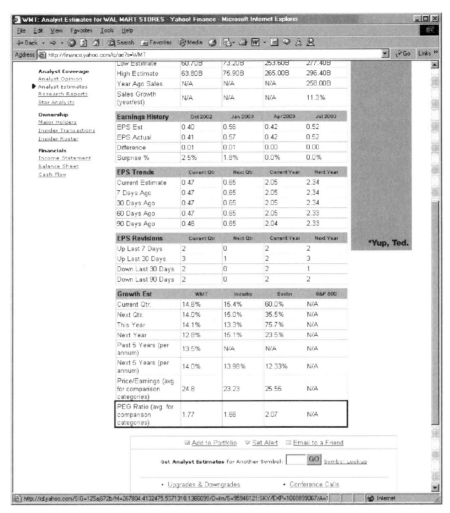

FIGURE 3.5 Yahoo.com PEG Comparison

companies in the same industry for a general idea of where the sector average PEG ratio should be. Yahoo has a great PEG industry comparison reference at the bottom of the Analyst Estimates page. Figure 3.5 shows just what I am talking about.

P/E ratios and PEG ratios are to pairs trading as chalk is to a weightlifter. To the champion weightlifter, chalk is a tool that only assists in gripping (literally and figuratively) the situation at hand. However, true strength comes from within, from many years of hard work. Thus, P/E and PEG ratios help us confirm or negate our thoughts, but are not part of our inner fundamental strength.

Understanding just how much cash a company has is vitally important to short-term investing. Cash-poor companies will generally always receive negative comments from analysts and find themselves out of favor with investors. Bottom line: Cash is the big kahuna!

We will quickly examine a few ratios to understand how much cash a company has. First, the current ratio equals current assets divided by current liabilities, and is meant to measure how effectively a company can measure its short-term obligations. It is often thought that the higher the current ratio, the less a company will have to worry about a cash crunch.

Current assets are defined as balance sheet items that are cash, cash equivalents, inventory, marketable securities, prepaid expenses, and accounts receivable. Current assets are generally all assets that can be converted into cash within one year.

Current liabilities are simply all liabilities (similar to accounts payable) that are short-term debts due within one year.

To find the current ratio, simply log on to Yahoo.com Finance and put in a ticker symbol. Then, click on "Profile" and voila—much of the company's financial health is at your fingertips.

The debt-to-equity ratio (EN 3.1) is vital in quickly understanding how a company is leveraging itself. The debt-to-equity ratio is calculated as a company's long-term debt divided by common shareholder equity, or equity available to common shareholders. Companies with higher debt-to-equity ratios are thought to offer greater returns to investors, but are normally riskier with larger liability obligations. The debt-to-equity ratio is also found under the Yahoo.com "profile" section.

TYING IT ALL TOGETHER

Many analysts may argue that the information cited in this chapter barely scratches the surface of a company's true financial health, and for all intents and purposes, I agree. However, for the average investor who does not have the luxury of countless hours to fundamentally pick apart every company he or she is considering, the information given here is designed to at least find a few red flags.

Let's examine a hypothetical scenario. Imagine that two companies, Crasher Inc. and Bumper Inc., are both in the business of manufacturing airbags. Demand for airbags appears strong; thus, an investor may be thinking about buying both stocks. However, when investigating the two companies with simple fundamental analysis, the investor finds the information shown in Figure 3.6.

	Bumper Inc.	Crasher Inc.	Industry Average
Cash	310m	220m	N/A
Income growth % 1yr	22.00%	15.00%	19.00%
Sales growth % 1y	13.00%	16.00%	12.00%
Current ratio	4.2	2.3	3
P/E ratio	34	23	19
PEG ratio	1.8	1.6	2.4
Debt-to-equity ratio	0.3	0.45	0.4

FIGURE 3.6 Crasher Inc. versus Bumper Inc.

Simple analysis discovered that Bumper Inc. has more cash to pay its bills, is currently exceeding the broader sector in income growth, and has less debt. What's more, even with lower sales growth, Bumper Inc. has greater income growth potential, which may allude to a more cost-efficient manufacturing process. Overall, the short-term trader not taking a long-term position in the stock may infer that the more soluble company (Bumper Inc.) embodies less risk during a near-term trade. Of course, this would also depend on both stock prices, for if Bumper Inc. was trading at $100 per share while Crasher Inc. had a present price of $10 per share, the conclusion might be different! Again, the previous analysis leaves much to be desired. However, for the investor who does not have the luxury of countless hours dedicated to research, the aforementioned fundamental analysis may at least offer some assistance in understanding equities.

You may now see that in the case of Crasher Inc. and Bumper Inc., if the stocks were presently trading at the same price, we may possibly infer that divergence is looming. Bumper Inc. might ascend and Crasher Inc. might decline. In short, by understanding fundamental analysis, we may be able to predict some of our statistics before they ever begin to unfold.

CHAPTER 4

Technical Analysis

*Candlestick Charting, Hammer
Bottoms and Hangman Tops,
Doji Star, Shooting Stars,
Engulfing Patterns, Support
and Resistance, Trend Lines,
Moving Averages*

To understand pairs, we must also understand technical analysis so that we can make more informed decisions when considering our positions. Technical analysis is simply the art of evaluating the historical price movements of a stock in an attempt to find information that may discern possible future direction. Usually, this is in the form of reading charts, coupled with assorted indicators such as: moving averages, stochastics, relative strength, and/or any other "indicator" that may map a stock's historical trading activity. Technical analysis can be both up to the moment, in "real time," or on a historical basis. However, I would like to point out that even real-time data is an event that has already occurred. Thus, all technical analysis is made up of *lagging indicators*, which presume future movements. For the swing trader, end-of-day (EOD) data will suffice to do proper analysis. End-of-day data is simply the open, close, high, and low of a stock's trading activity after any given trading day. Real-time data is generally needed only for day traders, institutional traders, or swing traders overly concerned about timing entries (or exits) in an effort to minimize slippage. (EN 4.1)

Again, it is important to remember that all technical analysis consists of lagging indicators because the data used denotes events that have already occurred. In short, technical analysis trys to map individual stocks, sectors, and indices using history as a potential guide to the future. Technicians attempt to find measurable patterns or "indicators," which may allude to possible future trading activity. In essence, it is said that technical analysis is the science of "self-fulfilling prophecies." By this I mean that technical analysis generally works only if many, many people follow similar indicators. As an analogy, when we go to buy tickets for an event, generally an orderly line forms as people wait their turn to get to the ticket window. The line itself is not mandated, but is honored by many people who are following the same rule of order. Technical analysis allows individuals to find benchmark rules of order on which to base market-oriented thought.

Fundamental analysts often scoff at technical analysis, saying that it has no true relevance to a stock's underlying value. While this may be true at the heart of the issue, fundamentalists seem all too quick to forget one important facet of technical analysis: If you have a stock that immediately begins to sell off and breaks critical support (explained later), one may assume that obviously someone's opinion of the stock has changed. Perhaps the altered opinion is that of a fundamental analyst who has sent out a research report downgrading the stock. The price activity of the stock recorded in technical analysis then simply alerts the average investor to a possible fundamental mindset adjustment, flagged by the technical breakdown observed on the actual chart. Regardless, the price activity witnessed in technical analysis is an extension of all the events surrounding a stock, including fundamental analysis, institutional order flow, earnings, rumors, and news. In a few words, the entire reason we are incorporating technical analysis in our pairs discussion is so that we may have an "alert" system to ideological or fundamental changes within a company. Technical analysis then becomes our road map to the market. In the chart in Figure 4.1, you will see a substantial

FIGURE 4.1 Technical Analysis Chart

breakdown in Microsoft. The actual sell-off was due to investor worries about Windows' security. In late October, there were many viruses splattering networks, all because of loopholes in the Windows code. Though Microsoft quickly developed patches to solve the problem, there was still selling in the stock. Even if you weren't in the real world and did not know of the viruses/worms, the chart would have alerted you that something big was happening. Thus, technical analysis is our eyes and ears to the market.

CANDLESTICK CHARTING

Candlestick charting is a method of charting dating back to the 1600s, when Japanese farmers would attempt to map the price action of rice futures. (EN 4.2) Each candlestick is comprised of four basic parts: open, close, high, and low. Each candlestick contains a "real body," which is the distance between the open and closing prices for the stock during the period covered. Although there are intraday candlesticks, we will use only daily candlesticks in this chapter (i.e., each candle equals a full day of trading activity). Each candle may also have a "wick," which is a line above and/or below the real body denoting the day's trading action higher than the open, or lower than the close. A stock can open at $20, trade as high as $21 during the middle of the day, then close at $19.50. This candle would look like Figure 4.2.

Each candle will either be green or red. Green candles indicate that the close ended higher than the open (the stock closed positive) and vice versa for red.

There are many different "patterns" of candlesticks, which are said to tell of potential future trading action. We will go over only a few basic patterns and then provide some additional resources to find more information.

As you read this chapter, please keep in mind that it may generally be a good idea to only use our candlestick knowledge on individual charts instead of the differential or ratio (explained later) for our pair. By being able to read the individual charts, we may again find ourselves ahead of our statistics as we potentially "predict" a move before it occurs.

Hammer Bottoms and Hangman Tops

In general, a hammer bottom is a candlestick that is at the bottom of a descending chart and denotes a potential reversal pattern. The hammer bottom consists of a small real body with little or no wick on top. The hammer has a very long tail underneath the real body, generally at least two times the real body. The greater the tail underneath the real body, the better the

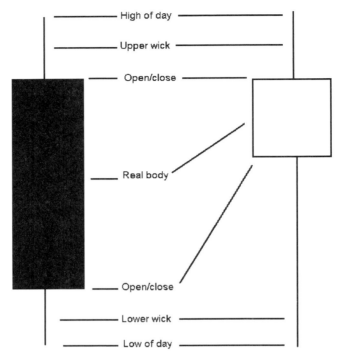

FIGURE 4.2 Candlestick Example

candlestick formation. It is also important to note that candlestick patterns usually require confirmation to ensure that the day's trading was not a "head-fake." (By confirmation I mean that the day following the hammer candlestick should have a close above the previous day's high, thus indicating a higher high in the relative range.) The hammer bottom combined with a second day of confirmation usually indicates that bears tried to take the bottom out of the stock but ran out of gas, and bulls recovered with strength. The resulting conclusion is that a substantial portion of weaker bulls were finally forced out of the stock and savvy bears realized that it is time to cover short positions. Thus, a potential reversal could be looming. Technicians often like to see a large volume spike on the actual hammer day, which is said to possibly confirm that the remaining bulk of frail buyers, or shorts, have exited the stock. Figure 4.3 displays a hammer bottom and the following day's confirmation.

The hangman top is exactly the same thing as a hammer bottom, but it is on the top of an ascending move. Much like a hammer bottom, a hangman top also has the tail underneath the candle. A hangman top with a large tail indicates that bulls may be growing nervous and could begin dumping their

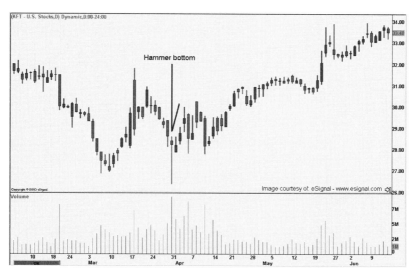

FIGURE 4.3 Hammer Bottom

positions. The close at the top of the tail signifies that even though bulls were able to hold ground, there are now many skeptical holders ready to drop the stock at the first sign of trouble. As with hammer bottoms, savvy technical analysts may also look for confirmation of a lower low in the subsequent trading day.

Doji Star

A doji star can be at either the top or bottom of a chart and may indicate that a stock is generally planning on making a new move. The doji is a day of consolidation, wherein a stock generally has a range above and below the open and close. Doji stars are characterized by tails on both the top and bottom of the real body. Consolidation days (otherwise known as doji stars, like the one in Figure 4.4) can produce intraday ascending and descending trend lines that day traders watch for potential breakouts.

Shooting Stars

Shooting stars are found on the top of a trend. The stock may trade above and below the open, but generally closes relatively near where the day commenced trading. The shooting star is similar to a doji, but with the upper wick resting at least two times above the real body. The theory behind a shooting star is that bulls gapped the stock up and tried to run it higher, but

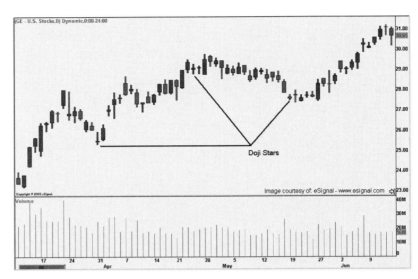

FIGURE 4.4 Doji Star

failed to hang onto gains. Then, if the following day closes below the shooting star's low, the pattern is said to have confirmation of bulls' lack of buying conviction. Figures 4.5 and 4.6 show two examples of shooting stars.

Engulfing Patterns

An engulfing pattern is a candle that literally engulfs the entire day's previous candle. A bullish engulfing candle opens lower than the previous day and then proceeds to close higher. The pattern is usually at the bottom of a descending move and can mean that traders are heavily covering shorts in anticipation of a possible ascending move. The bearish engulfing pattern is very similar but is on the top of an ascending trend and has an open and close at more extreme points than the previous session. Engulfing patterns are also called "outside" days by Western chartists, but generally mean the same thing. Much like all charting, engulfing patterns are best used when confirmed with the following day's trading activity. The chart in Figure 4.7 displays both bullish and bearish engulfing patterns.

Now that we have covered a few candlestick patterns, let's see how - this knowledge can apply to pairs trading. If our statistics are indicating that we should buy Stock A and sell short Stock B, we may want to check other information available, just to see whether our statistics agree with technical analysis. Then, by examining the charts, we may see that Stock A has just formed a hammer bottom (with confirmation), while Stock B has

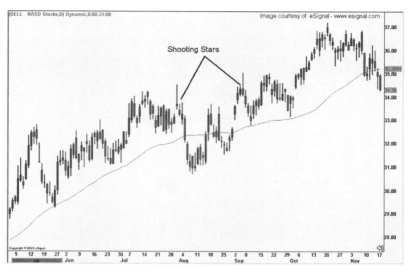

FIGURE 4.5 Shooting Star 1

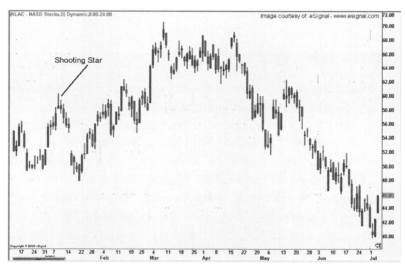

FIGURE 4.6 Shooting Star 2

created a shooting star (with confirmation), and we may feel more confident about entering our pair. The key to being an effective directional or pairs trader is to get as many different indicators on our side as we can. If our statistics coincide with the fundamentals and the technical charts, we have more favorable aspects of the trade working for us rather than against us.

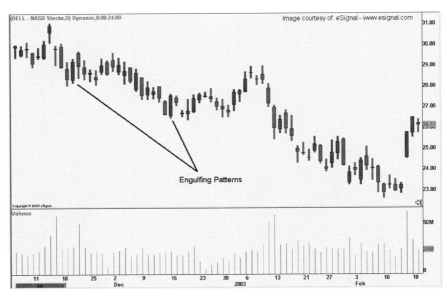

FIGURE 4.7 Bullish and Bearish Engulfing Patterns

SUPPORT AND RESISTANCE

While support and resistance are two very easy parts of technical analysis to grasp, they are also quite effective in predicting key levels of price action on any given chart. Support is simply the horizontal line among a series of similar points in a chart's history, drawn underneath the stock's current price. Horizontal support can date back anywhere from two ticks to an entire century, so long as there are multiple points that match up to form the support line. Support is said to be at levels *below* the current price of a stock, where bulls may attempt to hold the stock up, should it decline. Resistance is the same thing as support, with the exception that it is *above* the stock's current price. Resistance is a level where bears will try to keep the stock under, should the stock ascend. As a picture tells a thousand words, Figure 4.8 displays how support and resistance are drawn on a chart.

TREND LINES

Trend lines are another simple but crucial part of technical analysis and are often overlooked for more complicated indicators. However, at times technical analysis can be most effective by keeping things simple, rather than

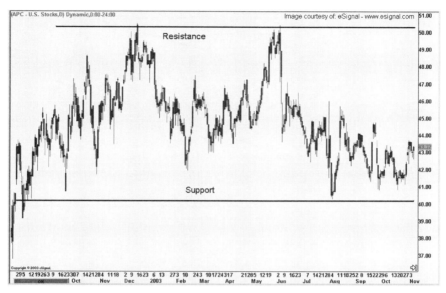

FIGURE 4.8 Support and Resistance

piling on tons and tons of confusing indicators. Why? In the industry this is called *analysis paralysis*, wherein one compiles too much information and is therefore not able to make any decisions at all. Basically, with too much information, one can become a "deer in headlights." In fact, sometimes the most effective information is the *most obvious* information that has been staring us right in the eyes the whole time!

Trend lines are just that: They are readily apparent—*angled*—support and resistance lines that denote the direction of a stock's trend. There are two types of trends: up and down. Ha! You have to be laughing to yourself, saying, "That was the most profound piece of trading information I have ever run across!" Okay, humor aside, it really is very important to understand the significance of trend lines. While the two directions I have just indicated seem incredibly simple, they are amazingly effective in predicting short- and long-term price movements.

Succinctly, an ascending trend line is drawn by connecting the low points of two or more candlesticks in a straight but elevating line. The line must be straight, not curved. The elevating line on the bottom of the upward-moving candlesticks (positive and negative days included) is known as ascending support. A descending trend line is exactly the same but is drawn using the highs of two or more days and slopes downward while producing

FIGURE 4.9 Ascending Support and Descending Resistance

lower lows. The downward-slanting line on the top of the falling candles is otherwise known as descending resistance.

If a stock has been moving upward for several sessions and ascending support is violated, the most obvious presumption is that (at least during the near term) the direction of the stock will turn. When ascending support is violated, a trader may be hoping the stock will pull back, while investors take profits off the table and wait for a more ideal long reentry point. However, if the stock violates ascending and horizontal support, more aggressive investors might attempt to short the stock in anticipation of a larger breakdown (see Figure 4.9).

Simply trading trend lines coupled with support and resistance is *not* recommended. Understanding this area of technical analysis certainly helps increase an investor's repertoire of analysis tools to make more informed and educated decisions, but is not enough information to base a trading strategy on.

However, I cannot pound the table enough for the average investor and even for the "master" technician to rethink the vitality and importance of trend lines!

MOVING AVERAGES

A simple moving average (SMA) is the average of a security's price over a specified period of time, represented in the form of a line on a stock's chart.

There are two major SMAs that traders observe: the 50-day moving average (50-SMA) and the 200-day moving average (200-SMA). Both moving averages are meant to serve as benchmarks around which individual stocks trade. A 50-SMA tends to be more volatile than a 200-SMA because the 200-SMA simply incorporates more data and thus has a smoother average. Some technicians view the 50-SMA crossing above the 200-SMA as bullish confirmation of a trend and vice versa for 50-SMA dip below 200-SMA. Moreover, both the 50-SMA and 200-SMA work as support and resistance for individual securities, sectors, and indices. Most charting programs are generally designed to add specified moving averages for many different periods. Figure 4.10 illustrates an example of a 50-SMA and a 200-SMA, while also identifying how a stock can bounce off the major moving averages as many different traders view the same benchmarks.

The second type of moving average is the exponential moving average (EMA). The EMA is generally the same thing as an SMA, with the exception that *recent prices* are more heavily weighted than the simple average of all prices. The resulting moving average tends to hover near a stock's actual price more closely than an SMA and can provide additional technical data to the analyst. Regardless, the effectiveness of moving averages is really only the product of many people watching the same thing at the same time. In English, moving averages are self-fulfilling prophecies because benchmark time periods are observed by large groups of investors who may be thinking

FIGURE 4.10 Moving Averages
Used with permission from Stockcharts.com.

the same thing at a similar moment. Though arguable, we might assume that the 50- and 200-SMAs hold more weight than the 50- and 200-EMAs because, most likely, a larger portion of the technical analysis investing public monitors SMAs instead of EMAs. What's more, a 50-EMA would likely be a more important level to watch than a 32-SMA, as more people will likely follow the 50-EMA over the obscure 32-SMA. (Incidentally, 32 is an arbitrary number used merely as an example.) Moving averages (much like a great proportion of technical analysis) come down to how many people are watching uniform numerical parameters. Obscure moving average time periods will generally not help when trying to predict future movements of a stock price.

Beyond moving averages crossing over and under one another, the averages are also used as support and resistance when monitoring charts. A 200-SMA is generally said to be a more significant benchmark of support (or resistance) than the 50-SMA. In addition, the 50-SMA typically stands as bolder support (or resistance) than a shorter-term moving average. When a stock begins to near a major moving average, typically traders may look for a bounce off the moving average, before the stock moves though or turns back. The theory is that many traders are watching the same average and (for an ascending stock) will sell their positions as the equity nears the benchmark moving average. This causes a complete ricochet off the moving average, or will at least "shake out" weaker buyers before the stock pulls through. The bottom line here is to watch for support and resistance–fueled trading activity when a stock nears a benchmark moving average.

For references on moving averages, see Appendix II.

CHAPTER 5

Technical Analysis Indicators

Stochastics
Chaikin Money Flow Oscillator
On-Balance Volume
Relative Strength Index

G etting into more complicated technical analysis, we will begin to look at indicators as an additional way of examining the present stock price, while deciphering historical price movements. Each of the indicators in this chapter can be applied to individual stocks, while also being used in conjunction with actual pairs. However, not all technical analysis programs offer the ability to track spreads or apply indicators to either a differential or ratio. Therefore, later in the book we will discuss how to build indicators in Excel. What's more, in Appendix II you will find a list of technical analysis programs that are pairs friendly, with a brief description of each.

STOCHASTICS

Our first indictor is called *stochastics*, which is an oscillator that is used to determine overbought and oversold conditions. Stochastics are lines that move up and down in a horizontal oscillator and are intended to depict when a stock is receiving excessive buying or selling pressure. Most stochastics consist of two lines called the %k and %d. The stochastics oscillator ranges from 0 to 100, where a movement below 20 is said to indicate selling pressure possibly leading to oversold conditions, while a number above 80 is thought to point toward buying pressure potentially alluding to overbought circumstances. When stochastics are in the overbought region, they also

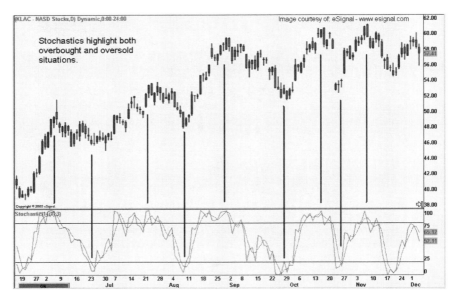

FIGURE 5.1 Stochastics

mean that bullish momentum is very strong and may continue. Conversely, when stochastics are in the oversold region, bears are thought to be applying significant pressure to security, which may continue to see additional downside trading. Figure 5.1 displays how a stochastics indicator appears on a chart.

Some technicians believe that when the actual %k and %d lines cross above and below one another they are alluding to potential buy and sell signals. Because %d is a moving average of %k, the actual signal is triggered when the %k line crosses above or below the %d line. Confirmation is thought to occur when the lower stochastics (that have just crossed up) begin to elevate out of the oversold region and vice versa for the overbought region. You will notice crossover and crossunder examples on the subsequent chart.

How are %k and %d calculated? The actual formula for a %k n interval is:

$$100 \times (C–Ll) / (Hh–Ll)$$

Where:
  Ll = lowest low for the last n *intervals*
  Hh = the highest high for n *intervals*
  C = close of the last interval

The %d line is a moving average or smoothed version of %k and is calculated as follows:

$$\%d = 100 * (HP/LP)$$

Where:
HP = n periods sum of (C − Ll)
LP = n periods sum of (Hh − Ll)

In addition to %k and %d, there are also slow %k and slow %d lines, which simply add more data into the equation in an effort to smooth out volatility. Sometimes, more savvy traders do not actually use stochastics as a leading indicator; rather, use the indicator as confirmation of the research and resulting thoughts that have already been constructed. For example, if an investor conducts fundamental research and discovers that a stock trading at $50 should really be trading at only $15, and then sees that the daily stochastics are painfully overbought, he or she might then infer that both technicians and fundamentalists may be seeking a pullback to bring the stock back to more sane levels.

CHAIKIN MONEY FLOW OSCILLATOR

To begin, we will briefly discuss the Chaikin Money Flow Oscillator developed by Marc Chaikin. In theory, the indicator is based on summing of the values of the accumulation distribution line for *n* periods (usually 21), and then dividing by the same number of periods. Overall, the indicator is meant to depict the strength of a stock movement. In general, a positive number indicates accumulation (buying), while a negative number is said to allude to distribution (selling). What's more, some technicians feel that the farther away from the zero line the money flow line moves, the stronger the signal. In addition, the indicator may add confirmation to a breakout or breakdown if the money flow line is above or below the zero line in the actual direction of the stock's contemporary move. Thus, if the stock breaks out above resistance and the money flow line is also above zero, technical bulls could very likely continue buying the stock. Also, if a stock is consolidating (traveling sideways) and the money flow indicator is increasing, bulls may be silently accumulating stock in hopes of a future breakout! Conversely, if the stock is trending laterally and money flow is decreasing, buying interest in the stock may be dwindling. Figure 5.2 displays a Chaikin Money Flow Oscillator with accumulation leading to a breakout.

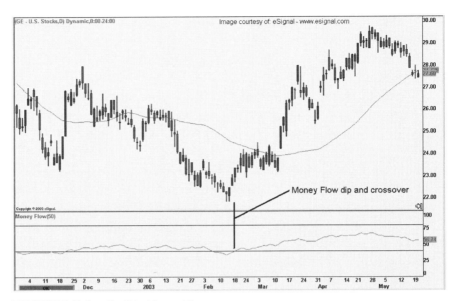

FIGURE 5.2   Chaikin Money Flow

ON-BALANCE VOLUME

On-balance volume (OBV) is an indicator developed by Joseph Granville that attempts to unveil trends in share accumulation (through volume) over time. Basically, OBV is a running total of all shares accumulated in one direction or the other, displayed in a cumulative oscillator. Simply put, each trading day's volume is added to the indicator if the day closes up, and is subtracted if the day closes down. Much like money flow, OBV is a trend confirmation tool, and can allude to either breakouts or breakdowns when the oscillator direction corresponds with stock price movement. If OBV is declining while a stock is rising, the oscillator may be signaling underlying weakness, thus potentially alerting technicians to hidden bearish pressure within the stock. Figures 5.3 and 5.4 display both OBV trend confirmation and negation.

RELATIVE STRENGTH INDEX

Introduced in 1978 by J. Welles Wilder, the Relative Strength Index compares a stock's recent ascending prices to its descending prices and converts the data into an oscillator that ranges from 0 to 100. The Relative Strength Index by Wilder is easily confused with other forms of relative strength that compare a company to its broader sector. Please do not confuse the two.

FIGURE 5.3 OBV Confirmation

FIGURE 5.4 OBV Negation

The actual formula for RSI is:

$$RSI = 100 - (100 / 1 + RS)$$

Where:
RS = *mean gain/mean loss*
Mean gain = *total stock price gains/n periods*
Mean loss = *total stock price losses/n periods*

Most technicians generally use 14 periods to compare data to, while using +30 and +70 as oversold and overbought settings on the actual oscillator. When the indicator drops below 30, the stock is said to be oversold and conversely overbought above 70. Though the actual use of the indicator differs from technician to technician, most agree that a move above 30 from within the oversold region (below 30) indicates bullish momentum fueled by possible short covering. When the oscillator falls beneath 70 from the overbought region, bears might begin adding supplemental pressure to the stock, and could bring additional sellers off the fence. Figure 5.5 displays both overbought and oversold conditions.

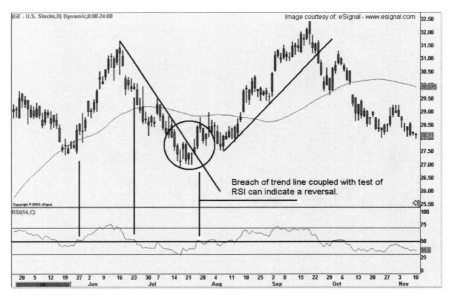

FIGURE 5.5 Relative Strength

At this point I would like to reiterate that it is very important to have a strong foundation of fundamental and technical information on which to base your pairs knowledge. Once we begin to statistically uncover the opportunities of pairs trading, it will be important to double- and triple-check all trades with fundamental and technical analysis. It is quite a bit of work, but the fact here is: If you don't do it, someone else will. And that person may uncover the one nugget of information that you don't know. After all, the point of trading is to make money, and to do so effectively, we must work hard, while leaving no stone unturned.

CHAPTER 6

Basic Pairs Terminology

*Understanding the Correlation
Spread, Differential, and Ratio
Spread, Differential, Ratio,
Divergence Trading
Convergence Trading*

Before we dive deep into the world of pairs, it is important to go over some rudimentary concepts of pairs. You may find that pairs terminology will change from author to author, mostly because the subject has relatively little material written about it. Moreover, because pairs traders seem to be a rare breed of their own, there isn't much communication between individuals. Thus, much of the lingo changes from person to person and office to office.

This chapter will cover:

- Basic understanding of correlation and why it is important
- Key terminology (differential, ratio, and intraday spread)
- Divergence trading
- Convergence trading

UNDERSTANDING THE CORRELATION

First, we must ask ourselves why the correlation itself is important. In short, the correlation is the glue of pairs; it is the measurement of relationship significance between equities (or other financial instruments). Later, we will get into correlation formulas and how to map out a correlation, though for the time being simply remember that -1 equals a perfectly negative relationship, while $+1$ should display a perfectly parallel liaison. By this I mean that two stocks with a +1 relationship would have *exactly* similar charts directly mirroring one another. Equities with a correlation of −1 would be comparable to positive and negative sides of a magnet. Even though they look similar on the surface, when you try to put them together, they force themselves away from one another. Sounds like a bad family reunion!

When we think of correlations, we consider not only the main correlation between two stocks, but also the correlation among any number of equities and other financial vehicles such as indices. For example, if you are an American, you have a relationship with not only the federal government, but your state government as well. While you may feel a stronger affiliation with your home state, everything that the federal government does likely affects you in one way or another. Thus, whether you like it or not, you have to pay attention to broader federal activities that *will* have an impact on your life. This would be the same as relating a sector to its corresponding index. Even if you believe that you have found the "perfect" pair in a relatively safe sector, it is still a good idea to know what the correlation is between your chosen stocks and the indices in which that they are listed. That way, if the market begins to dump, you may have a good idea of how your stocks will react. Another way of watching this may be to monitor beta, which will be discussed later in the book.

SPREAD, DIFFERENTIAL, AND RATIO

The differential, ratio, and intraday spread are simply three distinct ways of viewing and/or reading pairs. One point that often confuses people is the use of the term *spread*. All three terms used above describe a certain type of spread and are each calculated using different (though basic) math. However, the term *spread*, as it will be used in this book refers to the *intraday and closing pairs spreads only*. Intraday spreads are generally known as the difference between the bid and ask on an intraday basis. Thus, using the term *spread* only on an intraday basis keeps our terminology consistent with that of the broader market. (There are many circumstances in which the term *spread* applies to EOD [end of day—closing prices] data, though generally in the context of equities, *spread* refers only to the intraday difference between the bid and ask.) Normal investors buy stock on the ask and sell on the bid. If a stock were showing a spread of $1.20 by $1.40, then (if you entered a market order) you would buy the stock at $1.40 per share and sell it at $1.20. The spread would be $0.20 cents—and that, folks, is where market makers and specialists attempt to make their money. It is important to remember that spreads in pairs trading are vastly different than the typical bid/ask spread. Pairs spreads are described in the following paragraph. One last side note: With the exception of the term *spread*, when you hear either *differential* or *ratio*, assume that I am speaking about closing prices only. Other than the spread, any other data to be used on an intraday basis will be specifically denoted using the term *intraday* in the description.

Spread

In terms of pairs, an intraday spread equals the *intraday* change in Stock A minus the change in Stock B. For example, Intraday change during the present session (how much a stock is up or down) of Stock A – Intraday Change of Stock B = Spread. If last Monday, Stock A had gained $1.30 at the close and Stock B had lost $0.40, then the closing change spread would have been +$1.70. Yes, I know that "closing change spread" is confusing, but, stick with me for a moment. In general, when you hear someone say "What's the spread?", they will most likely be asking you during market hours when both stocks are live. Thus, you can look to see where both stocks are, quickly get out your abacus, and add or subtract the two numbers—then you will sound like a pro! However, when we are asked about the closing change spread, we are considering how much a stock gained or lost *within* that particular session. Some people will simply ask you "What was the closing spread?" You will then likely want to reply, "Do you mean the closing intraday spread or the differential?" It gets confusing, I know, but it is what it is.

Differential

The differential is simply one equity minus the other. For example, Closing price of Stock A – Closing price of Stock B = Differential. The differential is dissimilar to the spread, as it uses the pure closing price of both stocks and does *not* directly consider how much either stock gained or lost during the session. While a differential can be calculated for specified intraday periods, we will not do so in this book. The differential will primarily be used for EOD data and swing trading analysis.

Ratio

The ratio equals either the closing price or intraday change of the first stock divided by the second. For example, Intraday change of Stock A/Intraday change of Stock B = Intraday ratio. The ratio is generally used to measure the amount of one share needed to equal the value of another. Some traders

Differential	Ratio	Intraday Spread
Stock A - Stock B	Stock A / Stock B	Intraday change - Intraday change

FIGURE 6.1 Three Examples of Tracking Pairs

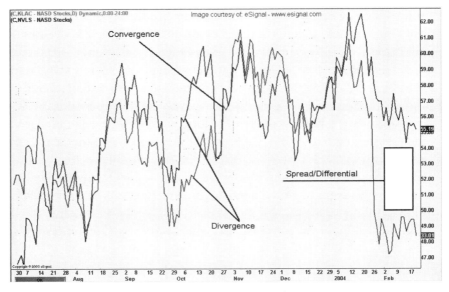

FIGURE 6.2 Diverged Equities versus Converged Equities

feel that using a ratio is more accurate than a differential, though much of this is simply personal preference. Moreover, the ratio allows the pairs trader to incorporate different facets of value analysis into the pair. We will go over the ratio in further detail in Chapter 13, where we will cover how to incorporate beta and earnings.

All three examples are shown in Figure 6.1.

DIVERGENCE TRADING

When we believe two stocks will diverge, we are betting that the differential, or ratio will grow apart. We are gambling that the two stocks will move away from one another.

Divergence traders are trading away from the statistical mean and/or believe that the fundamental valuation of two companies has changed. This belief denotes that the stocks will no longer trade together (at least in the short term) and will begin to separate. Imagine a rubber band expanding.

CONVERGENCE TRADING

Convergence traders believe that two stocks have already diverged to a point where the rubber band is near or at its maximum threshold, and will not grow apart any further. Thus, the convergence trader is betting that the two equities are going to come back together. Once again, equities reconverge for both technical and fundamental reasons, but can also simply have an independent event that sets one of the two equities in motion. No matter how you slice it, divergence is the rubber band expanding and convergence is the rubber band coming back together (see Figure 6.2).

Now that you have a general understanding of what pairs are and how they work, the most important concept to grasp is that of the rubber band. Pairs are simply a relationship of elasticity (not in the economic sense) where companies are bound by their correlations. As previously mentioned, correlations are the glue of pairs!

CHAPTER 7

Importing Data into Excel

Y ou may be asking yourself: Why Excel? Well, my friend, even if you have an advanced program that already calculates pairs, Excel will do wonders in helping you understand the internal workings of the strategy. This chapter is meant only to assist investors in creating a basic Excel spreadsheet for pairs analysis and learn how to import free (yes, free) end-of-day data from Yahoo.com.

The data we will be using is end-of-day (EOD) data. By this I mean that we will only be using each individual trading day's open, close, high, low, and total volume. This data is the same data used to make up daily charts for equities.

Also, the reason for a brief chapter on Excel is that we will be doing many of our calculations inside the spreadsheet program. In general, almost everyone has access to Excel; thus, it serves as an easily accessible platform to convey the pairs subject.

Step 1. Open Excel (any version will do) and create a new spreadsheet. Type "Main Spreadsheet 1" in cell A1, and then save the sheet as Example_pairs_sheet1. We will continue adding to this sheet as you work through the book, so by the end you will have your own spreadsheet. (As a side note, you will need Internet access to build your spreadsheet.)

Step 2. Once you have your spreadsheet ready to go, label the three tabs at the bottom of the sheet (each indicates a different sheet within the group): Main, Stock 1, and Stock 2 (see Figure 7.1).

Step 3. Once this is done, jump on the Internet and go to *www.yahoo.com.*

Step 4. Click on "Finance," or follow the link: *http://finance.yahoo.com/?u*

FIGURE 7.1 Excel Spreadsheet Example

Step 5. In the stock ticker entry box, put in the ticker KLAC for the company KLA Tencor.

Step 6. Next, look to the left of the screen and you will see a list of links. The fourth link down is titled "Historical Prices."

Step 7. Click on the link.

Step 8. From here you will see a table displaying the stock's closing EOD data, along with a date entry section at the top. In the date entry section use a start date of January 1, 2002, and an end date of July 31, 2003. Then click "Get Prices." Figure 7.2 shows what the screen should look like.

Step 9. Scroll to the bottom of the screen and click on the link titled "Download to Spreadsheet." You may have to save the data, but you should be able to just open it from the current location. The sheet should open an Excel spreadsheet with all of the historical data requested.

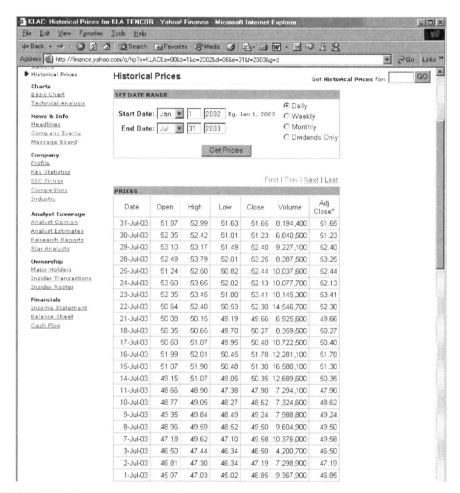

FIGURE 7.2 Historical Prices Screen

Highlight all of the cells that contain data. The easiest way to do this is to scroll all the way to the bottom of the sheet, click on the lowest right-hand cell that contains a value, then scroll up.

Step 10. Press Control C (Command C for Mac users) to copy the data (see Figure 7.3).

Step 11. Click on the Stock 1 tab in your spreadsheet, highlight cell A2, and press Control V (Command V for Mac users)to paste the data into the spreadsheet. Voila, you have just imported your first series of data.

Step 12. Repeat the same process for Novellus Corporation (NASDAQ: NVLS) and paste the data in the spreadsheet titled Stock 2. Now, both Stock 1 and Stock 2 should have historical data pasted into them. If you

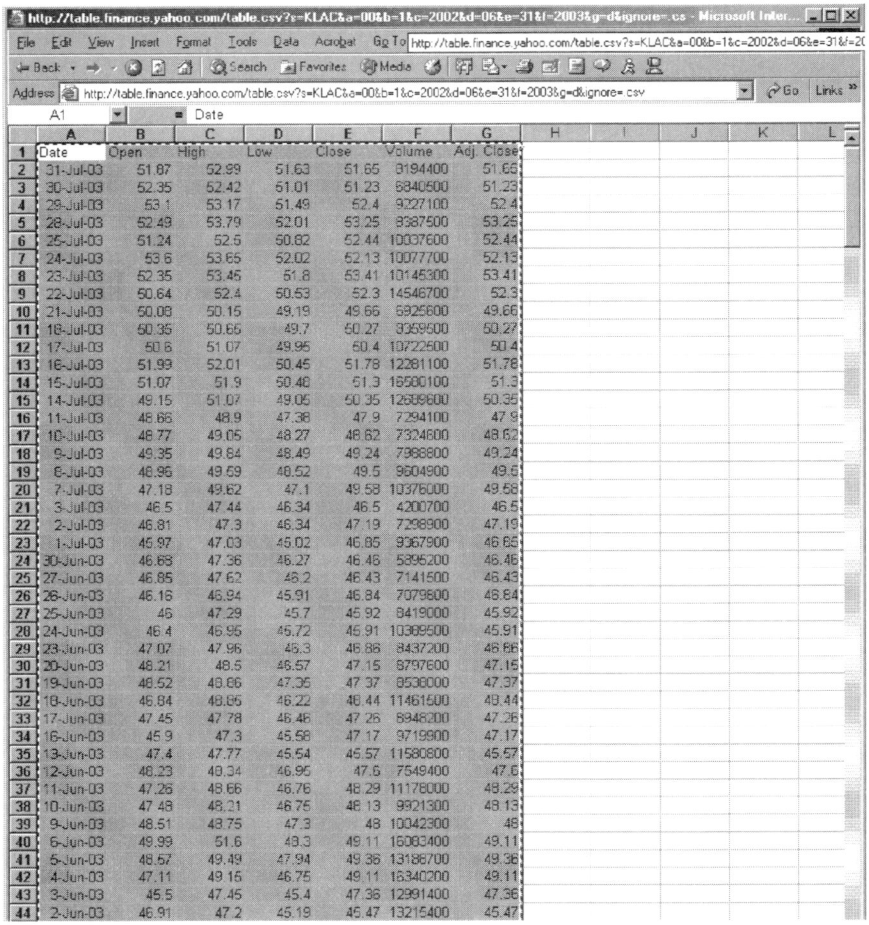

	A	B	C	D	E	F	G
1	Date	Open	High	Low	Close	Volume	Adj. Close
2	31-Jul-03	51.87	52.99	51.63	51.65	8194400	51.65
3	30-Jul-03	52.35	52.42	51.01	51.23	6840500	51.23
4	29-Jul-03	53.1	53.17	51.49	52.4	9227100	52.4
5	28-Jul-03	52.49	53.79	52.01	53.25	8387500	53.25
6	25-Jul-03	51.24	52.5	50.82	52.44	10037600	52.44
7	24-Jul-03	53.6	53.65	52.02	52.13	10077700	52.13
8	23-Jul-03	52.35	53.45	51.8	53.41	10145300	53.41
9	22-Jul-03	50.64	52.4	50.53	52.3	14546700	52.3
10	21-Jul-03	50.08	50.15	49.19	49.66	5925600	49.66
11	18-Jul-03	50.35	50.65	49.7	50.27	8369500	50.27
12	17-Jul-03	50.6	51.07	49.95	50.4	10722500	50.4
13	16-Jul-03	51.99	52.01	50.45	51.78	12281100	51.78
14	15-Jul-03	51.07	51.9	50.48	51.3	16580100	51.3
15	14-Jul-03	49.15	51.07	49.05	50.35	12689600	50.35
16	11-Jul-03	48.66	48.9	47.38	47.9	7294100	47.9
17	10-Jul-03	48.77	49.05	48.27	48.62	7324600	48.62
18	9-Jul-03	49.35	49.84	48.49	49.24	7988800	49.24
19	8-Jul-03	48.96	49.69	48.52	49.5	9604900	49.5
20	7-Jul-03	47.18	49.62	47.1	49.58	10376000	49.58
21	3-Jul-03	46.5	47.44	46.34	46.5	4200700	46.5
22	2-Jul-03	46.81	47.3	46.34	47.19	7298900	47.19
23	1-Jul-03	45.97	47.03	45.02	46.85	9367900	46.85
24	30-Jun-03	46.68	47.36	46.27	46.46	5895200	46.46
25	27-Jun-03	46.85	47.62	46.2	46.43	7141500	46.43
26	26-Jun-03	46.16	46.94	45.91	46.84	7079800	46.84
27	25-Jun-03	46	47.29	45.7	45.92	8419000	45.92
28	24-Jun-03	46.4	46.95	45.72	45.91	10389500	45.91
29	23-Jun-03	47.07	47.96	46.3	46.86	8437200	46.86
30	20-Jun-03	48.21	48.5	46.57	47.15	8797600	47.15
31	19-Jun-03	48.52	48.86	47.35	47.37	8538000	47.37
32	18-Jun-03	46.84	48.85	46.22	48.44	11461500	48.44
33	17-Jun-03	47.45	47.78	46.46	47.26	6948200	47.26
34	16-Jun-03	45.9	47.3	45.58	47.17	9719900	47.17
35	13-Jun-03	47.4	47.77	45.54	45.57	11580800	45.57
36	12-Jun-03	48.23	48.34	46.95	47.6	7549400	47.6
37	11-Jun-03	47.26	48.66	46.76	48.29	11178000	48.29
38	10-Jun-03	47.48	48.21	46.75	48.13	9921300	48.13
39	9-Jun-03	48.51	48.75	47.3	48	10042300	48
40	6-Jun-03	49.99	51.6	48.3	49.11	16083400	49.11
41	5-Jun-03	48.57	49.49	47.94	49.36	13186700	49.36
42	4-Jun-03	47.11	49.16	46.75	49.11	16340200	49.11
43	3-Jun-03	45.5	47.45	45.4	47.36	12991400	47.36
44	2-Jun-03	46.91	47.2	45.19	45.47	13215400	45.47

FIGURE 7.3 Data Highlighted

are having trouble, reference the spreadsheets located on the CD-ROM; however, I would highly recommend making sure you can build the spreadsheets yourself. Now that you know how to import historical prices into Excel, your analytical power has been substantially increased. We will get back to the spreadsheet in a little while, but first we will go over correlations.

CHAPTER 8

Understanding Correlations

Steven Price

A n investor looking to trade pairs may want a standardized method by which to compare the relationship between target stocks. Studying the recent spread or differential is one way to decide which stocks to play; however, knowing just how well correlated those equities are over time is a valuable tool that can contribute a historical perspective. Those that have shown a strong positive correlation over some historical period are more likely to do so in the future. Knowing this correlation may also open up a world of trading possibilities beyond simply stocks in related industries. For example, if a trader knew that two stocks were close to 100 percent correlated, would it matter whether one was American Airlines and the other was Wal-Mart? Probably not. What would matter is that those stocks, in addition to following other guidelines highlighted in this text, were also strongly matched with one another.

The mathematical calculation used by many fund managers as a risk management tool is the correlation coefficient. When a fund manager is looking for diversification, therefore reducing risk, he or she sometimes looks for stocks that are not closely correlated. This helps to ensure that a bad quarter for one of the fund's holdings can be offset by a good quarter for another holding. For a pairs trader, however, the reverse would be helpful. The more closely one stock is correlated to another, the more reliable is the movement in the same direction. The higher correlation also increases the

---

Note: If you find this chapter confusing, Chapter 9 simplifies the information using Excel; however, I highly recommend having a strong grasp of the correlation coefficient, as it is the foundation of pairs.

likelihood that a spread relationship will remain consistent and not break out beyond its historical value in opposing directions.

The correlation coefficient can be calculated on a spreadsheet, such as Excel (shown in the following chapter); however, an understanding of how it is measured will teach a trader just what he or she is looking at. We begin the search for a correlation coefficient by first looking at the activity of each individual stock.

The first measure we calculate is the variance, which is the square of the stock's standard deviation and a measure of how spread out the movement of the stock is. It is used as a measure of risk, but in our case, we will eventually use it as a standard of comparison between the two stocks. It is the measure of the stock's volatility from its mean, or expected return.

Let's say Stock A showed returns of 8 percent, 10 percent, 13 percent, and 17 percent over four periods. The first step in calculating the variance is to calculate the mean (μ) of these returns.

Step 1. $(\mu)_{\text{Stock A}} = \dfrac{8 + 10 + 13 + 17}{4} = 12$

The second step is to calculate the difference from the mean (return) in each period. In our example, this is:

Step 2. Calculate the deviation from the mean.

Period 1: $8 - 12 = -4$

Period 2: $10 - 12 = -2$

Period 3: $13 - 12 = 1$

Period 4: $17 - 12 = 5$

The first hint a trader can look for is the direction these values take. For instance, they move consistently from lowest (-4) to highest ($+5$), suggesting a consistently increasing return. This will be important when we begin to compare the two stocks.

For those unfamiliar with statistical analysis, the next step, which is to square the deviations, is done to avoid the canceling-out effect when attempting to define variance and standard deviation. If you look at the above values, you will notice that summing them will equal zero. Since we cannot divide zero by the number of terms in order to get an average deviation, we first square these values.

Step 3. Square the deviations.

$(-4)^2 = 16$

$(-2)^2 = 4$

$(1)^2 = 1$

$(5)^2 = 25$

We now sum these squared deviations and divide by the number of periods (n) minus one, or ($n - 1$). The reason we divide by ($n-1$), rather than (n), is to help get an unbiased estimator of variance and also because we cannot get the variance of a set of less than two numbers. This is the rule for sample data. For those traders who would like to delve further into this rule, a lesson in statistics is in order, which is beyond the scope of this text. However, for our purposes, we will simply follow the rule.

Step 4. Sum the squared deviations and divide by ($n-1$).

$$\text{Variance}_{\text{Stock A}} = \frac{16 + 4 + 1 + 25}{4 - 1} = \frac{46}{3} = 15.33$$

We now have the variance, but we will also need the standard deviation to eventually calculate the correlation coefficient. The standard deviation is the square root of the variance.

Step 5. Take the square root of the variance to calculate standard deviation.

$$\sqrt{15.33} = \text{Standard deviation}_{\text{Stock A}} = 3.92$$

We now have the basic mathematical components to calculate the correlation coefficient, but we need to first combine these to calculate the covariance between the returns. The covariance is the statistic that gives us a numerical value that tells us the actual correlation. It tells us if the target stocks are moving together, moving in opposite directions, or are unrelated. However, the covariance number is difficult to interpret, as it is inconsistent among stocks with different values. What does a covariance of 54 mean? What about −65? In general, a large positive number for covariance suggests that the stocks have a strong positive correlation (stocks that move in the same direction at the same time). A large negative number suggests a strong negative correlation (stocks that move in opposite directions in the same time period). Rather than trying to decipher the meaning of different covariance numbers that are based on differently priced stocks, we can convert that covariance term into a standardized value that applies to all pairs of stocks, known as the correlation coefficient.

In order to calculate the covariance, we subtract each return of Stock A from its mean, and then we subtract each corresponding return of Stock B from its mean and multiply the two values together. We then sum the resulting products and divide by ($n-1$). An example will make this clearer.

Rather than duplicate the same steps as above, assume the returns for Stock B are as follows: 1 percent, 2 percent, 4 percent, and 5 percent. This gives Stock B a mean (μ) of 3 percent, a variance of 3.33, and a standard deviation of 1.83.

Covariance Calculation

Returns

Period	A	B	$(A - \mu)$	$(B - \mu)$	$(A - \mu) \times (B - \mu)$
1	8	1	$8 - 12 = -4$	$1 - 3 = -2$	$-4 \times -2 = 8$
2	10	2	$10 - 12 = -2$	$2 - 3 = -1$	$-2 \times -1 = 2$
3	13	4	$13 - 12 = 1$	$4 - 3 = 1$	$1 \times 1 = 1$
4	17	5	$17 - 12 = 5$	$5 - 3 = 2$	$5 \times 2 = 10$
					Sum 21

Hint: Notice the difference in returns from stock B's mean also move from lowest to highest.

We take the sum of the products (21) and divide by $(n-1)$:

$$\text{Covariance of Stock A and Stock B: } \frac{21}{4 - 1} = 7$$

Now let's change some numbers around and look at another scenario. Suppose that instead of posting returns of 1 percent, 2 percent, 4 percent, and 5 percent in periods one through four, Stock B instead posted returns of 5 percent, 4 percent, 2 percent, and 1 percent in those four periods.

Period	A	B	$(A - \mu)$	$(B - \mu)$	$(A - \mu) \times (B - \mu)$
1	8	5	$8 - 12 = -4$	$5 - 3 = 2$	$-4 \times 2 = -8$
2	10	4	$10 - 12 = -2$	$4 - 3 = 1$	$-2 \times 1 = -2$
3	13	2	$13 - 12 = 1$	$2 - 3 = -1$	$1 \times -1 = -1$
4	17	1	$17 - 12 = 5$	$1 - 3 = -2$	$5 \times -2 = -10$
					Sum $= -21$

We take the sum of the products (-21) and divide by $(n-1)$:

$$\text{Covariance of Stock A and Stock B: } \frac{-21}{4 - 1} = -7$$

We can see that by reversing the order of the returns of Stock B, so that it declines as Stock A's returns increase, we get a negative covariance, implying stocks that move in opposite directions. Although we can see the difference in the direction of movement, it is difficult to know what exactly the values of 7 or -7 stand for in the world of all stocks.

The correlation coefficient standardizes this term to a value between 1 and -1. A correlation coefficient of -1 implies stocks that are perfectly negatively correlated, while a correlation coefficient of $+1$ implies stocks that are perfectly positively correlated. A correlation coefficient of zero implies no correlation. It is rare in the real world to find two stocks that have a perfect $+1$ or -1, but it is still much simpler to decipher a reading in this range than to decipher a reading of $+7$ versus a reading of $+26$.

The next step in the calculation is to divide the covariance term by the product of the standard deviations of the two stocks. In the case of the first distribution of Stocks A and B, we get:

$$\text{Correlation Coefficient: } \frac{7}{3.92 \times 1.83} = .976$$

In the second distribution, we get:

$$\text{Correlation Coefficient: } \frac{-7}{3.92 \times 1.83} = -.976$$

As you can see, the stocks that move in the same direction in terms of increasing returns have a high correlation coefficient $(+.976)$ close to $+1$. This would be true for stocks that also show an equivalent pattern of decreasing returns in the same periods. Instead of the variances in each period starting out negative (in relation to the mean) and turning positive at the same time, we would see these values begin positive (in relation to the mean) and turn negative in the same periods. Because we multiply these numbers together and then sum them, we will still get positive values for stocks moving in the same direction since multiplying two negatives gives us a positive number.

When we reverse the order of Stock B's returns to decrease as Stock A's returns increased, we end up with a correlation coefficient of $(-.976)$, which is close to a perfect negative correlation of -1.

Now let's try one more example. Instead of simply reversing the order of Stock B, let's use the same returns in no particular order. We'll assign values to the returns in periods one through four of 5 percent, 4 percent, 1 percent, and 2 percent. Let's go through the calculations once again.

Period	A	B	$(A - \mu)$	$(B - \mu)$	$(A - \mu) \times (B - \mu)$
1	8	5	$8 - 12 = -4$	$5 - 3 = -2$	$-4 \times -2 = 8$
2	10	4	$10 - 12 = -2$	$4 - 3 = 1$	$-2 \times 1 = -2$
3	13	1	$13 - 12 = 1$	$1 - 3 = -2$	$1 \times -2 = -2$
4	17	2	$17 - 12 = 5$	$2 - 3 = -1$	$5 \times -1 = -5$
					Sum $= -1$

By placing the returns from Stock B in no particular order compared to Stock A, we now get the following covariance and correlation coefficient.

$$\text{Covariance of Stock A and Stock B: } \frac{-1}{4-1} = -.333$$

$$\text{Correlation coefficient: } \frac{-.333}{3.92 \times 1.83} = -.05$$

As you can see, a number close to zero indicates very little correlation at all between the two stocks. This can be seen in the returns, where Stock A's returns are increasing and Stock B's returns first decrease, then increase, but show little similarity to Stock A.

Now let's say you were analyzing groups of stocks for the possibility of trading them in pairs and you got the preceding results of .976, −.976, or −.05 for your correlation coefficients of various comparisons. Which pair of stocks would you be more likely to choose, all else being equal? The high correlation of .976 would indicate that these two stocks are highly correlated with one another and that a temporary move in the spread between the two beyond historical values is more likely to correct itself than for either of the other two combinations.

A strong negative correlation might indicate that two stocks which are currently moving in the same direction could be due for divergence. In this case, the correlation coefficient would suggest that over the period of time for which you have collected data the stocks moved in opposite directions. If they have now converged, it may be an opportunity to trade the two on the expansion away from this convergence. Stocks that might exhibit this type of relationship could be gold stocks and banking stocks, which tend to move in opposite directions based on the strength of the economy.

One of the biggest factors to consider when calculating this coefficient is the time period and frequency of the sample data. If a trader is taking only quarterly results, the coefficient will measure only the end point at which these stocks finish four times per year. This would certainly allow for a great deal of movement in the interim periods and could be very costly for a trader with a rather short time horizon. Daily data is more accurate; however, it is also very labor intensive to compile and may show more extreme fluctuation than two stocks have exhibited over time, depending on the time period that is chosen. For instance, a trader who chooses a single month's worth of daily closing prices for his or her data sample may end up with a skewed picture of the relationship between two companies. If Stock A releases earnings mid-month and Stock B experiences little movement that month, the picture may be misleading.

The best way to address time and frequency of data sample collection would be for a trader to define the time horizon of his proposed trade and then pick a reasonable frequency by which to measure the two stocks' returns. The next step would be to go back far enough in time to smooth out the results of outlying blips in the data stream. If a trader is looking at a quarterly time horizon, he may want to take weekly data and go back 5 to 10 years to get an idea of just how correlated the stocks are. If a trader is looking at a time horizon of just a few days for his trade, it will be difficult to get a reliable coefficient; however, looking at daily data for the past few months may be more appropriate. The idea is to match time horizons and then extend back far enough historically to get a reliable number.

As mentioned earlier, the calculation for correlation coefficient can be done quickly and easily on Excel or another statistical program. However, a thorough understanding of how this is calculated can give a trader a better understanding of the data he is seeing and the ability to "eyeball" a set of returns . . . and get an idea ahead of time, whether he has found candidates for his pairs trading strategy before spending the time to enter the data.

CHAPTER 9

Correlation Simplified

What Is a Correlation?
Where to Find Correlations
Building a Correlation
Using Excel

WHAT IS A CORRELATION?

As previously explained, the correlation is the glue that holds a pair together. On a commonsense level, we might expect ExxonMobil (NYSE: XOM) and ChevronTexaco (NYSE: CVX) to have a higher correlation than ExxonMobil and Microsoft (NASDAQ: MSFT). Why you ask? Exxon and Chevron are both major oil and gas integration and refinery companies, while Microsoft is the root of all evil, er, um, sorry, I mean Microsoft is a software company. (Really, just kidding there.) All right, back on track, the main principle here is that comparable business models have higher correlations. Although there are a few exceptions, most companies will have the highest correlations with similar companies in their respective sectors; that is, trucking stocks will closely follow trucking stocks, while insurance stocks may faithfully pursue other insurance stocks.

WHERE TO FIND CORRELATIONS

While I highly recommend working through the previous chapter, I also have a shortcut. First, if you are willing to pay for data, the best resource available is *http://www.market-topology.com*. This site has already neatly mapped out the correlations for not only U.S. markets, but foreign markets as well. I am not completely sure what time periods market-topology.com is using for its correlation data, though I have noticed that the correlation numbers are identical to those retrieved on a Bloomberg terminal.

If you have access to a Bloomberg terminal (cost: around $1,400 per month), the command to find historical spread information along with correlation numbers is: Ticker EQUITY Ticker EQUITY HS GO. Using actual company tickers, the historical spread function would be entered as XOM EQUITY CVX EQUITY GO. Then, once the historical spread screen is displayed, hit "2" GO; you will then see the correlation number on the lower left-hand corner of the screen. Because Bloomberg never seems to change, I have a feeling that this spread command will be accurate for several years to come. (That's a good thing.) But what if you don't want to pay for the correlation data or do not have access to a Bloomberg terminal? No problem, we can build our own using an Excel spreadsheet.

BUILDING A CORRELATION USING EXCEL

Using the spreadsheet that we already created, the Excel syntax for calculating correlations is CORREL. Let's walk through how to calculate the aforementioned relationship.

A brief explanation of Excel syntax is needed before we go too far. Anytime you are putting a mathematical formula in a cell, if you click in the chosen cell, you will then see the label bar activated on the top of the screen. You can type the formula in either the actual chosen cell or the formula field at the top of the screen. Excel reads figures as a mathematical formula only if there is an equal sign (=) at the beginning of the syntax. After the equal sign, verbal functions must then come first before any actual cell values or mathematical equations. As an example of a verbal Excel function, when we type in *AVERAGE* before our designated numbers, the spreadsheet will know to automatically total all numbers in the specified period and divide by the total amount of cells read. After the function comes the actual math syntax. In general, Excel reads math much like college algebra. For example, *[A1 + (A1*B1)]* would mean that the spreadsheet would first multiply A1 and B1 and then add cell A1. When we put in syntax such as *=AVERAGE (A1:A100)*, we are asking Excel to return the mean of all cells summed from A1 to A100. If you find yourself confused at any time, simply click on the Help option on the toolbar and select the first option Microsoft Excel Help. You can type in key words like *standard deviation*, and Excel will bring up several options of topics to choose from.

Step 1. In cell A3 on the Main page, type in: Close Correlation. You will notice that the text we have just typed overlaps into cell B3. To separate

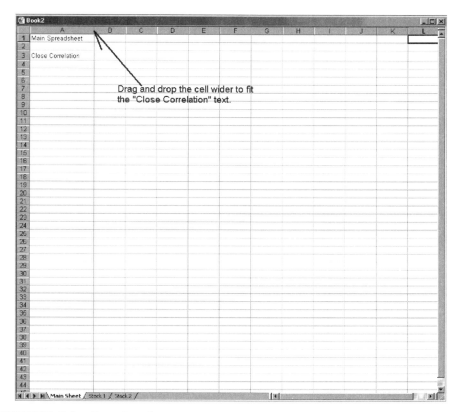

FIGURE 9.1 Close Correlation

cell B3, grab the cell divider on the top of the screen and widen the cell so that the text "Close Correlation" is only in cell A3 (see Figure 9.1).

Step 2. Highlight cell B3 and type =CORREL('Stock 1'!E2:E190,'Stock 2'!E2:E190). What we are asking Excel to do is to go into the Stock 1 spreadsheet and compare all the closing data to the closing data in the Stock 2 spreadsheet. (Notice that the syntax for making a formula in one spreadsheet look in another spreadsheet is denoted as 'Stock 1'!E2:E190.) Our resulting study has now allowed us to see that the correlation between Novellus (NASDAQ: NVLS) and KLA-Tencor (NASDAQ: KLAC) for our given time period is +.82! (As an arbitrary number, we are using only 188 days of data, just to make our initial analysis a little easier.) This is a very high correlation and denotes that our pair definitely has a tradable relationship. What this *does not* mean is that the pair will *always* diverge and converge. Even though our present data indicates that the two stocks have historically (in the period we measured) traded very similar to one another, the pair could still fall apart at any moment in the future. How? As we very well know, the semiconductor market is extremely fickle, with technology continually shaping how chip makers do business. Both Novellus and KLA-Tencor face technology risk, research risk, political risk, event risk, market risk, and generally just about any other type of risk we can think of. Thus, if one company finds itself the unfortunate recipient of (just for the sake of example) geographical risk, the pair could quickly blow up. For example, several semiconductor companies found themselves under the scrutiny of bears when the SARS outbreak in 2003 caused several domestic chip makers to halt production in Asian countries. If the correlation is true to its nature, then the two stocks will come back together once the geographical problem has been fixed. However, there is always the chance that whatever

FIGURE 9.2 Spreadsheet Example of Correlations

event drove the two stocks apart in the first place has now altered the business models to a point where the correlation will begin to break down.

Next, we will take a look at the daily change correlation to see how accurately the two stocks trade together on an end-of-day change basis. To do this, we will first need to set up a column to calculate each day's change from the previous session.

Using Excel:

Step 1. In the sheet Stock 1, label cell H1: Change.

Step 2. In cell H2, put in the formula: =G2-G3. This will calculate the change between the present day's closing price and the closing price of the previous day.

Step 3. Repeat for Stock 2.

Step 4. Once you have the changes in each cell, you will need to make sure that *all* the cells in column H have the same formulas. To do this, simply highlight cell H2 and press Control C (Command C for Mac users). Once you have done this, highlight (using your mouse) all of the cells vertically in column H starting with cell H3 to the bottom of the sheet—or at least to the bottom of the data. Press Control V (Command V for Mac users). This should paste the change formula respectively into each cell.

Step 5. In the main sheet, in cell A4, type in: Change Correlation. Then in cell B4, add: =CORREL('Stock 1'!H2:H190,'Stock 2'!H2:H190). This will

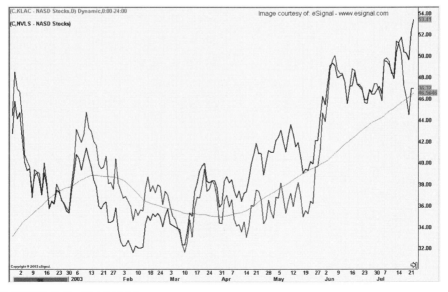

FIGURE 9.3 KLAC-NVLS

calculate the correlation of the day-to-day change between the two stocks. Figure 9.2 shows what your spreadsheet should now look like. If you prefer all the data from our time range, you can put in =CORREL ('Stock 1'!H2:H397, 'Stock 2'ᶜH2:H397). However, in the first CORREL example under Step 5 we are using much less data, again, just for the ease of analysis.

So what does this data mean? What these two correlations are telling us is that most likely KLAC/NVLS is a very viable pair to trade. Why?

First, the actual correlation between the two stock prices is (rounded) 0.82, and the change correlation is 0.90 for the period of our study. If the change correlation has a higher value than the EOD correlation, then we know that the two stocks are not only a good pair to trade on an EOD basis, but will also have some intraday opportunity as well. You can see that our correlation data has given us some food for thought.

Given the high correlation of our two stocks, we can also infer that the charts of the two stocks should look extremely similar. Figure 9.3 demonstrates exactly that. Take a close look and you will see that there is a remarkable similarity between the two. I'm not sure about you, but I smell opportunity here. When two stocks have a distinct relationship, then the "rubber band" theory is clearly in effect.

CHAPTER 10

Understanding Stock Correlations in Relation to Indices

Why an Index?
What Is Beta?
How to Apply Beta
Where to Find Beta

WHY AN INDEX?

In Chapter 1, I mentioned that an index is similar to a highway running through a small town. More than likely, many of the smaller roads in a town will parallel the larger road's general direction. This causes city planners to rethink the development of newer suburbs in an effort to make the city's streets congruous with the larger, immobile interstate. This principle is witnessed in the market, as investors realize that they are less able to have an impact on a large index, than on a single stock. Thus, as investors, we are forced to base our decisions (the planning of our portfolio development) in accordance with the greater direction of the corresponding index. Investors may then find information regarding a stock's movement within an index by using beta.

WHAT IS BETA?

Beta is the measurement of a stock's volatility in relation to a larger index, usually the Standard & Poor's (S&P) 500. Moreover, beta is said to be a measurement of market risk. Investopedia.com defines *risk* as: "The chance that an investment's actual return will be different than expected. This includes the possibility of losing some or all of the original investment. It is usually measured using the historical returns or average returns for a specific investment." Investorwords.com defines *market risk* as: "Risk which is common to an entire class of assets or liabilities. The value of investments may decline over a given time period simply because of economic changes or other events that impact large portions of the market. Asset allocation and diversification can protect against market risk because different portions of the market tend to under-perform at different times. This is also called systematic risk." In general, the S&P 500 is said to have a beta of +1; thus, any stock with a beta of greater than 1 should (in theory) have greater volatility than the broader market. In brief, the greater a stock's beta, the more amplified its price movement will be compared to the S&P 500, and the more market risk a security may face. For example, a stock with a beta of +1 would likely have percentage moves similar to the S&P 500. However, a stock with a beta of +1.5 would increase 50 percent when the S&P 500 was up 25 percent. The key in comparing beta is to understand that percentage moves are the great equalizer. Thus, even though the daily change in the Dow may be +200 points and the daily change for Microsoft may only be +1.3 points, if the percentage moves are similar, then the beta correlation will likely be near +1.

HOW TO APPLY BETA

If we look at Microsoft and Oracle, we know that there is a definite relationship between the two companies. The correlation coefficient displays a relationship of +0.82. The relationship discovered when looking on Yahoo.com is that Microsoft has a beta of 1.74, while Oracle has a beta of 1.88. Both stocks have high betas compared to the S&P 500! Taking this one step further, if we run a correlation study on both Microsoft and Oracle separately against the S&P 500, we end up with 0.87 and 0.66, respectively. These numbers validate our thoughts on beta, as the lesser-correlated Oracle has a higher beta, thus indicating greater volatility compared to everyday movements of the S&P 500. No matter how you slice it, though, because Microsoft and Oracle both have betas above 1, they are both more volatile than the S&P 500. For example, if S&P 500 moves (random number for the sake of argument) 0.03 percent in one day, Oracle should (in theory) close 1.88 times (on a percentage basis) above the closing price of the S&P 500. However, given that day-to-day order flow and news events can cause stocks to trade more erratically than the indices, the beta measure of intraday volatility does not always work. In fact, it's probably a good idea to never

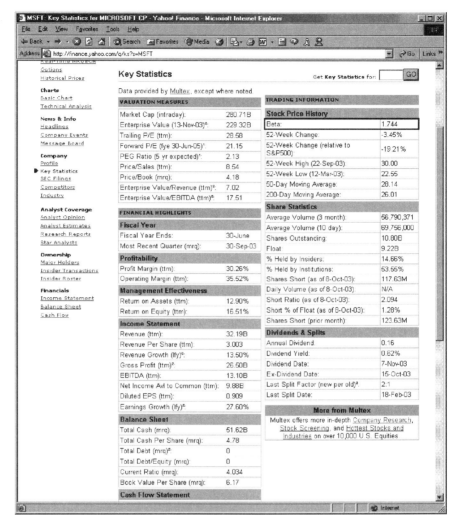

FIGURE 10.1 Yahoo.com and Beta

institute this theory in an actual trading system without some other type of data to improve the trading theory. And in the context above, that is exactly what it is—a theory. While it does not work very well by itself in reality, it is important to understand.

WHERE TO FIND BETA

Figure 10.1 displays the same Yahoo.com Key Statistics page that we looked at in Chapter 3. Beta is the first item down in the far right column.

CHAPTER 11

Basic Statistics

Frequency Distribution
Mean/Median/Mode
Mean Deviation
Variance
Standard Deviation

A lthough some statistics were discussed in Chapter 8, it is important enough to delve a little deeper into. A basic understanding of statistics will be the second layer of our pairs foundation, on which we build our knowledge. So what is statistics? Statistics is the study of numerical data in an attempt to find systematic patterns. Hyperdictionary.com defines *statistics* as: "The practice, study or result of the application of mathematical functions to collections of data in order to summarize or extrapolate that data." As a result, we will be using simple descriptive statistics in an effort to uncover reliable pairs data in hopes of finding possible trading patterns.

FREQUENCY DISTRIBUTION

To begin our tour in statistics, we will look at a frequency distribution, which is basically a table in which all data has been grouped in specific classes called categories. The frequency distribution has nonoverlapping data that can be seen and analyzed.

The following steps show how to create a frequency distribution:

Step 1. Define the classes in which the data will be sorted. A class is a level of prices that have definite upper and lower limits that do not overlap with other levels. This principle is known as making prices mutually exclusive, so they cannot show up in two separate classes.

Step 2. Assign the observations (stock prices) to their classes. Once all the prices are assigned to their respective classes, we may then find the midpoint for further data analysis. For the midpoint, subtract the lowest value of all classes from the highest value.

Step 3. Count the number of observations in each class.

How do we define the classes? When we have the total amount of observations in the entire population, we will attempt to find out what our class interval is. A class interval is the total distance from the smallest to largest values in any one class. To pick the size of the class interval, use this formula: Class interval = (Highest value − Lowest value) / Number of classes. But how many classes are there? To find the total number of classes, we will use the formula: $2^k \geq n$. In the aforementioned equation, k stands for the power to which 2 is raised and is the *smallest* integer that is greater than n, otherwise known as the total amount of observations. Hence, in a data set with 100 prices, our class size would be 7. This is because $2^6 - 64$ is less than 100, while $2^7 = 128$, which is greater than 100. We would then have seven total classes. Next, using our previous formula, we would then have Class interval = (100 − 1) / 7, which equals 14.14, or simply 14.

Setting up a frequency distribution allows us to actually see the pattern of the data we are analyzing. Let's construct a frequency distribution with the following closing prices: 5, 4, 6, 8, 12, 5, 6, 4, 9.

First, we have nine total observations. Thus, we find that k = 4, as $2^4 = 16$, and is the smallest integer equaling a sum greater than 9. Now, we know that we have four classes. To figure out the intervals within the four classes, we would use: (12 − 4) / 4, which equals 2. As a result, our classes and observations are:

4 − 5	4
6 − 7	2
7 − 8	1
8 − 9+	3

Using the frequency table that we have just created, we can then visually see how our data is skewed. The actual visual representation is called a histogram and is represented as a line that looks like an upside-down "U" on a chart. By skewed I mean what type of curve the data presents. Normal data is said to be "bell shaped" with the mean, median, and mode all in the center of the curve. A normal curve is a perfect upside-down U. Skewed data looks like a U stretched either to the right or left, and represents that there are more (or more extreme) values on one side of the data set. (EN 11.1)

MEAN/MEDIAN/MODE

Studying the mean, median, and mode, we will find basic relationships of where our pair has been trading.

- *Arithmetic mean*: The sum of all values divided by the total of all values, otherwise known as the average. Initially, we will be using only the arithmetic mean for our analysis.
- *Median*: The midpoint of all data when it is arranged in numerical order. For example, for four different closing prices of: $27, $28, $32, and $33, the median would be $30.
- *Mode*: The number in the data set that appears most frequently. In the set of closing prices: $23, $23, $23, $27, $45, $68, the mode is $23.

MEAN DEVIATION

The mean deviation and standard deviation are both measurements of dispersion that are meant to depict how the data is spread within a population. (By population, I am referring to all of the data we have to work with, not a select group within, which is known as a sample.) The mean deviation (also known as mean absolute deviation [MAD]) is an average of the absolute values of the deviations from the arithmetic mean. All deviations from the mean are in percentages and equal zero. Thus, the mean deviation only uses absolute values to get around the "zeroing out" problem.

To put this in mathematical terms, using the above numbers we can calculate the mean deviation from the average stock price. Our prices are $23, $23, $23, $27, $45, $68. Our mean or average price is $34.83.

To calculate the mean deviation, we subtract the mean from each value, sum the values and then divide by the total number of original observations.

VARIANCE

The variance is the mean of the squared deviations from the mean. The reason that we square the deviations is that when the numbers are not squared, the total of all deviations equals zero. By squaring the deviations, we then have positive numbers to work with. Don't worry too much about variance, as we will not be using it; however, just for the math buffs, Figure 11.1 shows the formula for a population variance. For sample variance look at Figure 11.2.

$$\frac{n \sum x^2 - \left(\sum x\right)^2}{n^2}$$

FIGURE 11.1 Population Variance

$$\frac{n \sum x^2 - \left(\sum x\right)^2}{n(n-1)}$$

FIGURE 11.2 Sample Variance

STANDARD DEVIATION

One step further is the standard deviation, which is the probability of deviation known as the square root of variance. In layman's terms, the standard deviation allows us to measure the data observations from the entire population, and map them in regard to the statistical mean. The actual formula for a population standard deviation is shown in Figure 11.3. For a sample standard deviation see Figure 11.4. Don't worry, we will let Excel do our calculations for us, however, for the time being it is important to understand what a standard deviation is.

How is the data measured? The empirical rule states that in a normal distribution:

- 68 percent of the data will rest within +/− one standard deviation of the mean.
- 95 percent of the data will lie within +/− two standard deviations of the mean.
- 99.7 percent of the data will sit within +/− three standard deviations of the mean.

Thus, once the standard deviation for a data set is known, the range that the data should fall within can be measured. Using the same prices—$23, $23, $23, $27, $45, $68—we know that the mean is $34.83. By plugging

$$\sqrt{\frac{n \sum x^2 - \left(\sum x \right)^2}{n^2}}$$

FIGURE 11.3 Population Standard Deviation

$$\sqrt{\frac{n \sum x^2 - \left(\sum x \right)^2}{n(n-1)}}$$

FIGURE 11.4 Sample Standard Deviation

the numbers into our formula for a population standard deviation, we come up with a population standard deviation of 18.36. What does this mean? The empirical rule would state that 68.3 percent of all prices reside within one standard deviation of the mean. Thus, 68.3 percent of all prices lye within one standard deviation of $34.83. If one standard deviation equals 18.36, then 68.3 percent of all prices should rest between $16.47 and $53.19. (Simply the standard deviation added and subtracted from the mean.) Our logic may then follow that 95 percent of the prices are situated within $0 (the value is zero, as stock prices cannot be negative) and $71.55. If we lived in a vacuum of pure statistics, we could then buy the stock any time the price traded near $0 or short sell it when the price nears $71.55. Although obviously the market is not quite that simple, you can still see that this is getting exciting!

So now you're sitting there saying "All right bub, enough of this statistics stuff, just show me how it works—show me the money." Before we begin, I would like to go over the following 10 statistical principals, just kidding, had you going there for a second. Instead, we'll now take the basic statistical information that we have and put it into practice with Excel.

CHAPTER 12

Excel and Statistics

Setting Up the Spreadsheet
Average, Median, Mode, and
Standard Deviation
Understanding the Present Data
How Do You Know Which Stock
to Buy or Short?
Charting the Data

SETTING UP THE SPREADSHEET

All right, back to our trusty spreadsheet! At this point we should already have data imported into our spreadsheet, so now we just need to begin applying our basic statistical functions to commence analyzing our pair.

Step 1. Bring up your spreadsheet and label cell A8 Mean, A9 Median, and A10 Mode. Then label B6 Differential, C6 Ratio, D6 Closing, and D7 Spread.

Step 2. Label cell A12 Average Deviation, A13 Standard Deviation, and A14 Population Standard Deviation.

Step 3. Right click on the Stock 1 spreadsheet tab and then insert a new worksheet. Label the worksheet Pair Data.

Step 4. In the Pair Data worksheet, label cell A1 Pair Data, then label the following cells: A4 Date, B4 Differential, C4 Ratio, and D4 Close Spread. (You may have to widen the cells, via drag and drop, to fit the text.)

Step 5. Next, click in cell A5 and hit the = key. Then, click on the Stock 1 worksheet tab, click once in cell A2, and hit Enter. What we have done is asked the Pair Data sheet cell A5 to always correspond the first date in the sheet with that of Stock 1. And because we will update the data in the Stock 1 sheet sometime in the future, we want the dates and data in the Main Sheet and Pair Data sheet to automatically update themselves. Next, copy and paste the Pair Data cell A5 all the way down the A column to cell A195. If you are using all of the data, then paste the data all the way through cell A400.

Step 6. Type in the following formulas in each corresponding cell:

B5: =('Stock 1'!E2-'Stock 2'!E2)

C5: =('Stock 1'!E2/'Stock 2'!E2)

D5: =('Stock 1'!H2-'Stock 2'!H2)

Step 7. Highlight cells B5, C5, and D5; then press Control C (Command C for Mac users) to copy.

Step 8. Using your mouse, highlight cells B6, C6, and D6 all the way through cells B400, C400, and D400; then press Control V (Command V

	A	B	C	D	E	F	G	H	I	J	K
1											
2											
3				Close							
4	Date	Differential	Ratio	Spread							
5	31-Jul-03	15.85	1.442737	-0.64							
6	30-Jul-03	16.49	1.474669	-0.68							
7	29-Jul-03	17.17	1.487369	0.44							
8	28-Jul-03	16.73	1.458105	0.33							
9	25-Jul-03	16.4	1.45505	0.17							
10	24-Jul-03	16.23	1.452089	-0.86							
11	23-Jul-03	17.09	1.47054	1.1							
12	22-Jul-03	15.99	1.440375	0.88							
13	21-Jul-03	15.11	1.437337	0.54							
14	18-Jul-03	14.57	1.408123	0.67							
15	17-Jul-03	13.9	1.380822	0.73							
16	16-Jul-03	13.17	1.341103	1.22							
17	15-Jul-03	11.95	1.303685	1.11							
18	14-Jul-03	10.84	1.274361	0.26							
19	11-Jul-03	10.58	1.283494	-0.72							
20	10-Jul-03	11.3	1.302787	0.21							
21	9-Jul-03	11.09	1.290695	-0.04							
22	8-Jul-03	11.13	1.29007	-0.21							
23	7-Jul-03	11.34	1.296548	0.26							
24	3-Jul-03	11.08	1.312818	0.03							
25	2-Jul-03	11.05	1.305755	0.81							
26	1-Jul-03	10.24	1.279705	0.43							
27	30-Jun-03	9.81	1.267667	-0.55							
28	27-Jun-03	10.36	1.287219	-0.2							
29	26-Jun-03	10.56	1.291069	-0.06							
30	25-Jun-03	10.62	1.30085	0.09							
31	24-Jun-03	10.53	1.297626	0.02							
32	23-Jun-03	10.51	1.289133	-0.07							
33	20-Jun-03	10.58	1.289308	-0.18							
34	19-Jun-03	10.76	1.293909	-0.14							
35	18-Jun-03	10.9	1.290357	1.28							
36	17-Jun-03	9.62	1.255579	-1.12							
37	16-Jun-03	10.74	1.294812	0.46							

Main Sheet / Pair Data / Stock 1 / Stock 2 /

FIGURE 12.1 Pairs Data Spreadsheet

for Mac users) to paste the data from Step 7 into all of the highlighted cells. You have now not only imported data into an Excel spreadsheet, but you have also begun your analysis! Figure 12.1 shows an example of what your Pair Data sheet should look like when you have completed Step 8.

A few quick Excel tips: If you prefer using the keyboard over your mouse, you can highlight cells B6, C6, and D6, then hold the shift key down and press the down arrow key. The three columns of cells will highlight all other cells in the three columns as you continue pressing the down arrow key. To highlight entire pages of cells, highlight cells B5, C5, and D5, then hold the shift key down and press the end key. Finally, if you highlight cells B6, C6, and D6, then scroll down in the spreadsheet without clicking on another cell, you can then hold down the Control and Shift keys while clicking on cells B400, C400, and D400. As a result, all cells between B5 through D400 should then be highlighted. Use these functions as shortcuts to copy and paste data between Excel spreadsheets.

AVERAGE, MEDIAN, MODE, AND STANDARD DEVIATION

Now that we have our Pairs Data spreadsheet formatted, let's put some simple descriptive statistics into our Main spreadsheet. The Main spreadsheet should be all ready to go, but double-check it using Figure 12.2, just to be sure.

Excel is straightforward in the use of terminology, so there shouldn't be much confusion. Here are the Excel commands that we will use and a brief explanation of each:

- *AVERAGE*: Returns the average (arithmetic mean) of the data.
- *MEDIAN*: Returns the median of the given numbers. The median is the number in the middle of a set of numbers; that is, half the numbers have values that are greater than the median, and half have values that are less.
- *MODE*: Returns the most frequently occurring, or repetitive, value in an array or range of data. Like MEDIAN, MODE is a location measure.
- *AVDEV*: Returns the average of the absolute deviations of data points from their mean. AVEDEV is a measure of the variability in a data set.
- *STDEV*: Estimates standard deviation based on a sample. The standard deviation is a measure of how widely values are dispersed from the average value (the mean).
- *STDEVP*: Calculates standard deviation based on the entire population given as arguments. The standard deviation is a measure of how widely values are dispersed from the average value (the mean).

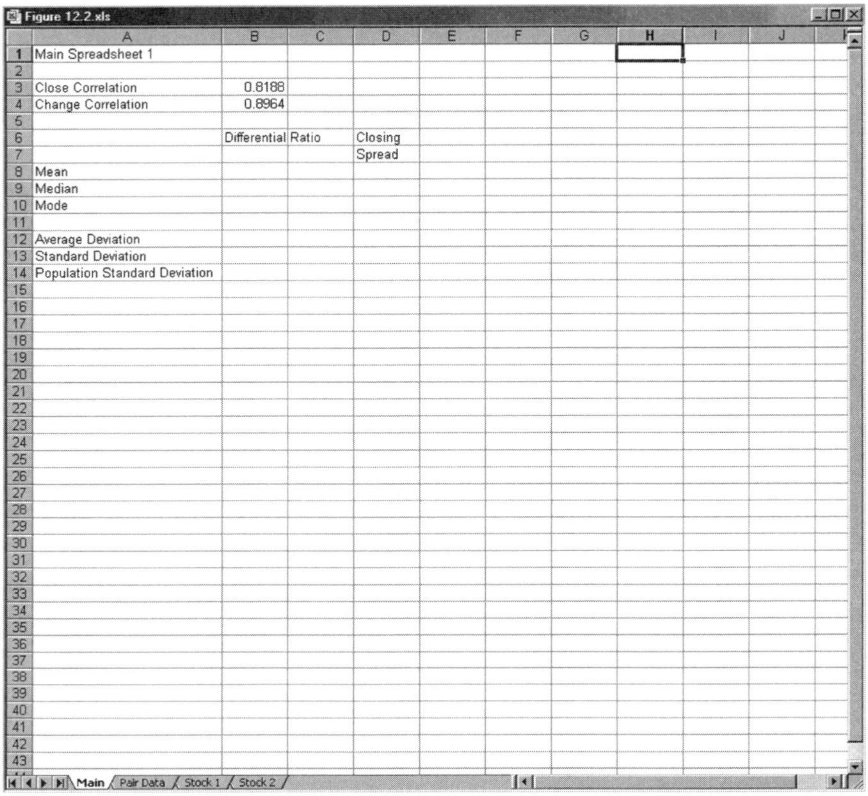

FIGURE 12.2 Main Spreadsheet

Now, let's plug in our actual Excel formulas in the Main sheet.

Step 1. In cells B8, B9, and B10, put in the formulas: =AVERAGE('Pair
Data'!$B$5:$B$195), =MEDIAN('Pair Data'!$B$5:$B$195), and
=MODE('Pair Data'!$B$5:$B$195). In cells C8, C9, and C10, type in:
=AVERAGE('Pair Data'!$C$5:$C$195), =MEDIAN('Pair
Data'!$C$5:$C$195), and =MODE('Pair Data'!$C$5:$C$195). (*Note:* Cell
C10 will return a N/A value; this is okay.) In cells D8, D9, and D10, enter:
=AVERAGE('Pair Data'!$D$5:$D$195), =MEDIAN('Pair
Data'!$D$5:$D$195), and =MODE('Pair Data'!$D$5:$D$195).

Step 2. In cells B12, B13, and B14, enter the following formulas,
respectively: =AVEDEV('Pair Data'!$B$5:$B$195), =STDEV('Pair
Data'!$B$5:$B$195), and =STDEVP('Pair Data'!$B$5:$B$195).

Step 3. In cells C12, C13, and C14, type in: =AVEDEV('Pair Data'!$C$5:$C$192), =STDEV('Pair Data'!$C$5:$C$192), and =STDEVP('Pair Data'!$C$5:$C$192).

Step 4. Finally, in cells D12, D13, and D14, type in: =AVEDEV('Pair Data'!$D$5:$D$192), =STDEV('Pair Data'!$D$5:$D$192), and =STDEVP('Pair Data'!$D$5:$D$192). (*Again, here you can make your data look all the way through the end of the worksheet if you wish to study a longer time period*).

At this point, we have some basic descriptive statistics entered into Excel, and we are beginning to paint a picture of what is happening within our pair. Follow these steps to see where the pair is:

Step 1. Label cell A18 Current Data, B19 Differential, C19 Ratio, D18 Closing, and D19 Spread.

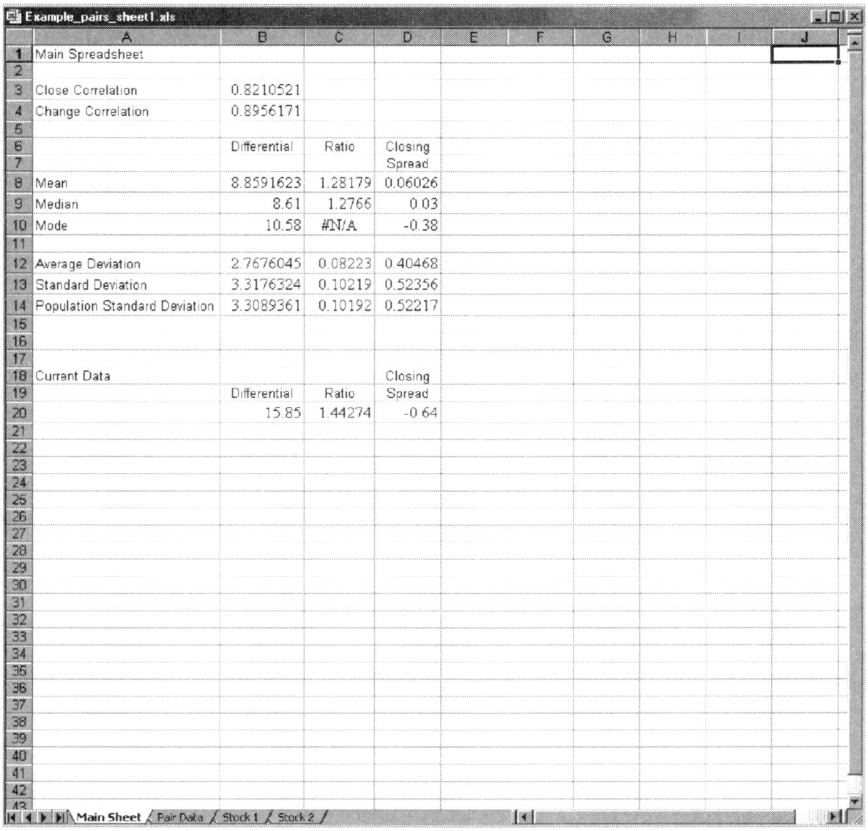

Example_pairs_sheet1.xls

	A	B	C	D
1	Main Spreadsheet			
2				
3	Close Correlation	0.8210521		
4	Change Correlation	0.8956171		
5				
6		Differential	Ratio	Closing
7				Spread
8	Mean	8.8591623	1.28179	0.06026
9	Median	8.61	1.2766	0.03
10	Mode	10.58	#N/A	-0.38
11				
12	Average Deviation	2.7676045	0.08223	0.40468
13	Standard Deviation	3.3176324	0.10219	0.52356
14	Population Standard Deviation	3.3089361	0.10192	0.52217
15				
16				
17				
18	Current Data			Closing
19		Differential	Ratio	Spread
20		15.85	1.44274	-0.64

Main Sheet / Pair Data / Stock 1 / Stock 2

FIGURE 12.3 Spreadsheet with Statistics

Step 2. In cell B20, put in: =('Pair Data'!B5); in C20, type: =('Pair Data'!C5); and in cell D20, enter: =('Pair Data'!D5)

Figure 12.3 shows what our spreadsheet should now look like.

UNDERSTANDING THE PRESENT DATA

Taking a brief moment to pause and understand the data that we have created, we can begin to see where our pair is headed. First, as we know from our Main page, the mean of the differential is 8.86, denoting that during the period we have studied, the two stocks traded (on average) 9 points apart. The data that we are studying goes back just under 200 days, which equates to slightly under one year's worth of actual trading sessions. Next, the pair is (in the period studied) trading just over two standard deviations from the mean. Thus, the statistics are telling us that that 95 percent the data falls within our present range. If we were to actually trade based on the data, we would short KLAC and go long NVLS—though the data presented does *not* necessarily present a good trading situation.

HOW DO YOU KNOW WHICH STOCK TO BUY OR SHORT?

To explain buy and sell sides of a pair it may be a good idea to first paint a picture on our spreadsheet so that we may get a visual idea of what is happening. Taking a look at the Main spreadsheet, we should have our basic statistics already formatted. The sheet should include our two correlations; the mean, median, and mode for the differential; ratio and closing spread; and average deviation, standard deviation, and population standard deviation. Figure 12.3 depicts a picture of a formatted version of our present spreadsheet. Incidentally, at this point you can always use the disk in the back of the book to load this actual spreadsheet onto your computer.

To further understand buy and sell sides, our goal is to add/subtract three standard deviations on either side of the mean to see where the pair is in regard to the mean.

Step 1. As a picture tells a thousand words, label cells F6 through I7 as depicted in Figure 12.4.

Step 2. Copy cells B8, C8, and D8 into cells G11, H11, and I11.

Step 3. In cell G10, enter the following formula: =$G$11+$B$13, so that we have the mean plus one standard deviation. In cell G9, enter the formula

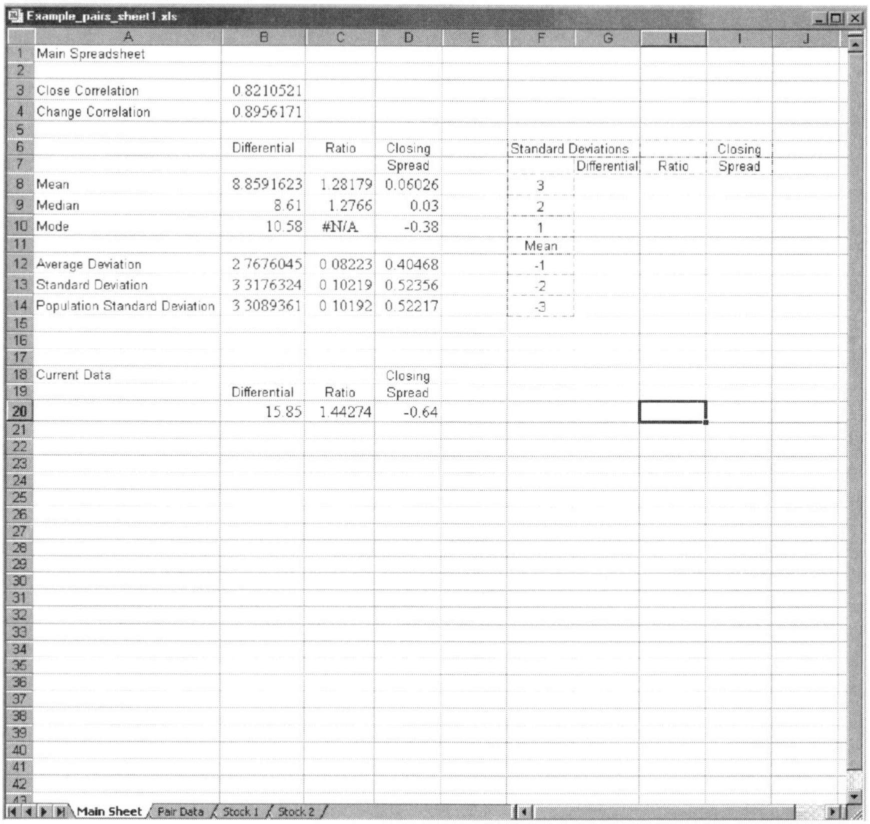

FIGURE 12.4 Spreadsheet Main Page

=$G$11+(2*$B$13). This gives us two standard deviations from the mean. In cell G8, do the same, except multiply cell B13 times three instead of two.

Step 4. Repeat steps 1 through 3 for all of the rest of the cells in this box, while remembering to subtract the standard deviation from the lower half of the cells. As a result, your standard deviations box should look similar to Figure 12.5. Keep in mind that columns G, H, and I are using the values from row 13 of B, C, and D. I know this is confusing, so you can always reference the spreadsheet in the CD-ROM. However, if you can struggle through this and build the sheet, you will only empower yourself later on.

It is important to always keep track of which stock came first in your data analysis. This is because when we refer to buying and selling a spread, we are assuming that there is a set structure for each of the equities involved. And indeed there is! Because KLAC comes first in our worksheets

Example_pairs_sheet1.xls

	A	B	C	D	E	F	G	H	I	J
1	Main Spreadsheet									
2										
3	Close Correlation	0.8210521								
4	Change Correlation	0.8956171								
5										
6		Differential	Ratio	Closing		Standard Deviations			Closing	
7				Spread			Differential	Ratio	Spread	
8	Mean	8.8591623	1.28179	0.06026		3	18.8121	1.588367	1.630942	
9	Median	8.61	1.2766	0.03		2	15.4944	1.486175	1.107382	
10	Mode	10.58	#N/A	-0.38		1	12.1768	1.383983	0.583822	
11						Mean	8.85916	1.28179	0.06026	
12	Average Deviation	2.7676045	0.08223	0.40468		-1	5.54153	1.383983	-0.4633	
13	Standard Deviation	3.3176324	0.10219	0.52356		-2	2.2239	1.077408	-0.98686	
14	Population Standard Deviation	3.3089361	0.10192	0.52217		-3	-1.0937	0.975216	-1.51042	
15										
16										
17										
18	Current Data			Closing						
19		Differential	Ratio	Spread						
20		15.85	1.44274	-0.64						

Main Sheet / Pair Data / Stock 1 / Stock 2

FIGURE 12.5 +/− 3 Standard Deviations in Spreadsheet

and all of our pairs calculations, the terms *buy* and *sell* will relate directly to KLAC. To be brief, when we refer to "buying or selling" a spread, we are making direct reference to the direction of the first stock in our pair. If the differential were above the mean, we would say "Sell the pair"; conversely, if the differential were below the mean, we would "buy the pair." Thus, as KLAC/NVLS is above the mean, we would refer to the pair as being on the "sell side." On a normal distribution, the buy side of the pair would be on the left of the mean, while the sell side of the pair would be on the right. In essence, the higher the value, or more overbought a pair is, the further up (or right) it would be on sell side of the statistical mean. Figure 12.6 displays the buy and sell side of the mean on our spreadsheet and in reference to the Gaussian curve.

At present, we may assume that the pair has made significant divergence over the last three months. How do we know that the pair has been diverging over the last three months? We can do one of two things to find this

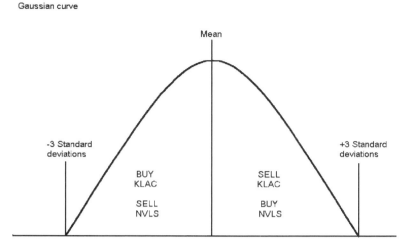

FIGURE 12.6 Buy/Sell Spreads and Gaussian Curve

information. First, we can look through the information on the Pair Data sheet, where our manual investigation will allow us to see the actual historical numbers diverging, or we can create a chart that will allow us to quickly decipher the present and historical trends.

CHARTING THE DATA

Follow these steps to chart the data:

Step 1. On the bottom of the spreadsheet, create a new worksheet (by right clicking on the spreadsheet tabs and then highlighting the "Insert" option) and label it Pairs Charts.

Step 2. In cell A2, key in the title Differential.

Step 3. Highlight cell A3, then click on the chart wizard icon on the top of the screen. Choose the B&W Line–Timescale chart under the Custom Types tab. Press Next.

Step 4. Click the Series tab on the top of the chart option screen, and then choose "Add" to insert the data to be charted—only if there is not a blue highlighted bar named Series to the left. If there is, disregard this step. (*Note*: If there is any other data already selected, delete it by highlighting the unwanted series and then clicking the Remove key.) Once the Series One data is highlighted, then label the data in the Name box as Differential Chart.

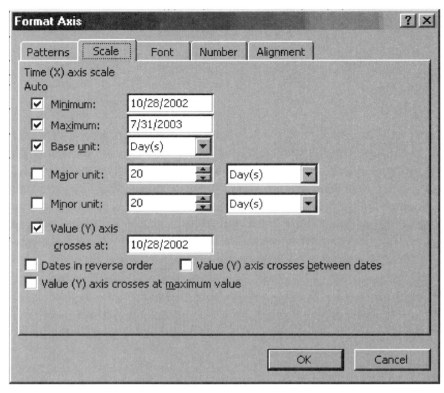

FIGURE 12.7   Format Axis Box

Step 5. In the Values field, either highlight the first 195 days of
differential data in the Pair Data spreadsheet, or type in ='Pair
Data'!$B$5:$B$400.

Step 6. On the bottom of the present chart wizard screen, you will see
another field titled Category (X) axis labels. In this field, enter the data
range that will correspond with the differential data within our new
chart. To do so, either highlight cells A3 through A195, or type in
='Stock 1'!$A$3:$A$397. Click Next, Next, and Finish to complete the
chart.

Step 7. From here you might need to resize and move your chart to get it
into place. To do so, highlight the entire chart and simply drag and drop
the borders into place.

Step 8. We might now need to reformat our X axis to make our dates
appear properly on the chart. On the lower portion of the chart, right
click on the date range, then select Format Axis. Under the Scale tab,
uncheck the Major Unit and Minor Unit boxes. Then, for the Major Unit

and Minor Unit boxes, replace the numerical value with 20. Figure 12.7 displays the box.

Step 9. Next, click on the Alignment tab at the top of the Format Axis screen. You will see a text orientation dial on the left portion of the screen. With your mouse, grab the actual dial and point it upward so that the text reads vertically from the bottom to top. You have just created your first pairs chart! Figure 12.8 displays how the new chart should appear in the spreadsheet.

Now we can visually see where the differential has been for the last year. What may jump out at us right away is that the differential has been expanding for quite some time. Then, if we hop over to the Pair Data sheet, we can see what the *actual* high value was for the period we see on the chart!

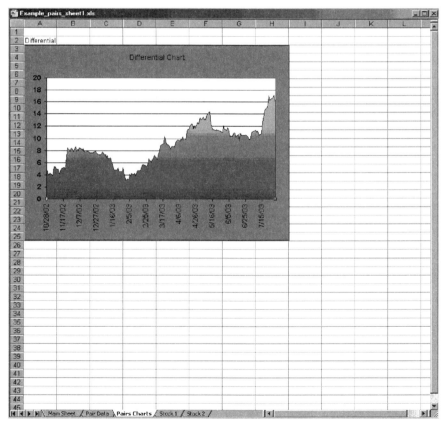

FIGURE 12.8 Differential Chart

The highest value for the differential was (for the period studied) on February 6th, 2002 (cell 377), when the two stocks were trading 18.04 points apart. Further scanning the data chronologically backwards, we can see that the spread hit a low of 3.19 on January 31, 2003. Thus, if history and statistics are any indication of what could happen in the future, we may deduce that the differential of 15.85 on July 31 may be nearing an actual trading point. One quick word of caution: Even though our initial data is pointing toward a nearing sell signal, we still have more work to do!

CHAPTER 13

Differential versus Ratio

Differential
Ratio

Before getting too far into analyzing the present data, I will take a moment and make sure that we have a full understanding of how we are gauging our pairs. We are presently using the two simplest methods: differential and ratio. Each has its own merit for the pairs analyst, though the bulk of the pairs community seems to prefer a ratio over the differential. In this book, we are mainly using the differential for the sake of simplicity, though as you begin to move further forward in pairs research, it may be a good idea to switch over to using a ratio. In the next few chapters, we quickly go over both in hope of grasping a deeper understanding of each method.

DIFFERENTIAL

First and foremost, it may be a good idea to simply use the differential as trend confirmation of the ratio. While the differential is useful in gauging where two stock prices are closing, it also lacks the ability to encompass valuation calculations like the ratio. Usually, when I am looking at a differential, I am only scanning a historical pairs chart to see just where the two stocks have traded in recent history. Generally, I can usually get a good idea where the visual mean is just by taking a moment to look over the chart. I do not want to discourage you entirely from using the differential as a way of reading your pairs data; however, there might be added benefits when using a ratio. For the purposes of this book, we will mainly concentrate on the differential, but will use the ratio as confirmation of our feelings.

RATIO

When using a ratio, we may obtain a better comprehension of the actual valuation of each stock. How is this so? If we use exterior data like earnings, beta, float, and dividends paid in our ratio calculation, the resulting number becomes more than simple division. For example, if one stock is trading at $100 and another at $50, the ratio is 2.0. This information indicates that for each single share of the $100 stock that we buy, we may want to purchase two shares of the lesser-valued security. On paper, the simple ratio appears to be a good idea, but unfortunately, we still leave out further valuation.

To get a better idea of how we could weight our pair, we can add in fundamental concepts to tweak our position valuation. For example, when adding volatility into our equation, we can divide each price by beta and then divide the results from one another. As an example, on any random date, suppose stock A is trading at $45, while stock B is trading at $60. Calculating a simple ratio (dividing Stock A by Stock B), we come up with 0.75. What this is telling us is that for every one share of the less expensive stock, we would purchase .75 shares of the more costly security. However, to measure Standard & Poor's (S&P) 500 volatility, we can add in the beta numbers to find an entirely new ratio. Assume that the beta for Stock A is 1.43, while the beta for Stock B is 1.62. Our new equation would be $[(45/1.43) / (60/1.60)]$, which equals 0.83. Remember that we are always using the denominator as the subject stock. Thus, incorporating volatility, we would actually purchase slightly more of Stock B than with the simple ratio division model.

CHAPTER 14

Applying Statistics to Pairs

Density Curve
Understanding the Data

Next, we will work on further breaking down our data, where we will attempt to zero the mean. This is the most important part of the book and will be the ultimate "trigger" for where we enter and exit our trades. Our goal is to try and pinpoint entry and exit points for our pair, while taking little pain and having tight stop loss points. The tool that we will use is called a density curve, the formula is shown in Figure 14.1.

DENSITY CURVE

By definition, a density curve is "the graph of a nonnegative function called a density function. The area between the graph of the function and the x axis is 1." Generally, normal density curves have many different functions, including characterizing probabilities; however, we will use it in a different fashion. A density curve looks similar to a bell curve, with the data evenly distributed around the mean. However, our curve will actually show up as more of a moving histogram, depicting where our current and historical differential or ratio are in regard to the mean. The density curve itself will yield a value between zero and positive one. Our buy signals will typically (though this changes from pair to pair) be triggered when the pair is within 0.003 thousandths of zero. Conversely, the density curve will indicate a potential selling point when our data nears 0.997 thousands of positive one. Let's set up the normal density curve in our spreadsheet.

$$f(x, \mu, \sigma) = \frac{1}{\sqrt{2\pi}\sigma} e^{-((x-\mu)^1/2\sigma^1)}$$

FIGURE 14.1 Normal Density

Step 1. In your Pairs Data spreadsheet, label cell E3 Density and E4 Curve.

Step 2. Then, we will need to import a little data from the Main sheet to make this work. This might get a little confusing, so I'll try and explain it very plainly. Click once in cell B1 of the Pair Data sheet. By doing this we have merely selected the cell.

Step 3. In cell B1, then hit the = (equal) key.

Step 4. Without hitting enter or clicking on another cell in the sheet, click on the Main sheet tab to revert to our first page. Click once in cell B8 to highlight the cell, and then hit Enter. The sheet should automatically flip back to the Pairs Data sheet, and the value in Main sheet B8 should now be in the B1 cell.

Step 5. Now, do the same for cell C1, except use the Main sheet cell B13 instead of B8.

Step 6. In cell E5, put in the formula =NORMDIST(B5,$B$1,$C$1,TRUE).

Step 7. Copy and paste the data through cell E400. Your Pairs Data sheet should mirror Figure 14.2.

Step 8. Add a graph of the data in the Pairs Charts spreadsheet.

As a quick explanation of the formula we have just entered into our spreadsheet, what we have done is entered three variables with a condition. We made the spreadsheet look for the first variable (our differential) chronologically through all 400 cells. The second and third variables are the mean and standard deviation from our Main spreadsheet.

What we are now discovering (as we visually look at our chart) is that the present value of the density curve is quite elevated, yielding 0.982. While this seems very high, it is not within the aforementioned 0.003 thousandths of positive one. Perhaps looking back through history will give us a better idea of why we are seeking such extreme values.

To do this accurately, we will need to look further back into history than just 400 days. Thus, go back to your spreadsheet and import 1,000 days of

	A	B	C	D	E	F	G	H	I	J
1	Pair Data	8.8591623	3.317632							
2										
3					Density					
4	Date	Differential	Ratio	Close Spread	Curve					
5	31-Jul-03	15.85	1.442737	-0.64	0.982449					
6	30-Jul-03	16.49	1.474669	-0.68	0.989278					
7	29-Jul-03	17.17	1.487369	0.44	0.993878					
8	28-Jul-03	16.73	1.458105	0.33	0.991164					
9	25-Jul-03	16.4	1.45505	0.17	0.988486					
10	24-Jul-03	16.23	1.452089	-0.86	0.986849					
11	23-Jul-03	17.09	1.47054	1.1	0.993448					
12	22-Jul-03	15.99	1.440375	0.88	0.984198					
13	21-Jul-03	15.11	1.437337	0.54	0.970226					
14	18-Jul-03	14.57	1.408123	0.67	0.957407					
15	17-Jul-03	13.9	1.380822	0.73	0.93567					
16	16-Jul-03	13.17	1.341103	1.22	0.903092					
17	15-Jul-03	11.95	1.303685	1.11	0.824239					
18	14-Jul-03	10.84	1.274361	0.26	0.724768					
19	11-Jul-03	10.58	1.283494	-0.72	0.698013					
20	10-Jul-03	11.3	1.302787	0.21	0.769049					
21	9-Jul-03	11.09	1.290695	-0.04	0.749341					
22	8-Jul-03	11.13	1.29007	-0.21	0.753163					
23	7-Jul-03	11.34	1.296548	0.26	0.772702					
24	3-Jul-03	11.08	1.312818	0.03	0.748381					
25	2-Jul-03	11.05	1.305755	0.81	0.745489					
26	1-Jul-03	10.24	1.279705	0.43	0.661372					
27	30-Jun-03	9.81	1.267667	-0.55	0.612791					
28	27-Jun-03	10.36	1.287219	-0.2	0.674503					
29	26-Jun-03	10.56	1.291069	-0.06	0.695908					
30	25-Jun-03	10.62	1.30085	0.09	0.702204					
31	24-Jun-03	10.53	1.297626	0.02	0.692737					
32	23-Jun-03	10.51	1.289133	-0.07	0.690615					
33	20-Jun-03	10.58	1.289308	-0.18	0.698013					
34	19-Jun-03	10.76	1.293909	-0.14	0.716661					
35	18-Jun-03	10.9	1.290357	1.28	0.730772					
36	17-Jun-03	9.62	1.255579	-1.12	0.590694					
37	16-Jun-03	10.74	1.294812	0.46	0.714616					

FIGURE 14.2 Pairs Data

data (up to July 31) for each stock. If you prefer not to take the time, you will find the worksheet on the CD-ROM labeled Example_pairs_sheet2.

Historically, we see that the density curve traded within 0.003 thousandths of one in February 2002. To be precise, the density curve hit a high of 0.997 on February 6. At the same time, our pair hit an almost exact near-term high of $18.04. What is truly remarkable about this data is that the spread did not diverge any further (during this time period) and then yielded a gain of 10 points over the next few months. What becomes even more amazing is that if you look farther back through the data to see if the pair ever yielded another buy or sell signal, we unearth more startling information.

In February 2002, the density curve hit 0.997 when the pair was trading 18.04 points apart. The following day, it collapsed to 0.995, with KLAC/NVLS converging to post a differential of 17.34. The gain equated to 70 cents, and the spread continued to buckle over the next month. By May, the differential had fallen to below 10. Farther down the road, the pair continued to decline all the way to just above 3 the following year. Clearly, the trade would have

Density Curve

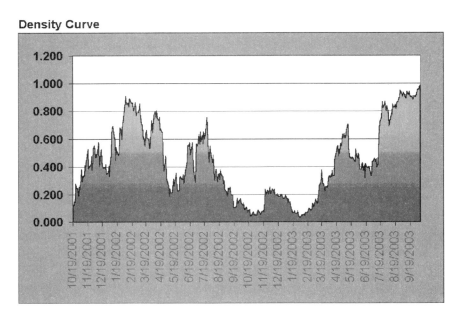

FIGURE 14.3   Density Curve

been a winner. However, don't get too optimistic yet—there is plenty of room for error, as you will soon see. (Examine Figure 14.3.)

UNDERSTANDING THE DATA

In the above examples, if we had bought and sold the pair when the density curve pulled within 0.003 thousandths of zero and one, we would have had a large winner. However, I would like to again reiterate that pairs trading is not this simple! The fact of the matter is that we are dealing with moving numbers. Our mean, median, and mode all shift as each trading day presents additional data. This causes our standard deviations, charts, and density curve to also change positions. For example, on August 1, 2003, our density curve was at 0.982. However, if we update the data through August 31, the density curve for August 1 then shifts to 0.985. We must understand that the data is constantly changing, making it a necessity to translate all numbers surfacing each day. Simply put, if we are to trade pairs with real money, we will not have the luxury of looking back into history to see whether we were right or wrong. Because of this truth, it is important to have several parameters that constitute a trade instead of one or two simple numbers.

If we revert to our data ending on July 31 and analyze the pair data sheet, we can make a few decisions. First, we know the density curve is at

0.982, not quite within the 0.003 thousandths of one that we would like to institute a trade. However, at the same time, the differential is trading at 15.85, coming off a near-term high of 17.17 on July 29. For all practical purposes, our gut instinct may be telling us that the pair has expanded. In fact, if we look at the differential chart, it appears as if KLAC/NVLS may definitely be at a potential sell signal. We infer this visually, with the differential chart indicating that the pair is at an extreme point of expansion. What's more, the ratio chart appears overbought, and is also displaying a possible sell signal as well.

The pair is currently at 15.85, trading over two standard deviations from the mean at 8.86. If the empirical rule has any merit, then we are presently trading with 95 percent of the total data. While the data seems exciting at first glance, we must ask ourselves about that other 5 percent—or at least the other 4.7 percent that could pull the spread apart over three more points before we hit the third standard deviation at 18.81! The point of the entire last paragraph is that regardless of how close our density curve is getting to zero or one, we may want to double-check our other descriptive statistics for additional confirmation before we take a position.

CHAPTER 15

Taking a Step Back for a Moment

We have built our spreadsheet up to where we have a useful tool in analyzing our pair. What's more, we also have some fundamental and technical information to also compare each individual stock with, just to double-check the statistics that have been presented. So now we ask, what constitutes a decent convergence pair's setup?

We would like to see our pair trade very close to (if not at) three standard deviations, while our charts confirm extreme expansion at the same moment. I usually only take a position if the differential is within 10 percent of the third standard deviation. Second, ideally the density curve will be within 0.003 thousandths of positive one, thus inferring that we are very close to maximum spread expansion. You *must* change the density curve entry signals for the type of pairs you are trading. What I mean here is that if you are trading KLAC-NVLS, I would actually recommend waiting until the density curve is pegged out at 0 or 1. The reason is that the entire sector and two stocks are *much* more volatile than other, slower-moving equities like energy stocks. When trading slower oil stocks, I will use the 0.003 rule, but only after I have scanned the historical data to see if entries of 0.003 thousandths of zero or one proved to be profitable. The pairs information contained in this book leaves much to the decision of the individual trader, and there is no single hard number that works in every case. This is very important to remember: If you simply build a spreadsheet and wait for a 0.003 or 0.997 entry without doing technical, fundamental, and commonsense analysis, *you will lose.*

I would like to take a step back and briefly discuss a losing situation with our present data. If we take another look at our Pair Data spreadsheet, we will find some disturbing information. Peeping farther back into history to

April 2000, we see that the density curve was trading on the upper end of the scale pegged near 1.00. Keep in mind that, at this time, the market was completely wacko, and it would have been a good idea not to trade at all, but for the sake of example, I will use this time period to completely dissuade you from trading pairs. On March 10, 2000, the density curve hit 1.00, a dead-on trade trigger. On that day, the differential closed at 21.18. The following day, the density curve began to drop very fast, bobbling around and showing extremely erratic trading. Ideally, we would have taken a position on the 13th, when the differential was at 17.91. The result would have been a gigantic losing trade, as the pair opened up another 10 points. In fact, on April 7, the differential hit a high of 38.94 before falling. I think it is safe to say that if you did not have a money management plan in place, you could have lost a ton of money. It would have been very important to double-check all events surrounding the trade, while also taking notice of all descriptive statistics. I cannot reiterate how important it is to have a solid money management plan in place with tight stop losses *before* a trade is ever entered! We will go over money and risk management later in the book, but for now please just keep in mind that no system is completely foolproof and, thus, we must always keep the worst-case scenario in mind. What's even more amazing, as the bear market began to ravage portfolios when the bubble burst, the density curve quickly sank to 0.001 on May 4. Had we taken a position, we might have made a little money if we had scalped, but more than likely, we would have lost our shirts. By October, the differential had fallen to under 10. This is just food for thought. Though the market and pairs have calmed down considerably, it is *very* important to note the possibility of losing megabucks if tight stops are not in place.

CHAPTER 16

Moving Average and Normalized Standard Deviation

Differential Moving Average
Normalized Standard Deviation

DIFFERENTIAL MOVING AVERAGE

Much like technical analysis, pairs trading benefits from using moving averages to uncover trend-trading possibilities. As mentioned earlier in Chapter 4, a simple moving average (MA) is the average of a security's price over a specified period of time, represented in the form of a line on a stock's chart. Thus, for further statistical analysis, we will determine a 90-day MA, and then calculate standard deviations from the mean. The principle behind calculating an MA is so that we can gain additional statistical confirmation when entering a position. If you imagine the differential drawn as a thick line on a chart, the MA would then be a more erratic line trading around the differential. Figure 16.1 depicts the differential and MA together on a chart.

What we are looking for is a standardized sell signal on the MA at the same time as the longer-term statistics (differential or ratio) are also indicating that the pair is nearing a sell point. Conversely, we would like the MA to be on the buy side when we are purchasing the pair. The reason we are trying to line the two up is that it is possible to get a moving average buy signal when the longer-term statistics are indicating a sell signal. When convergence trading, we want to make sure that all facets of the rubber band's expansion are on our side before we take a position. Figure 16.2 depicts how we can be on the wrong side of a trade if we buy a pair based on short-term statistics, even though the long-term data points toward selling.

Differential

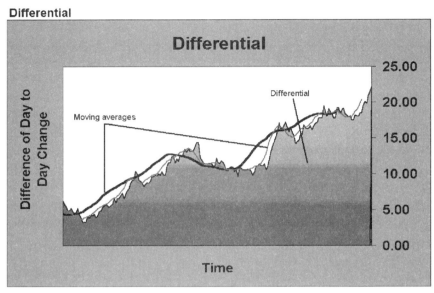

FIGURE 16.1 Moving Average and Differential

Differential

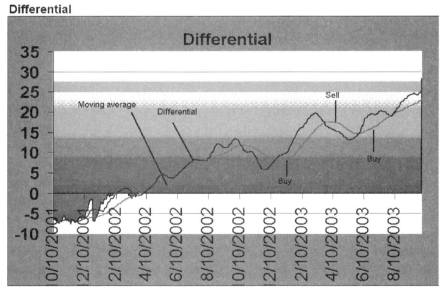

FIGURE 16.2 Moving Average and Differential with Buy/Sell Explanations

NORMALIZED STANDARD DEVIATION

In *The Complete Arbitrage Desk Book*, Stephane Reverre describes how to normalize "the value of the difference." (EN 16.1) By normalizing a value, Reverre is referring to changing data to a point where it is later represented with a base value. In essence, we will take our moving average data and "normalize" the result on a histogram with a base of zero. Thus, we will be able to measure the movements of the standard deviations as a histogram. Our goal is to use this data as an overlapping indicator and confirmation of our density curve.

Follow these steps to set up the moving average in Excel:

Step 1. Right click on the spreadsheet tabs at the bottom of our worksheet tabs and insert a new spreadsheet.

Step 2. Label cell A1 Differential Data, A3 Date, B2 and B3 90-Day MA Differential, C2 and C3 160-Day MA Differential, and D2 and D3 250-Day MA Differential.

Step 3. In cell A4, type ='Stock1'!A2 to import the date. Copy and paste cell A4 through the bottom of the cells that contain data.

Step 4. In cell B4, put in the formula =('Pair Data'!B5-(SUM('Pair Data'!B5:B95)/90))/STDEVA('Pair Data'!B5:B95). (EN 16.2) In cell C4, type in: =('Pair Data'!B5-(SUM('Pair Data'!B5:B165)/160))/STDEVA('Pair

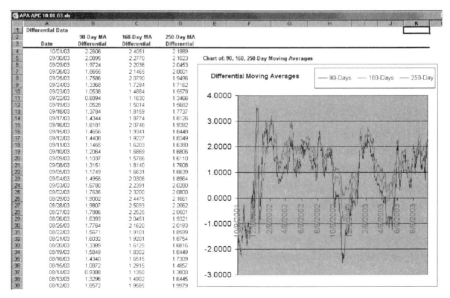

FIGURE 16.3 Chart of 90-, 160-, and 250-Day Normalized Standard Deviations

Data'! B5:B165). In cell D4, add: =('Pair Data'!B5-(SUM('Pair Data'!B5:B255)/ 250))/STDEVA('Pair Data'!B5:B255).

Step 5. Chart the data from column B, C and D beginning in column E.

The resulting chart (like the one in Figure 16.3) has variables that hover both above and below zero. Different pairs can produce diverse numbers, though in general the histogram should usually be fairly insightful as to a pair's range. If you have trouble setting up the data, please refer to any of the spreadsheets in the back of the book.

Now, returning to our empirical rule, we remember that:

- 68 percent of the data will rest within +/− one standard deviation of the mean.
- 95 percent of the data will lie within +/− two standard deviations of the mean.
- 99.7 percent of the data will sit within +/− three standard deviations of the mean.

Ideally, we would like to see all three of our normalized differentials trade above 2.0 standard deviations before selling a pair and conversely below 2.0 standard deviations before buying the pair. Going back to our density curve data from Chapter 14, we can now find new information that may have helped us make more informed decisions.

Generally, the rules for taking a trade are:

- The differential (or ratio) must be within 10 percent of the third standard deviations (in real data) when the pair is instituted.
- The differential chart visually displays that the pair is trading away from the mean.
- The density curve must be printing within 0.003 of the high and low values for the pair. Keep in mind that to substantially minimize risk you could scale your entry signals back to 0.000 or 1.000 on more volatile stocks, like tech stocks.
- The 90-day, 160-day, and 250-day normalized standard deviations (NSDs) must all be above +2 or below −2.

If any one of the above indicators is not within the parameters that we have mentioned, we will usually not take the trade, meaning that we will *not* purchase or sell short either stock.

CHAPTER 17

Money Management

Why Money Management?
Psychology of Money
Management
Understanding How Pairs Can
Be Dangerous

WHY MONEY MANAGEMENT?

This chapter may be a little premature; however, at this point I would like to slow down and take a moment to understand the risks involved with trading pairs, while discussing how to protect ourselves with money management. Even though pairs trading is essentially a hedge, the strategy involves more risk than directional trading, as each trade consists of two positions instead of one. Thus, if a position goes against us, we have double the exposure of a normal directional trade, not to mention we are paying twofold more commissions than a regular trade. If we are successively wrong on several positions, our transaction costs can further erode our account. What's more, if we do not have a firm understanding of both technical and fundamental analysis, we can endlessly watch our trading capital go down the drain while our pair creates a statistical anomaly.

PSYCHOLOGY OF MONEY MANAGEMENT

One of the most incredible traders I have ever met has a great way of approaching money management psychology. Kevin Cuddie says, "If you do not honor your stops you are lying to yourself and stealing from your family." While this is extremely harsh, it is exactly true at the heart of the issue. By not honoring our stops we are lying to ourselves from the moment we enter a trade. It is our duty as individual traders and investors to strictly adhere to the trading plan and rules we have already set forth—before we ever enter a single trade.

When Mr. Cuddie says you are stealing from your family, he is also right on the money. This sentence is very hard to swallow, but if you take a moment to consider the reality of the situation, you may find yourself having an incredible epiphany. Think about it for a moment. When you are investing, whether it be directional or pairs trading, you are working with your (or your firm's) hard-earned money. As students of the market, we already have many things against us, including order flow, news, insider knowledge, earnings, and, of course, our own emotions. It is necessary to understand that if you trade, you *will* lose from time to time, perhaps even all the time if you are not careful. Simply put, being able to cut your losses short is the name of the game. If you do not cut your losses when your stop loss points are triggered, you are taking your own money out of your own pocket. And if you have a family to take care of, you are taking money away from your family's livelihood, simply because you could not cut your own losses. It is generally true that we all want to progress both emotionally and financially forward; accordingly, if we waste our resources on losing positions, we hinder our ability to advance.

If you have a $100 account and you let a loss in one trade wipe out half of your account, you are in big, big trouble. Why? To recoup your original principal of $100, you now have to make 100 percent in the next trade to offset your original 50 percent loss. How many trades have you ever made that earned 100 percent? If you are like me, probably not many. Thus, we strive to take small loss after small loss, to then yield a large winner. Moreover, when we do not accommodate stops and take large losses, we only breed fear. And when you trade with fear, you might as well not be trading at all. When you fear losing money, you will find yourself with analysis paralysis and not be able to pull the trigger to enter a trade, or fear losing the rest of your money and not be able to close a losing trade.

The game blackjack has some interesting principles of money management that we should strive to learn from. First and foremost, when you place a bet on a blackjack table, you have specified your exact money management plan (in advance) for that particular trade. Unless you double down or split cards somewhere in the middle of the hand, you have specifically stated how much you are willing to risk. When the hand is over, if you have lost to the dealer, your money is taken by the house. At that point, you may be very happy that you didn't bet more! Unfortunately, when an equity trade goes against us, we do not have the luxury of a set loss unless we are dealing in options or some other financial instruments. If we continue to play the hand, our losses can go on inevitably, or at least until we are completely broke. What's worse is that if you are trading on margin, you can lose even more money than your account has, and actually end up owing money—clearly not a predicament that any us of want to be in!

Once our losing blackjack trade is over, it is then our responsibility to stop trading. As individuals, we must be accountable for our own decisions. No system in the entire world is completely foolproof; therefore, it is crucial that we understand losses *will* occur. Much like the blackjack table, we must stop trading when we are down and review what went wrong. Further, if we do not have expendable capital to step back up to the table with, then we should just walk away. Trading, much like gambling, is not for everyone. More importantly, pairs trading may also not be for all individuals, especially anyone who does not have the time to conduct the proper research and analysis. The information in this book is only as effective as the investor who individually pulls the trigger to enter a trade. Again, the statistics in this book will be wrong from time to time, consequently leaving us (as individuals) to know when to stop the bleeding.

UNDERSTANDING HOW PAIRS CAN BE DANGEROUS

While we have already gone over both technical and fundamental analysis to assist our pairs knowledge, the crux of this book is based on statistics. As I have already mentioned, our statistics can fail us from time to time. How? First, there is always the risk of human error. What if you build a spreadsheet and have the formula in just one key cell wrong? The result could be detrimental to your account if the mistake is not caught before a trade is entered. Second, pairs are only as strong as the statistics that back them. In all statistics, there is always the risk of an anomaly that skews the data. Thus, if our pair is at an outlying point where we receive a buy or sell signal, the trade is definitely not a sure thing. Despite the hedge, we must understand that the pair has diverged for a reason. It is our job as pairs traders to figure out why and then attempt to understand whether the correlation is strong enough to draw the two stocks back together. Take, for example, the buy signal for KLAC/NVLS that we received on October 3, 2002. In an independent event that affected our pair, Advanced Micro Devices (NYSE: AMD) had warned on October 2, 2002, while the broader chip sector seemed to be rapidly falling to the wayside. Then on October 8th, when we took our position, Lehman Brothers analyst Edward White announced that the semiconductor sector could see weaker order trends throughout 2003. However, Mr. White stated that he expected a few stocks to hold up well, specifically mentioning KLA-Tencor, the buy-side stock in our pair. While this news event helped to drive our pair in the right direction, consider the other side of the coin. It is very possible that White could have upgraded Novellus instead of KLA-Tencor. If such had happened, our pair could have quickly slipped further into the bowels of the investing earth, while we sat by in a losing trade. Also, during early October 2002 we were in the middle of warnings season, when many chip companies were announcing that they would miss their numbers. The event risk that we faced was that KLA-Tencor, could have announced either tragic earnings numbers or guided lower for the coming quarters. Either incident would have caused us to lose money in our trade. The point here is that statistics got us in the trade, while positive current events helped us get out with a winner. If you are *not* shaking your head at this very moment saying "I will never trade pairs, ever," then I am not sure what more I can say to convince you of the danger you face by trading statistical arbitrage.

My intent during this chapter is purely to talk you out of pairs, for if you are nervous after the last few sentences, perhaps pairs are not for you. If this is the case, please believe me when I say "no big deal." As traders, we find ourselves adapting to investment styles that fit our personalities much like different artists use different painting techniques. If you are a market impressionist, please do not try to fit in the box of surrealists. Your style is your style, and for many, the risks associated with pairs simply do not fit in their money management plan or psychological profile.

CHAPTER 18

Money Management II

Fundamental Principles
Know Yourself
The Plan

FUNDAMENTAL PRINCIPLES

The fundamental principles behind money management are very simple. However, as people with emotions driven by fear and greed, we can have an incredibly hard time sticking to our strategy. The foremost principle is don't lose money—ever. While this many seem a little elementary, it is a much harder task to implement than we perceive. Have you ever let a trade go against you thinking it will come back? Were you a part of the bull market bubble that blew up in all of our faces?

Let me tell you a little story about one of my more fantastic moments. While in college, I had the opportunity to participate in a pre–initial public offering, about which I knew almost nothing. However, it seemed like a fantastic deal at the time, so I put my hard-earned money to work. The company was/is called Homeseekers.com. At the time it was named something else, but the actual name no longer matters. I invested $10,000 in roughly 5,000 shares of this wonderful company at $2 a share. What a deal for a dot.com. I sat on the stock all through school, waiting for something to happen. Then after I was finished with my degree, the stock went public and I had the opportunity to exercise an additional 5,000 shares at $3. At the time it seemed like another wonderful opportunity, as the stock was trading at roughly $4. I scraped up the money and put my capital to work. I now had 10,000 shares in my account. Going into December 1999, the stock fired up to $15 a share, where I took some profits out. I think I cashed out about $70,000 worth and decided to let the rest ride. I was sure I would be a millionaire before I was 30. Then, just after January 2000, the stock began rapidly descending. I kept telling myself, just a pullback, just a pullback, just a pullback, which it wasn't. I never sold the remaining position of my shares, and at last glance the stock was trading on the NASDAQ bulletin board at 0.001 cents a share. If I just cashed out all of my position near the top, I would have made over $250,000. But I didn't; I rode it into the ground, just like any self-worthy Wall Street cowboy should. The bottom line: I had no plan and gave up a lot of money because of it.

If we are going to understand money management, we have to have a plan—any plan, just have a plan.

KNOW YOURSELF

To have a money management plan, you must first take a moment and get to know yourself. Ask yourself: Am I driven by a trading goal? Am I driven by the success of the trade or by the fear of losing money? Either way, are you driven by fear or greed? If you are driven by greed, then you must make sure you have an excellent money management plan with tight stops. However, if you are driven by fear, then you may want to loosen your stops a little, to ensure that when you do have a winning trade, you can hang on to it for a larger winner. No matter which end of the spectrum you are on, it's important to understand that all negative actions lead not to greed but, rather, fear. And fear is the ultimate trading destroyer. There is a fine line between being a responsible money manager and trading with fear. If you trade with fear, you close every trade that goes against you, if even by a few pennies. This is good, as you will never lose large amounts of money; however, you will never be able to make any real money or make rational, unbiased decisions. The best money managers in the world understand that there is a middle ground, where trades are closed when they violate preset technical, fundamental, or statistical levels. Thus, the shortcut to becoming a great money manager is to simply have predetermined stops before you ever take the position. Then, you have removed yourself from the trade and are unbiased about the trading action that follows your entry. And this is how to get to know yourself. If you rationalize your stops before you take the position, you can record your emotion when your stop nears. Do you want to leave the trade open to make more money, or close it out of the fear of losing?

THE PLAN

First and foremost, you should never, ever, ever take more than an $8\frac{1}{2}$ percent loss on each side of your pairs trade. The total capital lost equals 17 percent and can still be devastating to an account. When you calculate an

entry, one of your stops should always be 8½ percent per side. And if
either side hits, close the position. The fundamental idea here is to never
let a trade go against you endlessly. For more conservative traders, you
may want to actually lower the loss percentage to 2½ to 5 percent, thus
protecting yourself from unnecessary losses. The fundamental crux here
is that the lower your loss risk percentage, the better timed your entry
must be. If you only want to risk 2½ percent, then the wisest decision may
be to bump your density curve entry up to 0.000 or 1.00. Of course, this
means that you will hardly ever get into a trade, but it also means that you
will risk much less in terms of the statistical entry. What's more, for more
conservative traders of 2½ percent, you may want to also move your
standard deviation entry up either near or above three standard deviations.
The bottom line: The more conservative you wish to be, the pickier you
must be.

Second, it is vitally important to have technical stops as well. Review
your charts and find points where either stock is staging a technical breakout or breakdown that will cause one half of the position to fly out of whack.
If that point is breached, close the trade. Figure 18.1 gives a good example.
Using a simple trend line, we can see that Dell Computer was headed down
during the first part of 2003. The chart also displays a clearly marked trend
line that you could have used as a short stop for either pairs or directional

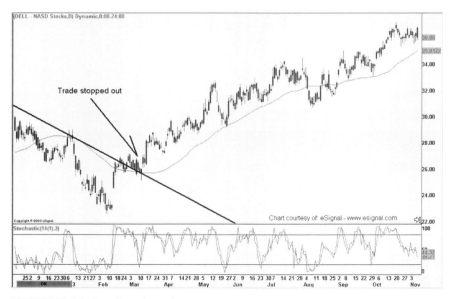

FIGURE 18.1 Dell Technical Stop

traders. Once the stock closed above the descending resistance line, it was off to the races. It is vitally important to have technical stops on your chart as well as capital percentage loss stops in your account.

Third, statistical stops should also be set hard and fast for any trade. I generally use the third standard deviation as a good point to close positions, should the trade go against me. However, if I am taking a position on the second standard deviation, the third standard deviation can be quite a ways away, and can infer substantial losses if the losing trade is held that long. Thus, I use the third standard deviation as an actual stop only when I implement a trade within 10 percent of the same standard deviation. More conservative traders may want to decrease this number significantly, though remember that to do so also means you must time your entry properly in order to avoid being quickly stopped out.

CHAPTER 19

The Reality of Pairs

Do Pairs Really Work?
Trader or Investor?
Making the Style Work for You
Intraday Pairs

DO PAIRS REALLY WORK?

The answer to this question is as rhetorical as the question itself. Pairs trading is not a system that will automatically fill your account with endless amounts of easy money. In fact, pairs trading might actually be more difficult than regular trading. Think about it. If you are a directional trader investing in only one stock, then your research is fairly limited. You only do fundamental research on the stock, sector, and market. Then, look at the stock's technical indicators, while also taking notice of historical news and pending events. After this is completed, you may then have a good idea whether the stock is worth trading. However, if you are a pairs trader, you have to conduct the same amount of research on two stocks instead of one. You can now see that this is not for the faint at heart.

Pairs do work; however, trading pairs is only as effective as the investor executing the trades. If you are willing to do only half of the research, then you will likely lose half (if not all) of your money. If you put in 100 percent, you will likely break even. The only way to make your account grow is to put in more effort than your competitor—and in the market, you are competing against everyone else. This may sound discouraging, but it is a market truth that will not go away. We cannot deny our responsibilities of hard work and expect to get lucky. Thus, if we really want to trade our own money and be successful, we have to put in 150-plus percent.

If used correctly, pairs can hedge your risk in times of uncertainty. You may be tempted to trade pairs with sexy, high-flying stocks. However, if you instead stick to slower-moving, more fundamentally sound companies, you may very likely have greater results. Take energy stocks, for example. Some of the larger energy companies have moved incredibly slowly over the past decade, while paying out consistent dividends. These stocks rarely have any volatility of divergence, unless some sort of scandalizing event or crisis occurs. Many institutional investors have valued these stocks to the penny and know exactly what each is worth. Thus, as long as the event that triggered divergence is not caused by an event that is incredibly scandalous, the two stocks will likely return to their original value, which are exactly the opportunities that you and I, the pairs traders, are looking for.

Do pairs ever fail? I can only answer this question with a resounding "heck yes!" During 2000 to 2001 I traded an account that had a 100 percent win/loss ratio. This means that we had *no* losers. Let me rephrase that to be more correct: We had many pairs trades that had both a winning side and a losing side. However, the winners always exceeded the losers; thus, the overall pairs positions were winners.

Then, going into the first few weeks of September 2001, we found a wonderful position, with two large companies that appeared to present less risk than other flamboyant high-flying stocks. The two companies were Boeing and Lockheed Martin. To be exact, the two companies were trading apart two and a half standard deviations. As a result, we bought Boeing and sold short Lockheed Martin. The trade looked amazing, and we anticipated that the position would yield at least 10 points.

Then, on the morning of September 11, 2001, I left for work slightly later than usual. I needed to give my wonderful better half a ride to work. After dropping her off at her office building, I pulled into traffic and heard what I thought at the time was a joke: "A plane has hit the World Trade Center in New York." I switched the station once, twice, three times—and then I knew it was for real. What I also then realized caused me to pull over for a moment and take a deep breath. I formed a hypothesis in my mind and drove to the office. When I arrived on the trading floor, all of the traders were not at their desks, but rather, were standing in front of the TVs watching CNBC and CNN. I knew what was going to happen and prayed for the market to open for just one minute—all I needed was one stinking minute to get out of our positions. Then, when the New York Stock Exchange did not open and the second plane hit, I knew our fate was sealed. I left work that morning and went home for what would turn into a week off while the markets stayed closed. As the week progressed, I listened to the news and realized more and more each day that the account that I put the Boeing/Lockheed Martin trade in was now on fire also. It was kind of like standing in front of a firing squad for days on end; waiting for the inevitable, and then waiting some more.

The problem was obvious: Though Boeing had a substantial amount of business from defense, it also heavily relied on selling jets to commercial airlines. And when a terrorist attack comes in the form of commercial airlines turning into hellish missiles over your own country's soil, people stop flying. When people stop flying, the airlines stop ordering jets. And when the airlines cease purchasing or discontinue current leases, the companies that manufacture planes (Boeing) take a huge dive. Conversely, Lockheed was completely exposed to defense; thus, the attack was sure to bring about immediate defense budget increases. And it did. Shortly after, the defense budget packed full of cash for research, development, and production for military/defense weapons and technology was passed. Washington soon after passed a fiscal stimulus package that amounted to $75 billion, of which many defense companies like Lockheed Martin received a good portion. The future was imminent, when the market opened again, I was sure Boeing would gap down and Lockheed Martin would gap up. And that's exactly what happened.

When the market reopened on Monday, September 17, 2001, the Boeing/Lockheed Martin pair gapped against us 14 points. Everything we had made for the entire year (and then some) went up in smoke. The account was devastated.

I had never expected this situation to occur and had no idea whether the correlation would hold. In short, I had no idea if the trade would come back, but knew that the account could not stand to lose one cent more. The account had grown 33 percent for the year prior to September 11. When the market then opened on September 17, the losses totaled almost 45 percent of the September 10 close. Just to get the account back to where we had started for the year, I needed to make 37 percent, and to get back to the level where the account closed on September 10, we needed to book 82 percent. I'm not sure which was more devastated—the account or me.

This is where I learned the most important lesson of my entire trading career. When you are down and out and are thinking about batting for the fences to recover losses, stop trading and take a break. Write down exactly what went wrong, or at least what you *think* went wrong, and put that piece of paper away for a while.

The irony of the situation is that the pair *did* come back, and if I had just left the trade open, it would have returned to its original value. However, even though I took a huge loss, I did the right thing. The situation was an anomaly and presented more future risk than it did reward. Had I not been in Boeing/Lockheed Martin before September 11, it would have been a great opportunity to take a position on the 17th. But then again, my 20/20 hindsight account never loses a trade.

What I did after September 11 was keep trading. And from there I managed to give up another 6 percent in the following six months. At that point I took a break, and thank God I did.

I decided to take some time off from trading during the late spring and summer of 2002. In fact, I don't think I actually placed a single trade until September 2002! During that time, I left the trading firm I had been at to go write for a financial newsletter. My timing when I stopped trading was one of the most lucky events of my entire life, as another market anomaly was about to take place, and at the time I did not see it coming—nor would I have known how to deal with the situation that would be presented.

During the summer of 2002, the market completely fell apart when the Dow Jones Industrial Average, NASDAQ, and Standard & Poor's (S&P) 500 all made fresh bear market lows. If there was one prominent theme to the market that summer, it was scandal. Companies like Enron, Citigroup, and Tyco were littered with corruption and accounting scandals. And investors quickly learned that if you can't trust a company's officers and accountants, just get the heck out. The resulting action triggered mass selling in a variety of different companies, and the selling generally appeared overnight. If at that time you were trading pairs based on statistics and/or correlations, then you most likely got killed. Thankfully by pure chance, I was not. And, when I went back and began reviewing trades that I might have taken, I was very pleased about my decision to take a break. September 11 and the summer of 2002 taught me two very important things.

First, statistical arbitrage is only as good as the legitimacy of the correlation supporting the trade. I am mostly speaking of convergence trading here, though this also stands true for divergence trading as well. Basically, when the events that pull companies apart are so extreme that companies are filing for bankruptcy, corporate insiders are being made to do the "perp walk," or class action suits are beginning to rise—just stay out. Of course, some argue that the aforementioned events create a perfect situation for divergence trading. However, I have yet to meet anyone who can accurately predict such events on a consistent basis and make money. When in doubt, stay out.

The second lesson is that when the market begins to capitulate or is at an extreme level, that is, the Market Volatility Index (EN 19.1) is above 40, it may be a good idea to sit on the sidelines. After all, if we are divergence trading, then we want to wait for the rubber band to completely expand, versus trying to time the trade before the pair has capitulated. Of course, we won't always be correct, but, when significant moments of substantial uncertainty arise, it may be in our best interest to pass for a more reliable opportunity.

After all this, what I am trying to say is that pairs do work; however, much like any other trading style, there will be times when the bottom falls out. From here, we will soon see that money management is the name of the game.

TRADER OR INVESTOR?

This is a question we must all ask ourselves. My advice in answering this question is to simply ask yourself how much time you have every day to watch the market. If you are not in a position to watch the intraday movements, you are an investor, not a trader. This is not a bad thing at all actually! In fact, this is absolutely outstanding, as most intraday traders (day traders) take on the most risk. I know, because I've been there. The problem with trading pairs on an intraday basis is that if two stocks are separating, they're doing it for a reason, and could very likely close at a high. This means you lose. Though we only briefly went over intraday pairs, I would not recommend day trading for the average Joe. Being an investor and trading with longer-term data, you have the ability to analyze your data and are not fighting against intraday order flow that you have no idea about.

To be an investor or, should we say, "swing trader," is most likely the better bet. When we hold a position for a shorter amount of time, as in two days to two months, we are keeping our capital at work, while not exposing ourselves to long-term risk.

There is a concept known as churning, which is also branded as overtrading. A broker who is trying to make money on commissions typically does this; however, swing traders who move in and out of their positions excessively can also be guilty of churning their own account. As pairs traders, we must be careful not to overtrade, as each pair has a long and short position, and thus, double the commissions. This is another reason I do not recommend intraday pairs trading, as the commissions can be horrendous.

MAKING THE STYLE WORK FOR YOU

To make the style work for you, you must stay abreast of your data. You must update your data daily and watch for opportunities. What's more, to be an effective pairs trader, we must also watch the news events surrounding us. If we are trading pairs into earnings season, and the companies that trade with our pair begin warning, it is a good idea to examine the possible outcomes for our stocks. Despite correlations, our pair can make dramatic swings during times of tribulation, like earnings. The last thing we want to do is wake up to a poor earnings report for the stock that we are long in. Even if the correlation is strong, the stock we are short may not react the same as the stock we are long. In this scenario, I highly recommend looking through each company's earnings estimates and searching for analyst guidance for the pending announcement. If our long stock has recently lowered earnings guidance and our short stock has not, it may be a good idea to exit the position as a precautionary measure to potential losses. After all, missed money is much better than lost money.

Please also keep in mind that each investor's risk tolerance is much different than the next. Thus, while I may have mentioned an 11 percent stop (5.5 percent per stock) for KLAC/NVLS, the same risk may not be acceptable for an investor with a smaller account. Think about it for a moment. If you lose 20 percent on $1,000, then you have to make back 25 percent to break even. Every time you lose money, it becomes harder and harder to make the money come back. I know that I have outlined this point twice in this chapter, but that's how vitally important it is to remember.

One of the most incredible slogans of trading I have ever heard is "80 percent of success is just showing up." I cannot commend this statement enough. As an example, in the summer of 2001, I was in a pair of trucking stocks. At the time, I was not using the density curve, and had not figured out how to accurately time the entry of my pairs yet. What I quickly discovered was that often, I had to sit on losing trades before they came back and made money. Fortunately, all did; however, I partly attribute the winning streak to dumb luck. Anyway, I had been sitting in the trucking pair for about six weeks and was approximately five points out of the money when an anomaly occurred. The NASDAQ had a plethora of problems with its systems and decided to keep the market open for an extra hour to allow traders a chance to make up for the lost time during the trading day. When 4:00 P.M. EST rolled by (the normal closing time for the exchanges) I looked around the trading floor and discovered—to my dismay—that almost every single other trader had already left for the day. The lack of liquidity before the close gave the other traders an excuse to go play golf. However, I stayed because I remembered reading about low-volume days before holidays when the markets went haywire, and I was already losing huge in my trucking pair and didn't want to come into any nasty surprises the following day. So I stayed and watched. Amazingly, the electronic communications network (ECN) activity was incredibly robust for both of my stocks. I began to see bids and asks build like the trucking stocks were tech highfliers. By this I mean that the buyers and sellers were stacking up tremendously on the bid and ask in both stocks. My first thought was: Can this be real? Then I surmised that there must have been institutional players out there who either had some huge orders to run—and saw the late day as an opportunity to move some serious volume—or that someone, somewhere was panicking.

Regardless, the bids were building on the stock I was long, and the asks were piling up in the stock I was short. My heart began racing—the pair that I had just been five points out of the money on was now three points in the money . . . then four points, then five points. I immediately marketed out of half of both positions, and put the other two halves further out of the money to see if I would be hit. Amazingly, my orders were immediately taken, and I walked away with a huge 10-point profit. Next thing I knew, I was standing on the top of my desk swinging a golf club, screaming at the top of my lungs in victory elation. I had just recovered 15 points. When I came to my senses, you could hear a pin drop. The only people in our office were the branch manager and compliance director, who were staring at me like I was a mad-man. And I was. I quietly put down my golf club, stepped off my desk, and left as quickly as possible.

The most amazing part of the whole experience is that I learned you can't make money if you aren't there. I later thought about the situation, and also realized that I didn't have to be there at all. I should have had orders outstanding in our system at my profit levels, whether I was out of the money or not. After all, that is the one benefit that computers give us: the ability to ease our day-to-day activities. No matter how you slice it, though, I was there when the other traders went home, and I made money because of it. When I got into the office the next morning, both stocks opened at where they had been trading at noon the previous day. It was like nothing had ever happened. I waited all morning for our manager to come inform me that the trades were unreasonable and that they had been broken; however, such never occurred. I won because I was there, I won because I was there, I won because I was there. And you will too.

INTRADAY PAIRS

Intraday pairs often involve more risk than normal pairs, as intraday movements can be less correlated than longer-term swings. On a valuation level, two stocks may trade closely together over a long period of time. This is because the stocks may have similar business models, assets, price-to-earnings (PE) ratios, earnings, or a variety of other congruous items that cause institutional investors to see the companies as complementary.

Regardless of fundamentals, however, during intraday trading, the stocks may be at the mercy of order flow. Order flow, as I define it, is all intraday buying and selling that affects the price of a stock significantly in one direction or another. Order flow is similar to the current of a stream; it is what pushes a stock. Much like a flat stream can meander, or a rapid stream can have many different sets of underlying currents and movements, it is extremely hard to predict the precise currents when you are in the water. The only thing you are sure of is that you are at the mercy of the flow of currents. And while swimming downstream in the water, you can get stuck in an eddy or smash into an unseen rock at any moment.

When you are transacting a 100-share trade, you are not adding substantial order flow to a stock. However, when your 100 shares coupled with 100 other people's 100 share orders decide the direction of a stock, the result is order flow. Keep in mind that this definition differs from person to person. The problem is that order flow is nearly impossible to figure out. If you watch a level II screen and look for larger buyers and sellers, you will almost never be able to see who is doing what. Five years ago, trading was a different story; however, now with many ECNs (e.g., Island, Instinet, Brut, Arca), market makers, specialists, and traders, the game has become very complicated. Seasoned traders may disagree with me, though for the average trader, order flow is impossible to accurately predict 100 percent of the time. As a result, it may be better for us to sometimes step away from the stream to observe the overall direction. Then if we can map out a safer course from afar (swing trading), we may then have less misfortune running into unseen obstacles when we are in the water.

The intraday pairs trader is at the mercy of order flow, which is the primary catalyst behind his or her trading actions. He or she is seeking to capitalize on order flow that drives two stocks apart or brings them back together. The main issue here is that as an individual trader, you will *never* know when substantial market moving, or individual stock-punishing order flow will begin. Why? Simply put, you are not on the trading desk at Morgan Stanley, Goldman Sachs, Merrill Lynch, Janus, or any other financial institution that runs huge orders. And even if you are on one of those desks, you still cannot predict what will happen with order flow, unless one of your buddies on another desk calls you and tells you. And that's one of those little illegal things the Securities and Exchange Commission (SEC) and the National Association of Securities Dealers (NASD) highly frown on!

Say we are trading a hypothetical intraday pair that has spread wide open, and we think it's going to collapse back into the mean by the end of the day. The hypothetical pair of stocks we are trading are: long Reported Miserably Inc. (NYSE: RMI) and short Beat Estimates Corp. (NYSE: BE). The pair has spread open—meaning that even though RMI missed earnings estimates and BE came in above estimates, the stocks are doing the opposite of what they should. By this I mean that your gut instinct tells you that RMI should go down, while BE should ascend. Even though you may perceive that the two stocks "ought to" move in one direction or another, they certainly don't have to.

In another scenario, what if Crazy Hedgefund X has been building a short position for months on end in a stock that is about to report, because their analyst knew the stock would miss earnings estimates? This is a "buy the rumor, sell the news" scenario for Crazy Hedgefund X, and now the traders will cover their huge short position into weakness, betting that suckers like you and me will be shorting after earnings. The end result of your intraday trade is that the stock may never come back and you will have to close your trade out a big, fat, stinky loser. What if we leave it open thinking that it has to recover some of the lost ground in the next few days? After all, we're hedged—right? Wrong again.

What if you are on the losing side of a larger pairs move and it's beginning a two-month divergence away from you? You would then be horribly wrong and have to sit in your losing trade until it either comes back or a margin call sells you out of the position and you lose all your money. Do you see the risks here? Intraday trading is extremely dangerous and should be left to the pros who have outstanding money management skills, plenty of expendable dollars to throw away (and the understanding that they probably will), a highly advanced technical analysis program, outstanding trading platform (like Tradestation), and nerves of steel. I'm not saying you are not this certain well educated, or well-tooled person; after all, you might be! However, for most people, intraday trading can be far above the acceptable level of risk tolerance!

CHAPTER 20

Trading an Actual Pair

Introduction
Trading Diary—The Beginning
Historical Time Line of
Divergence Events

INTRODUCTION

The next portion of the book was a bit of a gamble. With only a few weeks left to my publishing deadline, I decided that drab information presented in typical book form no more helps you learn how to trade pairs than reading a VCR manual does in helping you be actually able to program your VCR. Thus, I decided to switch directions and discard a good part of the book and put a trading diary in place. Here, I will walk you through a pairs trade—day by day—to show you exactly what I am looking for when I approach a pair and how I trade it. Furthermore, we will track the pair with real money on a daily basis. This is a real pair, with real money, and I will tell you play by play exactly what I am thinking—win or loss. At the point when I am writing this, I have no idea whether the pair will be a winner or loser by the time I close the position on November 14, 2003. I will use everything that I have brought forward in this book in the upcoming trade. Moreover, we will look at the trade on a statistical, fundamental, and technical basis, and will incorporate *all* of our market knowledge in an attempt to make money. I would like to again reiterate that this is a gamble, as I do not know what the outcome of the trade will be by the time this book goes to print. However, the lessons here should be timeless and invaluable, as we will work with two oil companies—an industry that really doesn't change all that much. This is a little nerve wracking, but exciting at the same time. As a trader, I have built my career on taking calculated chances, so this trade will be very interesting, as it is calculated chance as well. Here we go!

September 26, 2003: Today, I was looking around the market and noticed a possible pairs divergence that may be worth looking into. I used to trade this pair quite a bit, but have not looked at it in about two years. The two stocks I noticed were Apache Oil (NYSE: APA) and Anadarko Petroleum (NYSE: APC). I absolutely cannot believe the divergence of these two stocks! When I traded them in 2000 and 2001, they were one of my best pairs with a correlation of just under 90 percent. However, it now appears the correlation must have dropped substantially, given the immense amount of divergence that appears to have taken place. Looking at Figure 20.3, you can clearly see that throughout 2001, Apache and Anadarko traded quite closely to one another. The chart says a few important words about the two companies: "similar business models." However, the chart also shows that around January 2002, the two stocks began a divergence that would carry both equities far apart. We must try and figure out what happened at the time— and why Wall Street perceived so much change. Our goal is to then seek to understand whether the two stocks will come back together and, if so, when?

First, let's begin try to understand the two companies themselves, and see if we can uncover any similarities in their business models or financial statements. According to a press release distributed by the company, Apache is "a large oil and gas independent with core operations in the United States, Canada, the UK North Sea, Western Australia and Egypt." According to Yahoo.com, at of the end of 2002, Apache had 637 million barrels of crude oil in reserves, along with just over 4 trillion cubic feet of natural gas.

Anadarko Petroleum's press releases say it is "one of the world's largest independent oil and gas exploration and production companies. Houston-based Anadarko is active in the U.S., Canada, Algeria and Qatar and is executing strategic exploration programs in several other countries." At the end of 2002, Anadarko had 2.3 billion barrels of oil equivalent proved reserves. Taking a look at the balance sheet, as of June 30, 2002, Anadarko had over $20 billion in assets, while Apache had just under $12 billion.

Our immediate impression here is that both companies are independents with relatively similar goals. While total tangible balance sheet assets differ, both companies are operating in the same independent oil ballpark. Thus, we know why the charts have historically been quite comparable to one another—the companies were both pursuing similar types of business.

Looking back in time, we will scan the news around the beginning of 2001 to see if there were any apparent signs of the divergence about to take place.

At the beginning of 2001, oil began to climb back over $20 per barrel, based on a possible U.S. oil workers' strike and an explosion at a Kuwait oil field. However, just prior to these events, both Apache and Anadarko had reported earnings for the fourth quarter of 2001. Apache matched Wall Street's earnings estimates and announced a 31 percent climb in 2001 production, which was the largest production increase Apache had ever seen. In addition, despite an annual 16 percent decline in oil prices, Apache also mentioned that cash flow from operations increased by just under $2 billion. Investors happily embraced the news reported by Apache as a sign of stability and growth. The actual date that Apache reported on was January 31, with the stock closing at $48.49. After Apache reported, there were no significant up or down grades that immediately drove the stock in one direction or another.

Anadarko, however, warned a few weeks earlier, painting a different picture than Apache's optimistic outlook. One difference that Anadarko already faced going into earnings was that the company had recently begun slowing its drilling program in July 2001. The result was slower fourth-quarter volumes and not so stellar earnings. Then, one day before earnings were to be released, Anadarko announced that it would correct a 3Q01 accounting error, which amounted to just over $1 billion. For the 4Q01, though, Anadarko reported 41 cents a share, with a 41 percent decline in revenue. Anadarko cited the tough year as being mostly caused by lower energy prices. In addition, Anadarko also stated that it would push some of its natural gas developments to the side and wait for prices to become more attractive. Then, to add icing on the cake, the company forecasted 1Q02 earnings of 25 cents a share, versus the consensus expectation of 34 cents. Not good.

This was the beginning of Anadarko and Apache's divergence, though it would take a little time still before the two stocks really began to build momentum away from one another. In fact, if we take a moment and look at our spreadsheet to analyze the pair using only the price data up to January 31, 2002, we will see some pretty amazing things. Figures 20.1, 20.2, and 20.3 show the Main page, the Pair Data page, and the Individual Charts page. You will quickly notice on the main page that the two stocks were 66 percent correlated at the beginning of 2002. You can also see this directly on the Individual Charts page, where the two charts give an immediate visual representation of how closely the two traveled together.

On the main page of the spreadsheet, we know that the two stocks were 66 percent correlated, while also trading in between the mean and +1 standard deviation. The differential mean on January 31, 2002, was −4.55, while the actual differential was −0.64. If we had been extremely watchful of the pair, we would have been able to infer that with the difference in earnings news

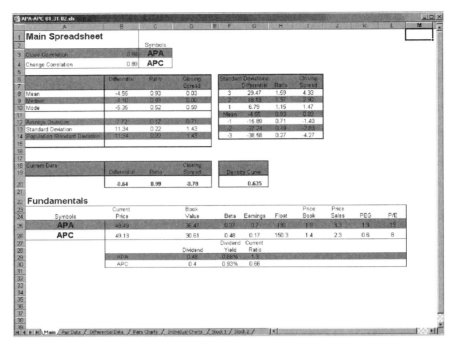

FIGURE 20.1   Main Page

(both stocks were trading just above the sell side of the mean) that divergence was about to take place.

Just to clarify, when I say sell side of the mean, what I am saying is any value above/greater than the mean. All differential and ratio values above the mean infer that the pairs trader would sell Apache Oil and buy Anadarko. Conversely, any number below the mean would allude to buying Apache Oil and selling short Anadarko. Thus, because the differential and ratio are presently above the mean, we will think only about shorting Apache and buying Anadarko. The setup for these two stocks in January 2002 proved to be the *perfect* divergence situation, where two companies with an extremely high correlation would begin to change not only fundamentally, but also in the eyes of Wall Street investors. We will continue to walk forward in time, while going over the news that surfaced, to see if we could have perceived more divergence.

HISTORICAL TIME LINE OF DIVERGENCE EVENTS

4/8/2002:   Apache fires its auditor and hires Ernst & Young, while also selling $400 million worth of 10-year notes.

	A	B	C	D	E	F	G
	APA-APC 01.31.02.xls						
1	Pair Data	-4.55	11.34				
2							
3				Close	Density		
4	Date	Differential	Ratio	Spread	Curve		
5	1/31/02	-0.64	0.99	-0.78	0.635		
6	1/30/02	0.04	1.00	1.03	0.657		
7	1/29/02	-1.02	0.98	-0.32	0.622		
8	1/28/02	-0.62	0.99	-0.38	0.636		
9	1/25/02	-0.19	1.00	0.61	0.650		
10	1/24/02	-0.82	0.98	-0.44	0.629		
11	1/23/02	-0.44	0.99	0.91	0.642		
12	1/22/02	-1.46	0.97	-0.07	0.607		
13	1/18/02	-1.35	0.97	0.59	0.611		
14	1/17/02	-1.94	0.96	0.58	0.591		
15	1/16/02	-2.38	0.95	0.33	0.576		
16	1/15/02	-2.67	0.95	-0.24	0.566		
17	1/14/02	-2.48	0.95	-0.26	0.572		
18	1/11/02	-2.21	0.95	1.10	0.582		
19	1/10/02	-3.22	0.94	0.82	0.547		
20	1/9/02	-4	0.92	-0.05	0.519		
21	1/8/02	-3.94	0.93	0.81	0.521		
22	1/7/02	-4.7	0.91	0.53	0.495		
23	1/4/02	-5.31	0.90	0.77	0.473		
24	1/3/02	-6.14	0.89	-0.42	0.444		
25	1/2/02	-5.6	0.90	1.40	0.463		
26	12/31/01	-6.97	0.88	0.04	0.416		
27	12/28/01	-6.98	0.88	-0.63	0.415		
28	12/27/01	-6.4	0.89	0.12	0.435		
29	12/26/01	-1.67	0.97	-0.46	0.600		
30	12/24/01	-1.43	0.97	0.34	0.608		
31	12/21/01	-1.85	0.97	0.09	0.594		
32	12/20/01	-2.02	0.96	0.28	0.588		
33	12/19/01	-2.4	0.95	0.25	0.575		
34	12/18/01	-2.83	0.95	0.74	0.560		
35	12/17/01	-3.9	0.92	0.63	0.523		
36	12/14/01	-4.46	0.91	-0.07	0.503		
37	12/13/01	-4.56	0.91	0.61	0.500		
38	12/12/01	-5.12	0.90	1.23	0.480		
39	12/11/01	-6.24	0.88	-0.25	0.441		
40	12/10/01	-5.88	0.89	-0.21	0.453		
41	12/7/01	-5.52	0.90	-0.18	0.466		
42	12/6/01	-5.35	0.90	0.89	0.472		

Main / Pair Data / Differential Data / Pairs Charts /

FIGURE 20.2   Pairs Data

4/16/2002:   Anadarko files to sell a $1 billion mixed shelf offering. According to CBSmarketwatch.com, the company would "offer shares of common and preferred stock, debt securities, depositary shares, warrants, and purchase contracts and units." Anadarko intended to use the proceeds for "general corporate purposes." However, anytime you have an offering, you generally have more stock, which means added saturation, translating into sluggishness for the stock price.

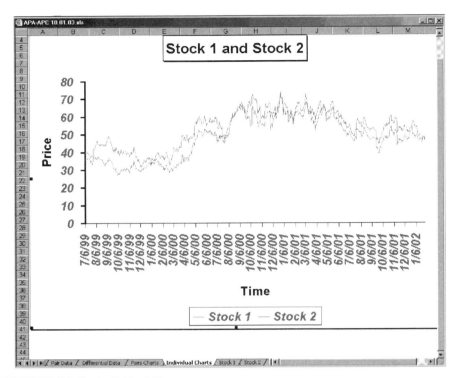

FIGURE 20.3 Individual Charts

4/23/2002: Apache is upgraded to Strong Buy by A.G. Edwards.

4/25/2002: Anadarko reports wounded 1Q02 earnings, still citing the same excuse of lower energy prices. Apache also reports lower earnings on a year-over-year basis. Crude oil had been falling and was near $27 per barrel.

5/15/2002: Coverage of Anadarko initiated at Prudential with a Hold rating.

I would like to take a moment and comment on the general crude situation in the spring of 2002. The price of crude had been struggling, as inventories seemed to be building on a national level. There was concern that OPEC (Organization of Petroleum Exporting Countries) nations were cheating on their quotas, and supply seemed to become more and more abundant. Despite specific news related to crude, Apache and Anadarko were definitely heading down different roads, as Apache seemed to be finding upgrades, while Anadarko was not quite earning a windfall of compliments from analysts. At the time, it felt like Anadarko didn't see much hope for future gains in crude, and thus preferred to taper its drilling operations more than Apache. The two companies' divergence felt motivated by Apache's hunger to succeed and Anadarko's complacency to just barely get by.

6/17/2002:   Anadarko announces that it unearthed gas wells in Louisiana and Texas.

7/10/2002:   The price of crude continues to bobble, trading under $27 per barrel. Halliburton (NYSE: HAL) came under scrutiny about possible accounting fraud issues. First Albany makes comments that the firm expected several independent oil companies to beat earnings, including Apache.

7/25/2002:   Finally, an upgrade for Anadarko by Salomon Smith Barney, which upped the company after it announced that it had beat earnings. However, Anadarko also stated that its second-quarter profit had declined 40 percent due to lower natural gas prices. Looking forward, the company lowered its 3Q02 earnings estimates to 60 cents a share, while analysts had previously been anticipating 77 cents. No matter how you slice it, July's earnings for Anadarko were not all that bright. Apache Oil also reported on the same day, singing tune of lower revenue. However, Apache's production declined only 5 percent year over year. The company went on to state that it was expecting its twenty-fifth year of growth, while also focusing efforts on expanding its drilling prospects. Purely from an investor's perspective in late July, it seemed that Apache's attitude toward business was aggressive and optimistic, while Anadarko's was complacent and passive. Further divergence would continue.

9/30/2002:   Anadarko Petroleum offers to buy Howell (NYSE: HWL) for $265 million. Anadarko intended on putting $200 million into one of Howell's Wyoming properties to increase reserves by 150 million barrels. In the long run, this appeared to be a good move by Anadarko; however, in the near term, investors smelled cash outlay.

10/24/2002:   Apache reports in line with Wall Street estimates at $1 a share. Though Apache did not blow away investors' expectations, the silver lining was that the company had drilled 259 wells during the quarter. Even more incredible, Apache's president mentioned that the total expense for the 259 wells was the same as what 200 would have cost in 2001. Apache was becoming more cost efficient and was taking advantage of higher crude prices to explore for more energy resources. (EN 20.1)

10/31/2002:   Anadarko Petroleum beat earnings and then raised its 2002 profit target. However, cash flow declined to $539 million from $735 million one year earlier.

11/22/2002:   In the article "Apache Oil-Drilling's Outspoken Captain," by CBSMarketwatch.com's Lisa Sanders (EN 20.2), the following appeared: "Plank has an avowed distaste for carrying debt. At a time when many energy companies are battling to shore up their standing with Wall Street's strict credit-rating agencies, it's the only one of its peers that can boast an 'A' rating, thanks to its 33% debt-to-capitalization ratio. By comparison, Anadarko Petroleum's debt ratio is at 45%, Burlington Resources is 51%, and Devon Energy weighs in at 61%, according to Standard & Poor's. All three are rated in the 'BBB' category." Clearly, we can see that Apache's dedication to aggressive, low-debt growth was separating it from the pack, and Figure 20.4, a chart of Apache and Anadarko from 1997 to December 2002, shows exactly what I mean.

1/13/2003: Apache enters an agreement to purchase Gulf of Mexico and North Sea property from BP for $1.3 billion. Though the acquisition is heavy in the cash outlay department, it will increase Apache's year-end assets by 14 percent. Though this is good news in the log run for Apache, investors may think otherwise and begin to drive the stock down.

1/30/2003: According to Yahoo.com, Apache earned $1.24 a share, versus 53 cents a share in the 4Q01. Unfortunately, analysts were expecting $1.28 a share; thus, Apache did not meet its earnings mark. However, investors continued to cheer the stock, which closed positive on the day, despite lackluster earnings.

1/31/2003: Anadarko reports earnings for the fourth quarter, stating that earnings more than doubled from the previous year. In 2001, Anadarko earned $108 million, or 41 cents a share. In 2002, the company reported $309

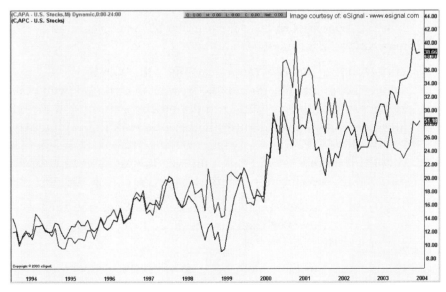

FIGURE 20.4   Apache Oil versus Anadarko

million, or roughly $1.20. However, sales volume equaled 197 barrels of oil-equivalent products (including natural gas), down from 199 million barrels in the prior year. Obviously, higher energy prices helped to bolster Anadarko's bottom line. Looking forward, Anadarko mentioned that sales volume for 2003 would come in 2 million barrels below previous estimates of 203 million. Anadarko was having production trouble because of the Venezuelan oil workers' strike. In addition, Anadarko expected first-quarter earnings to come in at $1.15 a share, or 5 cents below the consensus estimate.

Toward the end of January, the United States was urging the United Nations to seek a resolution that would authorize military action against Iraq, and war uncertainty was causing the price of oil to rise.

03/18/2003: Coverage is initiated on Apache by Bank of America with a Buy rating.

03/25/2003: CEO John Seitz resigns from Anadarko and is replaced by Robert Allison. Seitz's resignation came under extreme scrutiny of Anadarko's lagging stock price. However, Seitz's sudden resignation with little explanation spooked investors, who were already concerned with the weak stock price during times of rising energy prices. In addition, Allison is 64, and the company has a mandatory retirement policy at age 65. Speculation that Anadarko will become a takeover target begins to surface.

I would like to quickly mention that at this time, natural gas was on the move, trading at over $5 per BTU. Geopolitical tensions were causing fossil fuels to find strong gains. Concerning our pair, we can see that divergence will continue, while Anadarko has internal problems and Apache aggressively progresses toward becoming a more profitable company.

4/10/2003: Anadarko is upgraded to Buy at Prudential after the company increases its 1Q03 guidance from $1.15 a share to $1.35. However, analysts are still expecting the company to earn $1.48. Earnings per share aside, Anadarko expected $3 per share for cash flow in the first quarter, while the consensus estimate was $2.96. At this time, the new CEO announces that the company expects 5 percent production growth in 2003 and 12 percent growth in 2004. Also, he mentions that a 20 percent increase in drilling activity should result in a 20 percent increase in production volume for the fourth quarter over 1Q03. These are the first positive comments from Anadarko in a while!

4/24/2003: Apache reports that 1Q03 earnings more than quadrupled based on strapping oil and gas prices. Apache reported $2.10 a share, versus the expected $2.02. However, the stock drops two points over the next few days after investors infer that part of the quarter's results came from an earnings charge. The stock will not stay down for long, though, as the company expects to retire additional debt in the second quarter, giving it a debt-to-capital ratio under 35 percent, the lowest in the entire industry. (EN 20.3)

4/25/2003:   Anadarko reports that first-quarter profits have also quadrupled, with the company earning $1.45 a share, versus the consensus $1.43. Though Anadarko guided higher, investors let the shares slip over the next month on concerns of future falling oil and gas prices. In addition, Anadarko mentions that it expects to earn $1.15 a share in the second quarter, far below the consensus estimate of $1.43. However, the company also reveals that it expects full-year earnings to come in at $5.51, above analysts' estimates of $5.03. The stock will likely go nowhere on this news, as the common investor will probably ask him- or herself: "How can you beat estimates for the year, when you lowered expectations for the quarter?"

4/30/2003:   Anadarko updates its 2003-04 production volume forecasts and states that the company expects 2003 production growth to be about 5 percent, and 2004 to come in at 12 percent. CEO Allison makes positive comments that the company has reduced its drilling expenses by about 40 percent in certain areas. Anadarko's optimistic comments are good for the stock; however, the company still appears as if it has lost its hunger for growth.

5/01/2003:   Anadarko files to sell $350 million in five-year notes.

5/08/2003:   Apache Finance Canada issues $350 million in 12-year notes. Have you noticed some incredible similarities between these two companies yet?

05/23/2003:   Apache files to sell $1.5 billion in stock and debt (known as a shelf offering). Apache notes that the proceeds will be used for corporate purposes like paying down debt. While the move is good for the company, it can also translate to more supply in the stock and can drive the price lower.

At this time, the war with Iraq was coming to an "official" close, as stated by the White House. There was speculation that the war premium on oil would begin to evaporate, which would cause oil to lose as much as $4.00 to $5.00, to around $25 per barrel. Crude was trading at around $29 per barrel at the beginning of summer. However, weekly reports by the Energy Information Agency (EIA) and American Petroleum Institute (API) indicated a large divergence in supply levels for the week. Thus, crude was thought to still have some upside left, as there was still uncertainty in the market.

6/2/2003: Apache announces that the company is auctioning off 32 blocks in 18 western oil fields. The sale is part of Apache's plan rid itself of properties that can be sold to smaller companies.

6/5/2003: Anadarko announces that the company is raising its second-quarter forecasts and is also upping full-year guidance to $5.77 a share, far above the consensus estimate of $5.14. However, the company also lowers its 2003 production goals. At the same time, the company receives a down-grade from Merrill Lynch from Buy to Neutral. So much for good news—Anadarko is still in trouble.

6/9/2003: Amerada Hess (NYSE: AHC) announces that it has sold $260 million Gulf of Mexico assets to Anadarko.

6/24/2003: Apache announces that it will no longer have its natural gas marketed by Cinergy (NYSE: CIN) and will now take over its own marketing.

At this time, natural gas is over $6 per BTU, almost double where the price was in 2000.

6/30/2003: Tropical Storm Bill passes and does not affect the production of Anadarko's Gulf of Mexico's operations—a great break for Anadarko. However, the price of oil continues to stay high, as an oil strike in Nigeria gives investors more concern about supply issues.

7/11/2003: Gulf Storm Claudette causes Anadarko to evacuate some personnel from platforms, and eventually causes it to shut down 10 percent of its Gulf production. Claudette passes and operations are back to normal by the latter half of the month.

7/24/2003: Apache reports second-quarter earnings; the company discloses $1.76 a share, topping analyst estimates of $1.74. However, the company added in a one-time charge due to the weaker dollar; thus, the stock came under selling pressure after investors realize that the company really earned only $1.49 a share. The charge amounted to approximately $45 million in unrealized currency losses. Though investors were disappointed with the immediate outcome of earnings, Apache is still on track to higher production targets.

7/29/2003: Anadarko announces that it will begin shutting down some rigs to make sure it stays within its allotted 2003 budget. Didn't the company say in April that it had cut its drilling expenses by 40 percent in some areas? I guess this wasn't one of them. Expect more divergence from the two stocks.

7/31/2003:   In a further effort to trim costs, Anadarko announces that it is cutting 400 jobs and is closing some of its offices in Texas. The cost-cutting move is anticipated to save $100 million a year. One third of the jobs are being cut in the company's exploration and production division, with the rest of the jobs being slashed in departments that support the aforementioned unit. As a result, Bank of America downgrades the stock from Buy to Neutral, citing growth concerns for 2004 production. Anadarko also reports second-quarter earnings of $1.20 a share, below the consensus estimate of $1.25. In addition, the company trims its full-year guidance to $5.17 a share, down from $5.77. Remember on 4/25/2003, when we mentioned that the common investor might be asking him/herself: "How can you beat estimates for the year, when you lowered expectations for the quarter?" Well, the common (or should we say commonsense) investor was right.

At this time, speculation that Anadarko is for sale is gaining momentum. The CEO won't deny any possible takeover rumors of Anadarko. Analysts are also estimating that the company is worth only a price in the low $50s (as in $50 per share), as the bulk of Anadarko's assets are in the United States, and the company has roughly $5 billion in debt. However, with over 2 million barrels of proved oil and natural gas reserves, Anadarko would be a great asset to buy . . . and then tear apart.

8/15/2003:   Apache announces that the company is shutting down several platform valves in western Gulf of Mexico due to Tropical Storm Erika.

8/16/2003:   Apache returns workers to rigs one day after evacuation; no damages are incurred, just production losses.

There is speculation that Anadarko is talking to Italian firm Eni about a possible sale. Takeover rumors generally drive a stock price up. Also, Anadarko mentions that recent cost cutting has freed up capital to spend on exploration and development. The extra cash the company is talking about came from eliminating part of its exploration and development division and the jobs that support it. However, the company also attributes lower costs to discoveries and profitable developments.

9/12/2003:   Apache announces that the stock will split 2 for 1 early in 2004 and that it is increasing its dividend from 10 cents to 12 cents, payable on November 21 to shareholders on record October 22.

9/21/2003: The Sunday *Financial Times* reports that Royal Dutch/Shell Group is thinking about a $19.5 billion bid for Anadarko. Credit Suisse First Boston has been hired as the official negotiator for a possible deal.

9/25/2003: In response to an article earlier in the week by the *Financial Times*, Eni publicly announces that it is not in a partnership with Royal Dutch/Shell to purchase Anadarko.

And that brings us to where we are now—looking for a trade in this pair. We have to ask ourselves, why would this be the time when these two stocks have finally reached the maximum point of expansion, and what would drive them back together? When we review all of the events over the last two years, we can see why the two have diverged as much as they have. Apache has been a strong company, aggressively trying to expand its drilling operations, while paying down debt. Anadarko would like to do the same thing, but as a much larger company, it has had trouble gaining its footing. In addition, Anadarko has been fighting to keep investors happy with the stock, while trying to restructure the company to a more profitable entity. It would be a great surprise for Apache's stock to decline in the future, unless analysts or investors begin to view the stock as being overvalued. If the price of oil drops dramatically, the stock would fall, but then again, so would Anadarko's. In short, we are looking for an opportunity where Apache is overbought, while Anadarko is able to either solidify a merger or post some sort of decent news that shows the company is trying to do more than just hold onto its proven reserves.

You may be asking yourself: Why all of that? Why write all of the major events for both of these two companies for two years? Because when I invest money, I want to be sure I know what's going on in both the past and present. And this is the type of historical news and earnings research I do on all my pairs. The great part is that I will trade Apache/Anadarko again in the future, and because of my notes, the bulk of the research will have already been done. All I will need to do is update my files, check current events and earnings, update my spreadsheet, and factor in both technical and fundamental analysis—and I will be ready to trade. This may seem like a ton of work even for an updated pair, but we want to know everything that is going for or against us when we trade. Why leave any stone unturned?

CHAPTER 21

The Current Setup

*Understanding Where the Pair
Is Now
Apache Oil[1], Fundamentals,
Earnings, Technical Analysis,
Statistics, Summary
Anadarko Petroleum
Fundamentals
Earnings, Technical Analysis,
Statistics, Summary*

UNDERSTANDING WHERE THE PAIR IS NOW

Let's look at both of the companies now. We will make a checklist of what we are examining. We will look at:

- Fundamentals
- Earnings
- Technical Analysis
- Statistics
- Summary

Now that we have a plan, let's start with Apache Oil.

---

[1]*Note*: All charts for Apache Oil reflect post split prices, though the text includes pre-split numbers (the stock split 2-for-1 on January 15, 2004 after the text was written).

APACHE OIL[1]

Fundamentals

Unless noted otherwise all numbers are from Yahoo.com.

To begin, the stock is trading with a price-to-earnings (PE) ratio of 13, and a forward PE of 12. The difference between a regular PE (known as a trailing PE) and a forward PE is that a regular PE takes into consideration the last four quarters of earnings. A forward PE looks at the earnings estimates for the next four quarters that have yet to happen. Thus, we can assume that Apache is trading at 13 times earnings now, and will be almost the same in the next year. The industry average PE is 18; thus, on a valuation basis, our company is trading at fewer times earnings than its competitors. PEG (PE to growth) is 1.7, while the industry average is 1.5. The result here is that the market is expecting the earnings growth for Apache to be slightly greater than the industry average. While a PEG number above one indicates that the stock could be overvalued, Apache is not in this case, as the industry average is also greater than one. One quick point to note: I double-checked the PEG ratio on Smartmoney.com, which lists a PEG of 0.9. If this number is correct, then Apache is actually undervalued. The problem with forward-looking numbers is that different sources use different growth numbers. This is exactly the case in this situation. My general rule of thumb is to average the two numbers. In this case, it would be 1.3, a reasonable forward-looking number, but not completely accurate. However, more diligent investors can figure out what the PEG is by using the information in Chapter 3.

Next, Apache is trading at 3.3 times sales, while the industry average is 1.8. This number is concerning, and indicates that the company might be a little top heavy in regard to revenue, which is good considering that we are thinking about shorting the stock. Next, the book value of the stock is $36; thus, the stock is trading at 1.9 times book. Obviously, the actual value of the stock is less than the stock itself. Just for a refresher, book value is the net asset value of the company, minus intangible assets and liabilities. (EN 21.1) We will wait to see what Anadarko's book value is and compare the two. The current ratio is 1.3, indicating that if disaster struck, the company would be able to pay its bills 1.3 times over, before it runs out of current (liquid) assets.

Apache is reasonably valued at the current price, but may be getting a little top heavy in regard to future earnings. The stock can ascend only so far before institutional investors stop and ask themselves if the price is worth the risk. Long-term holders will not exit the stock unless fundamentals erode, which is not likely. So from a fundamental basis, we are counting on shorter-term money to sell the stock based on valuation. These types of institutional investors use a combination of market timing and fundamental valuation to protect profits while occasionally trading in and out of positions.

Earnings

In the second quarter, Apache reported earnings of $243 million, or $1.49 a share, up from $143 million, or 0.95 cents in the prior year. However, the company missed analyst expectations of $1.74 a share. Excluding charges, the company beat by two pennies, but in real terms, the company missed. The company cited fluctuations in foreign currencies as the cause for the shortfall; however, in the real world, things like currencies always fluctuate. What is important is that oil production rose by 40 percent in the quarter, while natural gas production leaped 15 percent. The company stated: "We had significant drilling successes and we have completed $1.5 billion in acquisitions year-to-date, the impact of which will be reflected in future quarters." (EN 21.2) Despite the optimistic view from the CEO, the company's one-time charge of $45 million—attributed to currency fluctuations—was due to a weaker U.S. dollar. This is significant because recently several Asian countries announced that they would stop artificially supporting the U.S. dollar to keep their currencies down. The reason Asian countries have been doing this is that when their currencies are low relative to the dollar, then they export more, which brings additional money into their countries. More exporting means increased manufacturing, which means more jobs overall. Thus, without artificial support propping the greenback up, the U.S. dollar is destined to fall lower in the near term. We know from the second quarter that a weaker dollar is bad for Apache. Do you see where I am going? We can generally assume that the company will have the same type of "charge" in the third quarter, unless the company has instituted some sort of currency hedge. However, considering that the Asian currency announcement occurred in September, we can assume Apache probably didn't see it coming. Thus, for the third quarter, I will bet that the company will miss estimates (after charges) again. And the company reports on October 23, just a few weeks from when this is being written. If I am correct, than the missed earnings will help the short side of our pair commence its decline. And none too soon!

Technical Analysis

Looking at the one-year chart for Apache (Figure 21.1), we can see several things. First, the stock is trading near resistance, which it has tested three

FIGURE 21.1 APA Chart

times and been unable to break through. Second, just two days ago, the
stock gapped up on news that the company was paying down more debt, but
has since been unable to hold onto gains. There are several implications
here. Generally, when a stock gaps up, it then falls back in the succeeding
days to close the window—fill the gap—and then resumes the previous up
trend. However, because the stock gapped up and immediately made a lower
low in the following session, the actual pattern is called an Evening Star,
where the three-day pattern indicates that buying orders did not support the
elevated price of the stock. Evening Stars are usually good indications of a
short-term reversal, assuming the stock breaches the gap window support—
roughly $68 in this case.

Third, we also like that the larger one-year pattern is an ascending
wedge, as the stock is trading right at resistance. Ascending wedges are
bullish patterns, but in our case, we are seeking another leg of consolidation. In layman's terms, we are looking for the stock to fall (consolidate)
back to the large rising line crossing the chart in Figure 21.1. Ascending
support is resting near $63, which would be very profitable for our trade,
should the stock fall that low. Daily stochastics are also indicating that the
stock may be overbought, and may need to cool off before heading higher.
This supports our theory that Apache will pursue one more leg of consolidation.

One trouble spot is the moving average convergence divergence (MACD), which has just witnessed a bullish crossover. We do not like this event and would like to see the 12-day moving average (12-DMA) quickly fall back beneath the 26-DMA. Given that the last two days have declined, and that MACD is a trailing indicator, it would be fair to assume the 12-DMA will decline.

Statistics

To bring the statistics as current in our spreadsheet, we will need to update our data through the close of September 26 for both stocks. Also, all of the spreadsheets for each day of the trading diary are located on the CD-ROM in the back of the book. I encourage you to pull up the spreadsheets on your computer and sift through the data as each day passes. After all, the entire trading diary is meant to be a "hands-on" experience to unveil the mystery of pairs.

Looking at the Main portion of our spreadsheet, we see that the pair is presently trading above two standard deviations on the sell side at 26.72. In addition, the ratio is also above two standard deviations at 1.64. However, we also see that the pair has gained risk over the last two years, as it is now trading with a correlation of 0.59.

In the Pair Data portion of the sheet, the density curve is the key to our trade. Over the past several years, the density curve has been slowly opening up and is now at 0.994. My concern for the sake of the book is that I will not get a sell signal before my publishing date. What's more, if the density curve wobbles in this area for the next three weeks and then we do get a signal, there may not be enough time before November 14 to allow the pair room to collapse. Though there are many risks here, my instincts tell me now that the density curve is above 0.990—after several years of divergence—we should get a signal fairly soon. Looking at our pairs charts, we immediately recognize the divergence that has occurred over the last few years. As a side note, you can also see how, if we had been on the ball fundamentally, we could have traded the divergence of these two stocks over the past few years. However, divergence is generally not measurable by statistics, as when a pair is trading on the mean, it can go either way. Statistically, our odds are no better trading the pair either way. Thus, when seeking divergence trades, we must be fully aware of the fundamental events that are transpiring. In short, convergence trading balances statistical odds against fundamental information, while divergence trading—from the mean—does not have the added benefit of trading on the outlying standard deviations.

Summary

We haven't unearthed any information indicating that Apache is an unhealthy company by any means. It is important to distinguish this point in our pairs trading mentality. On the contrary, the information we have found simply indicates that Apache has been extremely strong over the last two years. What we are looking for is an overvalued situation that will present a pullback for us to take advantage of as the stock falls to more reasonable levels. Thus, it is crucial to understand that by considering shorting this stock, we are going against the grain of "trading with the trend." We are contrarians and consequently have more risk. Our risk comes from the fact that we are trying to short a strong stock; we are in essence trying to pick a near-term top. Even with proper due diligence, this can be a losing battle simply because of investor's emotions. Overall, people prefer to buy stocks than short them—after all, many investors don't even know how to short a stock. The point I am trying to get across here is that even though we are trying to implement a hedge, we have considerable risk ahead. I know this is simply redundant rhetoric; I just want to make it extremely clear that we are betting against the flow of each stock.

The crux of our summary is that Apache is starting to look a little top heavy fundamentally, statistically, and technically. There is no doubt in my mind that the stock can go higher, but in the near term it's due for a pullback.

ANADARKO PETROLEUM

Fundamentals

We will begin with a little overview of Anadarko. The company is much larger than Apache, with balance sheet assets over $20 billion as of June 30. This company is almost twice the size of Apache in terms of financial statement assets.

Looking at fundamentals, the company has a PE ratio of 9 and a PEG of 0.86. While these numbers aren't exactly sparkling, they aren't exactly treacherous either. Just to start, we have to be encouraged at the fundamental numbers that Anadarko is posting. Both numbers are lower than Apache's, which is what we would like to see for our trade. What's more, the company has a price to sales of 2.2, and a price to book of 1.4. Figure 21.2 show Anadarko's fundamentals according to Yahoo.com.

Going over the numbers that we have just mentioned, we can assume that the company is fairly valued at present levels and is poised for gains,

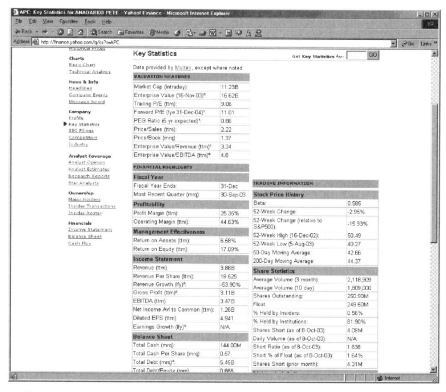

FIGURE 21.2 Yahoo.com Fundamentals

as news surrounding the stock improves. One of the most encouraging numbers is the PEG ratio of 0.86. This ratio lets us know that the stock has room to grow, as future earnings improve. One definite concern is the current ratio, which Yahoo.com (not shown) shows as 0.77. After entering the symbol for a quote on yahoo.com, we click on the "Key Statistics" tab to see the actual numbers. In the last earnings report, Anadarko reported current assets of $1,494 million versus $2,250 million. Thus, to get our current ratio, we divide current assets by current liabilities and we get a ratio of 0.66. Ouch, this is even worse than the number we had before. Our conclusion here is that the company would be pressed for cash if it had to cover *all* of its short-term liabilities at once. While this is not likely to happen, the company's lack of a heaping cash reserve may have investors on edge, and hence is part of the reason for the stock's lack of performance over the last few years.

The stock is well poised for gains, as it is trading at reasonable levels in consideration to valuation. However, investors may be slightly nervous with the company having grown to such a large entity that it does not have the expendable greenbacks to aggressively grow further. Regardless, the trading fundamentals (i.e., PE, PEG, and price to sales) are all well within our ballpark of acceptable numbers.

Earnings

In the most recent earnings report on July 31, the company announced that it had earned $300 million, or $1.20 a share, versus $240 million, or 93 cents in the same quarter 2002. The company fell short of analyst expectations of $1.25; it did, however, see increased net income year over year. The oil magnate attributed the gains to higher oil and natural gas prices. Despite the better-than-expected numbers, the company also mentioned that it was planning on cutting 400 jobs and closing several offices in Texas to save $100 million a year. While this was already mentioned earlier in the book, what was left out is that the company will take a $35 million charge in the third quarter because of the plan.

At the same time, the company also trimmed its full-year earnings outlook from $5.77 a share to $5.17. Obviously, the company is also having trouble with currency exchanges, cited as "falling commodity prices," and will continue to see weakness in future earnings unless the company intervenes in some type of currency hedging. Overall volume output for both natural gas and oil declined in the quarter. Looking forward, Anadarko needs to pull a rabbit out of its hat and either show some sign of an interested buyer, discover a few stellar oil fields, or figure out some way to increase oil production. Again, I am not an oil analyst and am simply making the same observations that the average Joe investor would make.

Technical Analysis

The technical picture for Anadarko looks slightly contrarian, but encouraging nonetheless. The stock is trading on the lower portion of its one-year range, shown in Figure 21.3. The stock has been trading between $40 and $50 since August 2002 and has most recently tested support in early August 2003. Over the last year, the stock has attempted twice to break through $50, but failed both times.

The technical picture depicts short-term descending resistance of the last four months at roughly $45. If the stock can break out above the $45 level, the short-term trend will have been reversed indicating another potential test of $50 on the horizon. Conversely, if ascending support just over $40

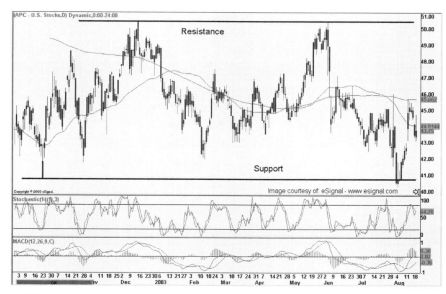

FIGURE 21.3 Anadarko Trading Range

and horizontal support (not pictured) at the $40 whole number is broken, we
may then want to close both sides of our position. Next, the slow stochastic
has been hovering near the overbought region and may now be indicating
that some additional profit taking is on the horizon. The MACD appears to
have been consolidating near the 0 line and has now started to edge higher.
Overall, the technical picture is good for our stock; we are trying to buy near
support with a tight stop just below the whole number. The MACD has
recently turned up and the stock is close to breaking a short-term trend line
that, if breached, would bring momentum traders in off the fence. I like the
technical setup—though not exactly a typical bullish chart, but good for our
pairs trading format.

Statistics

Refer to the statistics for Apache Oil on page 137.

Summary

The fundamental picture for Anadarko looks good; the stock is trading with
fundamentals that support the current price and possible gains in the future.

Most encouraging is the PEG ratio, which alludes to growth on the horizon. Earnings were decent due to higher oil and crude prices, and the company's restructuring program (including job cuts) will save money in the future. However, I am concerned that volumes for both natural gas and oil both fell in the second quarter and thus, have concerns about production growth. The company is obviously looking for a merger, which will be a positive if it surfaces, but is not something we can count on. The technical picture is good for our setup, as the stock is trading on the lower portion of the range, with a clear stop at the $40 whole number. Overall, the setup is ideal for this trade and is encouraging with the current statistical data as well.

CHAPTER 22

Trading Diary[1]

Friday, September 26

As you already know, I have just come across this pair and found that it may present some interesting opportunity in the near future. You may be asking yourself how I found the pair to begin with? I have a spreadsheet with over 200 pairs that I check every day. The sheet updates itself with a macro I had programmed that self-extracts data from Yahoo.com. While this portion of the program is proprietary and not available in this book, it should not stop you from finding great pairs. In fact, the macro is a recent addition to my trading, and only several months ago, I would scan charts each night to find possible pairs divergences. What I do is keep a running "watch list" of pairs that are beginning to separate with their correlations. Then, instead of scanning 200 charts a night, I can look through only 50 or so. When I hear news about two related stocks that may have diverged, I put them on the watch list and keep a close eye on them. What's more, every two weeks I go through my entire pairs universe of about 400 stocks to find possible convergence setups or fundamental events that could lead to additional divergence. In my scans, I ran across Apache/Anadarko, a pair that I have not traded in a long, long time. Obviously, I was not on board for the divergence (though I wish I had been) and am now trying to find a point where the rubber band will cease expanding.

Initially, I like the technical picture (see Figure 22.1) of the two stocks and the divergence that has occurred. Fundamentally, it feels like Apache is getting top heavy, while Anadarko has been suppressed because of managerial

---

[1]*Note*: All charts for Apache Oil reflect post split prices, though the text includes pre-split numbers (the stock split 2-for-1 on January 15, 2004 after the text was written).

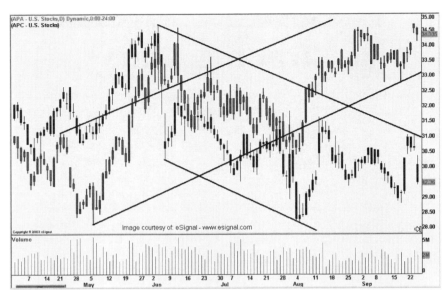

FIGURE 22.1 APC through 9/26

impotency. While I have no doubt that Apache will go higher in the future, a pullback seems right around the corner. And as for Anadarko, the largest independent oil company, the asset value of the company is sure to attract some type of merger-related news, and hence, gains for the stock.

In recent news, OPEC decided to cut the supply of oil by 900,000 barrels beginning on November 1. The news was quite amazing and points out that the OPEC cartel sees some type of oversupply surfacing, or simply cares only about keeping the price of crude artificially high. If oil continues to trade near or above $30 per barrel, both Apache and Anadarko will see improved profits in the quarters to come. The move outraged analysts and has sparked some debate as to what OPEC's true intentions really are.

Looking at the statistics of our trade, I am salivating at the setup. The density curve has now poked its head above 0.990, with it currently at 0.994. It's not every day that I get into a trade on the day it hits 0.997 or greater, but now that I am watching this pair closely, I will not miss a beat. I am concerned that the pair has been opening up for several years, and feel that it is quite pompous to think that my style will call the top of the spread to the day. However, I will wait patiently to take a position, and will then keep my stops tight. Once I have taken a position, I will set breakout and breakdown stops for both Apache and Anadarko (respectively) and close both sides of the position, should either stock betray me. After all, it's not about your entry, it's all about your exit.

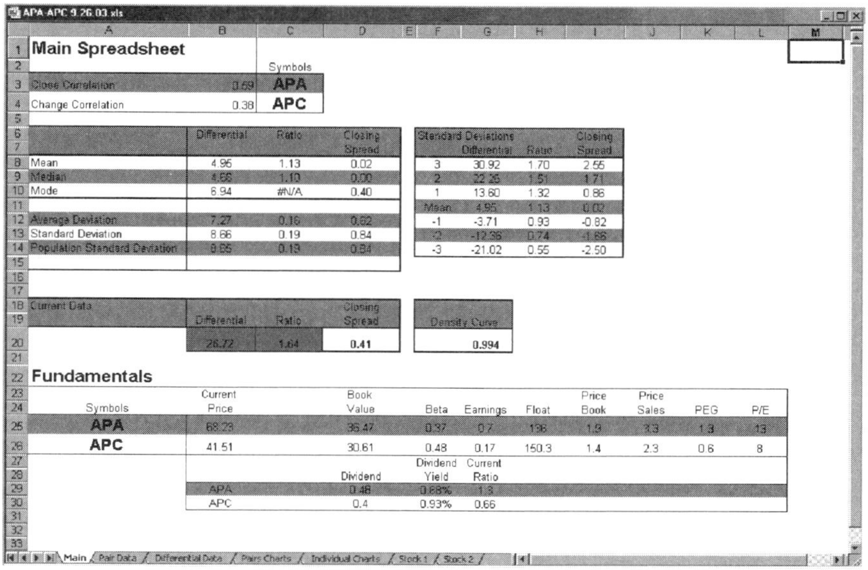

FIGURE 22.2 Main Spreadsheet

Figures 22.2 and 22.3 show the current density curve data and the Main spreadsheet with descriptive statistics.

My concern now (as I have previously mentioned) is that the pair will not open up to give us an entry signal with enough time to collapse before the book is published. However, it is my experience that once a signal is triggered, the trade moves fairly quickly. Also both companies report earnings in the next month, with Apache on the 23rd of October and Anadarko on the 31st.

Monday, September 29

Bingo! Our pair is continuing to open up, with the density curve now at 0.995. What I previously forgot to mention is that this pair is trading above two standard deviations, for both the differential and the ratio. The differential is currently 27.11, with the second standard deviation at 22.33, while the ratio is presently 1.65, and the second standard deviation (for the ratio) is 1.51. Thus, as long as the descriptive statistics indicate that the pair is above two standard deviations—and the density curve closes at or above 0.997—we will immediately take a position on the following day. Figure 22.4 shows how our density curve has been slowly opening up for the past two years and is now hovering very close to one.

There was no news today on either stock. I would like to take a moment and look at the technical picture for Apache. The stock has just concluded

APA-APC 9.26.03.xls					
	A	B	C	D	E	F
1	Pair Data	4.95	8.66			
2						
3				Close	Density	
4	Date	Differential	Ratio	Spread	Curve	
5	9/26/03	26.72	1.64	0.41	0.994	
6	9/25/03	26.31	1.62	1.38	0.993	
7	9/24/03	24.93	1.56	0.94	0.990	
8	9/23/03	23.99	1.54	1.20	0.986	
9	9/22/03	22.79	1.51	-1.11	0.980	
10	9/19/03	23.9	1.55	-1.01	0.986	
11	9/18/03	24.9	1.59	-0.10	0.989	
12	9/17/03	25	1.60	-0.54	0.990	
13	9/16/03	25.55	1.61	0.60	0.991	
14	9/15/03	24.94	1.59	0.17	0.990	
15	9/12/03	24.78	1.58	1.10	0.989	
16	9/11/03	23.67	1.55	-0.13	0.985	
17	9/10/03	23.8	1.55	0.44	0.985	
18	9/9/03	23.36	1.54	-0.66	0.983	
19	9/8/03	24.03	1.55	0.57	0.986	
20	9/5/03	23.45	1.54	-1.06	0.984	
21	9/4/03	24.52	1.56	-0.54	0.988	
22	9/3/03	25.06	1.57	-0.13	0.990	
23	9/2/03	25.19	1.58	-0.29	0.990	
24	8/29/03	25.48	1.59	-0.05	0.991	
25	8/28/03	25.53	1.59	0.89	0.991	
26	8/27/03	24.63	1.58	0.69	0.989	
27	8/26/03	23.94	1.56	-0.30	0.986	
28	8/25/03	24.24	1.57	0.87	0.987	
29	8/22/03	23.37	1.54	0.03	0.983	
30	8/21/03	23.34	1.53	1.00	0.983	
31	8/20/03	22.34	1.51	-0.67	0.978	
32	8/19/03	23.01	1.53	0.62	0.982	
33	8/18/03	22.39	1.50	1.20	0.978	
34	8/15/03	21.19	1.47	0.54	0.970	
35	8/14/03	20.65	1.46	-1.14	0.965	
36	8/13/03	21.79	1.49	-1.51	0.974	
37	8/12/03	23.3	1.55	0.64	0.983	
38	8/11/03	22.66	1.53	-0.28	0.980	
39	8/8/03	22.94	1.55	-0.40	0.981	
40	8/7/03	23.34	1.56	1.14	0.983	
41	8/6/03	22.2	1.55	1.50	0.977	

Main \ **Pair Data** / Differential Data / Pairs Charts

FIGURE 22.3 Pair Data

the third consecutive down day after the recent evening star candlestick formation. The stock has now fallen below the gap (or window) support, which is a good sign for our trade—with the exception that we need the pair to open up enough that an entry signal is created. Figure 22.5 shows that the stock has support at $66 due to the 50-SMA (simple moving average). A breach of the 50-SMA would likely bring the stock into ascending support at roughly $64, where we would like to see a further breakdown. I don't know about you, but this betting against a strong stock stuff is stressful.

Density Curve

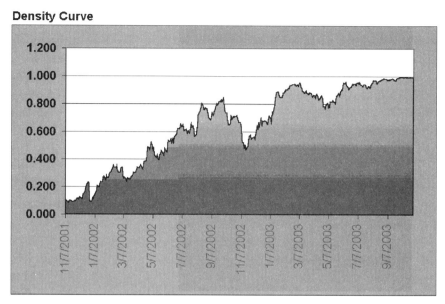

FIGURE 22.4 Density Curve

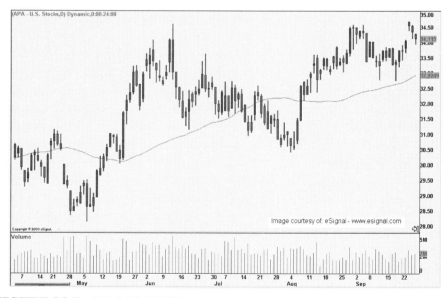

FIGURE 22.5 APA 9/26 50-SMA

Tuesday, September 30th

Standard & Poor's (S&P) announced that it would leave Apache's credit rating at A-/Stable/A-2, in light of the company's repurchase and retirement of preferred interests from three of the company's subsidiaries. The announcement by S&P has caused Apache to gain a little momentum and hold gap window support. This is good for our pair, as we would like it to open up slightly more or at least enough to produce an entry signal. The density curve data revised yesterday's data down to 0.994, with today at 0.995. The data expansion continues to move in the correct direction, and I have a feeling that either stock could now trigger the 0.002 move we need to enter the position. Figure 22.6 shows the density curve data over the last month.

Wednesday, October 1

Now I am getting really excited, as the pair has continued to open up, with the differential currently at 28.29 and the ratio at 1.68. The electrifying part here is that both the differential and the ratio are very close to the third standard deviation, which means that (if we ever take a position) we will be trading with nearly 99.7 percent of the pair's data. Generally, I like to find pairs with differentials and ratios trading as close to the third standard deviation as possible, without going over. The problem is that once the third standard deviation is violated, the remaining 0.3 percent of data can translate into infinite pain for our pair. Thus, I generally always use the third standard deviation as a secondary tier stop loss. Call it a reserve parachute, if you like. If I take a position close to the third standard deviation and it is subsequently violated, I then close the entire position, regardless of other stop loss parameters. Close the losing play, live to trade another day.

Addressing concerns that we have for the pair—even though we don't have a position yet—Anadarko was hammered lower in the last few days of September. I imagine that part of this was due to September being the last month of the third quarter, and many funds, institutions, and personal money managers did not want the stock to show up on their quarterly reports. Thus, they dumped Anadarko, as is did not perform very well in the third quarter. Coincidentally, the stock found support on the last day of the month and actually closed positive today. The buoying action of the stock insinuates that some investors who recently sold positions are now reclaiming them at a lower price for the fourth quarter. And, of course, some of the gains over the last two days can be attributed to short covering as well.

	A	B	C	D	E	F
	APA-APC 9.30.03.xls					_ □ ×
	A	**B**	**C**	**D**	**E**	**F**
1	Pair Data	4.98	8.71			
2						
3				Close	Density	
4	Date	Differential	Ratio	Spread	Curve	
5	9/30/03	27.58	1.66	0.47	0.995	
6	9/29/03	27.11	1.65	0.39	0.994	
7	9/26/03	26.72	1.64	0.41	0.994	
8	9/25/03	26.31	1.62	1.38	0.993	
9	9/24/03	24.93	1.56	0.94	0.989	
10	9/23/03	23.99	1.54	1.20	0.985	
11	9/22/03	22.79	1.51	-1.11	0.980	
12	9/19/03	23.9	1.55	-1.01	0.985	
13	9/18/03	24.9	1.59	-0.10	0.989	
14	9/17/03	25	1.60	-0.54	0.989	
15	9/16/03	25.55	1.61	0.60	0.991	
16	9/15/03	24.94	1.59	0.17	0.989	
17	9/12/03	24.78	1.58	1.10	0.989	
18	9/11/03	23.67	1.55	-0.13	0.984	
19	9/10/03	23.8	1.55	0.44	0.985	
20	9/9/03	23.36	1.54	-0.66	0.983	
21	9/8/03	24.03	1.55	0.57	0.986	
22	9/5/03	23.45	1.54	-1.06	0.983	
23	9/4/03	24.52	1.56	-0.54	0.988	
24	9/3/03	25.06	1.57	-0.13	0.989	
25	9/2/03	25.19	1.58	-0.29	0.990	
26	8/29/03	25.48	1.59	-0.05	0.991	
27	8/28/03	25.53	1.59	0.89	0.991	
28	8/27/03	24.63	1.58	0.69	0.988	
29	8/26/03	23.94	1.56	-0.30	0.985	
30	8/25/03	24.24	1.57	0.87	0.987	
31	8/22/03	23.37	1.54	0.03	0.983	
32	8/21/03	23.34	1.53	1.00	0.983	
33	8/20/03	22.34	1.51	-0.67	0.977	
34	8/19/03	23.01	1.53	0.62	0.981	
35	8/18/03	22.39	1.50	1.20	0.977	
36	8/15/03	21.19	1.47	0.54	0.969	
37	8/14/03	20.65	1.46	-1.14	0.964	
38	8/13/03	21.79	1.49	-1.51	0.973	
39	8/12/03	23.3	1.55	0.64	0.982	
40	8/11/03	22.66	1.53	-0.28	0.979	
41	8/8/03	22.94	1.55	-0.40	0.980	
42	8/7/03	23.34	1.56	1.14	0.983	
43	8/6/03	22.2	1.55	1.50	0.976	
44	8/5/03	20.69	1.51	-0.06	0.964	

Pair Data / Differential Data / Pairs Charts / In

FIGURE 22.6 APA-APC 9/30/03 Density Curve Data

The most important concern I have now is that the stock is trading just over $41, and only slightly above my stop at $40. As mentioned before, I will close the position if the stock violates the $40 whole number. The problem is that the stock is trading near our stop before the trade has actually been entered. Thus, if $40 is sullied and we still have not received an entry signal,

FIGURE 22.7　APC CHART 10/1

I will toss the trade in the dumpster anyway. The point here is that trading only with pure statistics rules out common sense. And discarding this trade if Anadarko falls below $40 is common sense.

Figure 22.7 displays Anadarko's trading action over the last few days. It also shows the descending resistance line that we would like to see the stock eventually ascend back over in order to indicate another leg of trading within the $40 to $50 range.

Thursday, October 2

And here we go! Are you nervous? I am. The pair finally received the buy signal today, so now it's time for me to put my money where my mouth is. This entire book comes down to today, the session that provided an entry signal for an actual pairs trade. What's more, this is the first time the Apache/Anadarko density curve has hit 0.997 in the history (over six years) of data we are covering. The closing differential today was 28.75, while the ratio was 1.69; both still above two standard deviations. Figure 22.8 shows our Pair Data sheet and the actual sell signal.

Incidentally, the signal was derived from Apache's move above $70, which was a new 52-week high. And so I am asking myself, "Why would I ever step in front of a stock trading at a new 52-week high—am I insane?" And while the answer may partially be yes, I know that I have done my research. Apache looks top heavy, and, statistically, the pair looks as if it

	A	B	C	D	E	F	G	H
				Close	Density			
	Date	Differential	Ratio	Spread	Curve			
1	Pair Data	5.01	8.76					
5	10/2/03	28.75	1.69	0.46	0.997			
6	10/1/03	28.29	1.68	0.71	0.996			
7	9/30/03	27.58	1.66	0.47	0.995			
8	9/29/03	27.11	1.65	0.39	0.994			
9	9/26/03	26.72	1.64	0.41	0.993			
10	9/25/03	26.31	1.62	1.38	0.992			
11	9/24/03	24.93	1.56	0.94	0.988		Sell signal	
12	9/23/03	23.99	1.54	1.20	0.985			
13	9/22/03	22.79	1.51	-1.11	0.979			
14	9/19/03	23.9	1.55	-1.01	0.984			
15	9/18/03	24.9	1.59	-0.10	0.988			
16	9/17/03	25	1.60	-0.54	0.989			
17	9/16/03	25.55	1.61	0.60	0.990			
18	9/15/03	24.94	1.59	0.17	0.989			
19	9/12/03	24.78	1.58	1.10	0.988			
20	9/11/03	23.67	1.55	-0.13	0.983			
21	9/10/03	23.8	1.55	0.44	0.984			
22	9/9/03	23.36	1.54	-0.66	0.982			
23	9/8/03	24.03	1.55	0.57	0.985			
24	9/5/03	23.45	1.54	-1.06	0.982			
25	9/4/03	24.52	1.56	-0.54	0.987			
26	9/3/03	25.06	1.57	-0.13	0.989			
27	9/2/03	25.19	1.58	-0.29	0.989			
28	8/29/03	25.48	1.59	-0.05	0.990			
29	8/28/03	25.53	1.59	0.89	0.990			
30	8/27/03	24.63	1.58	0.69	0.987			
31	8/26/03	23.94	1.56	-0.30	0.985			
32	8/25/03	24.24	1.57	0.87	0.986			
33	8/22/03	23.37	1.54	0.03	0.982			
34	8/21/03	23.34	1.53	1.00	0.982			
35	8/20/03	22.34	1.51	-0.67	0.976			
36	8/19/03	23.01	1.53	0.62	0.980			
37	8/18/03	22.39	1.50	1.20	0.976			
38	8/15/03	21.19	1.47	0.54	0.968			
39	8/14/03	20.65	1.46	-1.14	0.963			
40	8/13/03	21.79	1.49	-1.51	0.972			
41	8/12/03	23.3	1.55	0.64	0.982			
42	8/11/03	22.66	1.53	-0.28	0.978			
43	8/8/03	22.94	1.55	-0.40	0.980			
44	8/7/03	23.34	1.56	1.14	0.982			

Pair Data / Differential Data / Pairs Charts / Individual Ch.

FIGURE 22.8 PAIR DATA 10/2

is nearing maximum divergence. To tell you the truth, I generally prefer pairs in which both stocks are range bound, and neither are making a new 52-week high or low. Figure 22.9 shows just how strong Apache is.

The actual plan for the trade is this: Tomorrow morning, I will buy 1,000 shares of Anadarko after 10:00 A.M. EST and sell short 1,000 shares of Apache at the same time. The reason I am choosing after 10:00 A.M. EST is that I like to let some of the morning's order flow—and trading action—shake out before I put my money in. Usually, I actually look at the stocks in the morning and then make a decision to enter on the open or wait. However, for the

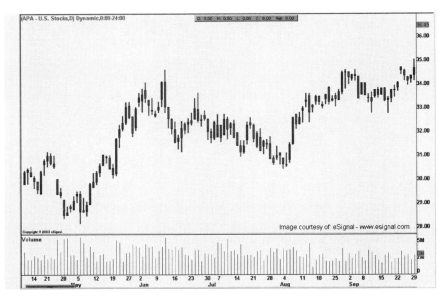

FIGURE 22.9 APA 10/2 New 52-Week High

sake of the book, I will wait until after 10:00 A.M. EST before taking my positions. Also, keep in mind that we are taking our position ahead of earnings. When I can avoid it, I usually try to not trade ahead of earnings announcements. However, in the case of Anadarko/Apache, as we already discussed, the upcoming earnings could actually help the pair reverse in our favor.

Friday, October 3

This morning I entered my position at the following prices (rounded to the nearest whole number):

- Anadarko Petroleum: Long 1,000 shares @ $41.60 = $41,600 in capital exposure.
- Apache Oil: Short 1,000 shares @ $70.50 = $70,500 in capital exposure.

Thus, I am risking $112,100 on this trade.

My stop parameters for the position are: First, if the position moves above three standard deviations, I will close the trade. The differential of my position is 28.90, and the differential of the third standard deviation is 31.41. Thus, if I am stopped out by this method, I stand to lose $5,020: [($31.41 − 28.90)*2,000] = $5,020. This would equate to a 4.5 percent loss of my trading capital.

	Shares	Entry	Total Exposure	Close	Dollar Gain/Loss	Percent Gain/Loss
Apache Oil (short)	1,000	70.5	$70,500.00	71.7	($1,200.00)	
Anadarko Petroleum (long)	1,000	41.6	$41,600.00	42	$400.00	
Differential		28.9		29.7		
Gain/Loss					($800.00)	
Total Exposure			$112,100.00		$111,300.00	
Commissions: # of trades * $20 per trade			2		($840.00)	
Total Gain/Loss including commissions			$112,060.00		$111,260.00	-0.75%

FIGURE 22.10 Trade Summary 10/3

Second, if Anadarko falls below $40, I will close the position. It is hard to figure exactly how much I will lose, but I can assume that it will be $1,600 from my entry on Anadarko, plus or minus any gain/loss from Apache.

Third, if we were not trading near the third standard deviation, I would not risk more than 8 percent of capital on each side of the trade. However, this is the most risky way of pairs trading, as it can wipe out 16 percent of your account. This is only to be used by investors who can afford to lose all of their trading capital. If you cannot afford to lose, *do not trade*. It's that important!

This trade has an unusually low risk-to-reward ratio for a pairs trade, as normally when we are risking 16 percent of our capital, we stand to barely make that much if the trade works out. Thus, what I do is put tight trailing stop losses on my positions once they begin to work in my favor. Also, another tactic I often use is to quickly close part of the position once it shows gains. That way, I make sure the commissions (which are double) are paid for, while trying to put a little dough in my pocket.

Figure 22.10 is a breakdown of where our trade stands. As you can see, we are already $840 out of the money including commissions. Ouch! The closing differential closed above our entry, which is not good for our pocketbook or peace of mind.

Monday, October 6

Our first reaction to today's trading is "oh no," as the pair has continued to open up against us. The differential is $29.79, and the density curve is still at 0.997. What's scary here is that the density curve could continue to open up to 1, where I would be stopped out at for a large whopper of a loss. And losing money is no fun. However, considering that the trade moved against us by only 8 cents, I am not worried yet. Also, Anadarko gained ground, which is a positive sign. Remember, we are hoping the stock will rise above

	Shares	Entry	Total Exposure	Close	Dollar Gain/Loss	Percent Gain/Loss
Apache Oil (short)	1,000	70.5	$70,500.00	72.9	($2,400.00)	
Anadarko Petroleum (long)	1,000	41.6	$41,600.00	43.12	$1,520.00	
Differential		28.9		29.78		
Gain/Loss					($880.00)	
Total Exposure			$112,100.00		$111,220.00	
Commissions: # of trades * $20 per trade			2		($920.00)	
Total Gain/Loss including commissions			$112,060.00		$111,180.00	-0.82%

FIGURE 22.11 Trade Summary 10/6

$45 to indicate a breach of descending resistance and a potential move to the upper end of the annual range. Currently, we are down 0.82 percent in our position, which translates to $920 dollars. What's more, the ratio is only 0.02 away from the third standard deviation, which is concerning, even though we are using only the differential as our third standard deviation stop. Figure 22.11 shows our loss to date, including commissions, of course.

There was no significant news today.

Tuesday, October 7

The trade moved in our direction today, with the differential coming in to 29.61. While I am still out of the money $750, the picture is getting a little brighter. Wachovia Securities upgraded Anadarko to Market Perform (EN 22.1), which is an outstanding sign for our trade. Though the stock did not gain any ground, Wachovia is likely seeking some sort of merger talk to help bolster buying sentiment.

Apache continues to gain ground and is picking up momentum. The stock closed at $72.51—another 52-week high. Thankfully, Anadarko is also hanging in there, closing at $43.02. While I am concerned that the trade is still negative, there is no reason to panic yet. Figure 22.12 displays the gains that Apache's stock has made.

My feeling is that if the stock wasn't top heavy before, it is getting there now. Also, this is the perfect scenario depicting how pairs trading can be frustrating and mind-boggling. I have attempted to short an incredibly strong stock and am paying dearly for it. My feeling is that investors are purchasing the stock ahead of earnings, which could lead to a "buy the rumor, sell the news" type of scenario.

Figure 22.13 shows the current trade summary.

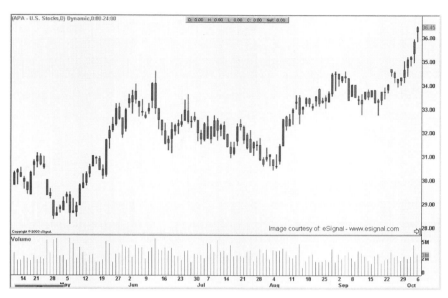

FIGURE 22.12 APA 10/7 New 52-Week High

	Shares	Entry	Total Exposure	Close	Dollar Gain/Loss	Percent Gain/Loss
Apache Oil (short)	1,000	70.5	$70,500.00	72.63	($2,130.00)	
Anadarko Petroleum (long)	1,000	41.6	$41,600.00	43.02	$1,420.00	
Differential		28.9		29.61		
Gain/Loss					($710.00)	
Total Exposure			$112,100.00		$111,390.00	
Commissions: # of trades * $20 per trade				2	($750.00)	
Total Gain/Loss including commissions			$112,060.00		$111,350.00	-0.67%

FIGURE 22.13 Trade Summary 10/07/03

Wednesday, October 8

The density curve has been pegged at 0.997 for the last four days; however, the differential has fallen to 29.42, which certainly bodes well for the trade. I am happy to see the position cool off, but will reserve my emotions until the differential falls below the entry point. The trade still has a considerable amount of risk, as any bad news for Anadarko at this point could quickly send my capital into someone else's pocket. In addition, the ratio is still at 1.69 and has not come in at all. I still maintain that Apache is overbought and that the current trading action is simply buying ahead of earnings. My biggest fear here is that Apache will consolidate for several days, then break

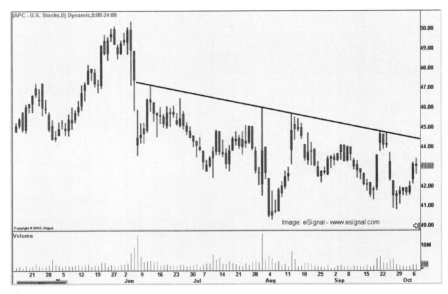

FIGURE 22.14 Anadarko through 10/8

	Shares	Entry	Total Exposure	Close	Dollar Gain/Loss	Percent Gain/Loss
Apache Oil (short)	500	70.5	$35,250.00	71.78	($640.00)	
Anadarko Petroleum (long)	500	41.6	$20,800.00	42.36	$380.00	
Differential		28.9		29.42		
Gain/Loss					($260.00)	
Total Exposure			$56,050.00		$55,790.00	
Commissions: # of trades * $20 per trade			0		($260.00)	
Total Gain/Loss including commissions			$56,050.00		$55,790.00	-0.46%

FIGURE 22.15 Trade Summary 10/8

out. Anadarko has been gaining some momentum and is moving away from the $40 stop, though until the stock actually breaches the short-term descending resistance line, I won't get to overzealous. Figure 22.14 displays Anadarko's current range, and shows that the stock is gaining momentum.

In news today, Apache announced that it made a second discovery off the shore of Western Australia. Though this news won't really affect the stock much, it is positive news indicating that the company is still aggressively finding new wells. If I wasn't short the stock, I would be very happy about the find.

As the following trade summary in Figure 22.15 depicts, we are still negative, with the position down $560, or one half a percent, "Apache fall, Apache fall, Apache fall," I am thinking.

Thursday, October 9

Wow! What a difference one day makes—the trade has come positive, and none too soon! The differential fell below my entry of 27.84. The catalyst for the decline came from Apache receiving a downgrade by CS First Boston from Buy to Neutral. In my opinion, the firm sees that the company is overvalued and has acted on such information. (Keep in mind that this just my guess.) One area of concern, though, is that the company has confirmed a shareholder meeting on December 18 for a previously announced stock split. While this news will not directly affect the price in the near term, stocks have a tendency to run up ahead of splits. Thus, I will be relieved to exit the trade early if the position falls farther in my favor. However, the lower lows created in the past two sessions have somewhat relieved my fear that the stock could be consolidating for another breakout. From here, the stock will likely fall into the $68 range, otherwise known as near-term ascending support. Figure 22.16 shows the density curve, which has fallen to 0.995—an excellent sign for our trade.

Also encouraging, the ratio has fallen to 1.65, thus backing off from the third standard deviation at 1.72. Sometimes it takes investors several days to digest up/downgrades, which could translate to more selling on the horizon. At the end of the day, the good news here is that in the last week, the trade has had one upgrade for our long position and one downgrade for the short side. This is a good sign that we are on the right side of the rubber band—the contraction side. The position is now positive $1,020, or 0.91 percent. If I were to close the trade here, it wouldn't be a bad take for only five days of trading. One percent every five days on $100,000 translates to 52 percent in gains each year. Not bad, but a completely unreal number. But then again, its okay to dream, isn't it? (See Figure 22.17.)

Friday, October 10

The differential popped back up to 28.69 and has eroded the bulk of the trade's profit overnight. But the important thing to remember is that the trade is still green, and that's all that matters. The density curve picked up a little momentum and has risen to 0.996, but isn't anything to worry about at this time. My only real concern is that the position collapses before I have to

```
APA-APC 10.09.03.xls                                          _ □ X
         A              B            C           D            E        F
1   Pair Data         5.10         8.92
2
3                                             Close       Density
4   Date           Differential   Ratio      Spread      Curve
5   10/9/03           27.84        1.65       -1.58        0.995
6   10/8/03           29.42        1.69       -0.19        0.997
7   10/7/03           29.61        1.69       -0.17        0.997
8   10/6/03           29.78        1.69        0.08        0.997
9   10/3/03           29.7         1.71        0.95        0.997
10  10/2/03           28.75        1.69        0.46        0.996
11  10/1/03           28.29        1.68        0.71        0.995
12  9/30/03           27.58        1.66        0.47        0.994
13  9/29/03           27.11        1.65        0.39        0.993
14  9/26/03           26.72        1.64        0.41        0.992
15  9/25/03           26.31        1.62        1.38        0.991
16  9/24/03           24.93        1.56        0.94        0.987
17  9/23/03           23.99        1.54        1.20        0.983
18  9/22/03           22.79        1.51       -1.11        0.976
19  9/19/03           23.9         1.55       -1.01        0.982
20  9/18/03           24.9         1.59       -0.10        0.987
21  9/17/03           25           1.60       -0.54        0.987
22  9/16/03           25.55        1.61        0.60        0.989
23  9/15/03           24.94        1.59        0.17        0.987
24  9/12/03           24.78        1.58        1.10        0.986
25  9/11/03           23.67        1.55       -0.13        0.981
26  9/10/03           23.8         1.55        0.44        0.982
27  9/9/03            23.36        1.54       -0.66        0.980
28  9/8/03            24.03        1.55        0.57        0.983
29  9/5/03            23.45        1.54       -1.06        0.980
30  9/4/03            24.52        1.56       -0.54        0.985
31  9/3/03            25.06        1.57       -0.13        0.987
32  9/2/03            25.19        1.58       -0.29        0.988
33  8/29/03           25.48        1.59       -0.05        0.989
34  8/28/03           25.53        1.59        0.89        0.989
35  8/27/03           24.63        1.58        0.69        0.986
36  8/26/03           23.94        1.56       -0.30        0.983
37  8/25/03           24.24        1.57        0.87        0.984
38  8/22/03           23.37        1.54        0.03        0.980
39  8/21/03           23.34        1.53        1.00        0.980
40  8/20/03           22.34        1.51       -0.67        0.973
41  8/19/03           23.01        1.53        0.62        0.978
    Pair Data / Differential Data / Pairs Charts / I
```

FIGURE 22.16 APA DENSITY CURVE 10/9

close it in November. I would feel silly to publish a loss, but I will record whatever happens, for better or worse.

Anadarko's chart in Figure 22.18 is cheering, as the stock is building a base above $42, which is now support. I hate to think the stock could be forming a bear flag (consolidation after a large downward movement) that may indicate another big drop coming up. While I don't think this is the case,

	Shares	Entry	Total Exposure	Close	Dollar Gain/Loss	Percent Gain/Loss
Apache Oil (short)	1,000	70.5	$70,500.00	70.67	($170.00)	
Anadarko Petroleum (long)	1,000	41.6	$41,600.00	42.83	$1,230.00	
Differential		28.9		27.84		
Gain/Loss					$1,060.00	
Total Exposure			$112,100.00		$113,160.00	
Commissions: # of trades * $20 per trade				2	$1,020.00	
Total Gain/Loss including commissions			$112,060.00		$113,120.00	0.91%

FIGURE 22.17 Trade Summary 10/9

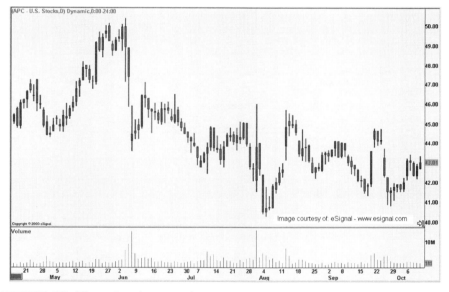

FIGURE 22.18 APC 10/10 Bear Flag

I must consider all possibilities of my trade, even the not-so-bright ones. Figure 22.18 displays the possible bear flag forming. Usually though, a bear flag forms only after a large vertical drop, which in this case the stock did not do. The bear flag is normally the first part of a "flag and pennant" pattern, where in a consolidating "flag" is first formed, followed by a substantial decline and then more consolidation.

The trade now has a meager profit of $170 after commissions, which would equate to $130 if closed. While it is a little discouraging to see the profit dwindle, I am very optimistic about the future of the trade. There was no notable news for either stock today. (See Figure 22.19.)

	Shares	Entry	Total Exposure	Close	Dollar Gain/Loss	Percent Gain/Loss
Apache Oil (short)	1,000	70.5	$70,500.00	71.7	($1,200.00)	
Anadarko Petroleum (long)	1,000	41.6	$41,600.00	43.01	$1,410.00	
Differential		28.9		28.69		
Gain/Loss					$210.00	
Total Exposure			$112,100.00		$112,310.00	
Commissions: # of trades * $20 per trade				2	$170.00	
Total Gain/Loss including commissions			$112,060.00		$112,270.00	0.15%

FIGURE 22.19 Trade Summary 10/10

	Shares	Entry	Total Exposure	Close	Dollar Gain/Loss	Percent Gain/Loss
Apache Oil (short)	1,000	70.5	$70,500.00	72.04	($1,540.00)	
Anadarko Petroleum (long)	1,000	41.6	$41,600.00	43.08	$1,480.00	
Differential		28.9		28.96		
Gain/Loss					($60.00)	
Total Exposure			$112,100.00		$112,040.00	
Commissions: # of trades * $20 per trade				2	($100.00)	
Total Gain/Loss including commissions			$112,060.00		$112,000.00	-0.09%

FIGURE 22.20 Trade Summary 10/13

Monday, October 13

Here I am, red again! The differential gained ground over the last day, and is now at 28.96, just above my entry. Overall, the trade is down $100—nothing to worry about. What I don't like, though, is that Apache looks like it is consolidating for another leg higher—yes, the thing I was worried about earlier. However, the density curve is still below our entry at 0.996, while the ratio is at 1.67 (see Figure 22.20). This is where I generally enlist faith in the statistics and hope that they will prove true. Incidentally, hope is the last thing you ever want in a trade. Maybe you should put the book down and go get a beer—I know I am.

Tuesday, October 14

I'm glad I had beers last night instead of worrying about my trade, and it seems to have paid off. The position is now working in my favor again, with the differential at 28.52. Given that the differential has been hovering around this area, and that the density curve has not been able to move higher, I have a feeling that the trade will begin to show some profit. The chart for Apache is still very strong, and I wouldn't put it past exuberant buyers to push the

	Shares	Entry	Total Exposure	Close	Dollar Gain/Loss	Percent Gain/Loss
Apache Oil (short)	1,000	70.5	$70,500.00	70.97	($470.00)	
Anadarko Petroleum (long)	1,000	41.6	$41,600.00	42.45	$850.00	
Differential		28.9		28.52		
Gain/Loss					$380.00	
Total Exposure			$112,100.00		$112,480.00	
Commissions: # of trades * $20 per trade			2		$340.00	
Total Gain/Loss including commissions			$112,060.00		$112,440.00	0.30%

FIGURE 22.21 Trade Summary 10/14

stock higher. My question now is: Who is the greater fool? Who is foolish enough to buy the stock here, thinking that someone else is going to buy it higher? I can see purchasing Anadarko at $46 or $47—higher than where the stock is here—but Apache? No dice. The risk to reward for the stock is getting too high for the average investor to stomach, and in my opinion, the company knows it. That's why we have recently heard talk of a split, to make the stock cheaper and more attractive for additional investment.

At this point our trade is positive by $340, and after taxes, I'm not sure if that's even a car payment, so we'll press on.

There was no notable news on either stock today. (See Figure 22.21.)

Wednesday, October 15

We're back in business. The differential fell to 28.07 and has our profit building once again. Though we haven't made any real money, the trade is encouraging. There was no significant news on either stock today; thus, the selling was due to the larger movement of the market. I am keeping a close eye on Anadarko, which has fallen to $41.56. If Anadarko falls beneath $40, the whole trade gets closed—win or loss. My reason for the $40 dollar stop is in the cliché "You don't have to buy, but you do have to sell." What this saying means is that it will be more difficult for Apache to ascend than for Anadarko to crumble. If the stock breaches $40, then many investors will say they've had it with the thing, and throw in the towel. Add in a couple of funds exiting their positions, and we could see an all-out dump in the stock equating to several points evaporated. I for one don't want to be along for the ride and, statistics aside, would rather sleep at night than spend my time wishing someone would realize the value of the stock and buy it back up. The bottom line here is that for every trade, you should have an "I've had it, sell the thing" stop. And for Anadarko, $39.99, one penny below $40 is my number. The reason I have chosen $39.99 is that I want the stock to print below the whole number before closing the position. Sometimes a stock will test a substantial support or resistance level and not penetrate it. Also of important note, more seasoned traders often prefer to put their stops roughly 25 cents above/below a whole number, just to ensure that a couple of cents on the opposite side won't wiggle them out of their positions.

Figures 22.22 and 22.23 voice both my concern and optimism for the trade. Figure 22.22 shows that Apache's stock fell beneath $70, which is critical support. I am very pleased with the trading action, as the stock is now resting near ascending support. If it continues to fall and breaks the ascending line, longer-term ascending support near $64 could quickly become a reality. This is good, good, good.

Figure 22.23 is bad, bad, bad. Anadarko's stock has made a bold move downward and could be heading toward $40. In addition, the stock has violated horizontal support at $42, which does not bode well for bulls. My thinking here is that the stock will hold above $40, as institutions buy the dips. Even though Anadarko hasn't reported any good news lately, my instincts tell me that somewhere out there lurks a merger rumor. However, we could be long gone from the entire trade before any such news surfaces.

The trade is now up $790, or 0.70 percent. I would like to close the trade within the next three weeks, and to do so I will need some negative news from Apache, while Anadarko struggles to hold ground. (See Figure 22.24.)

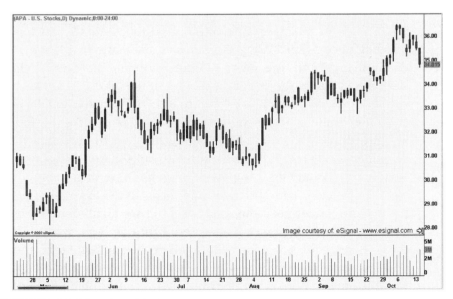

FIGURE 22.22 APA 10/15

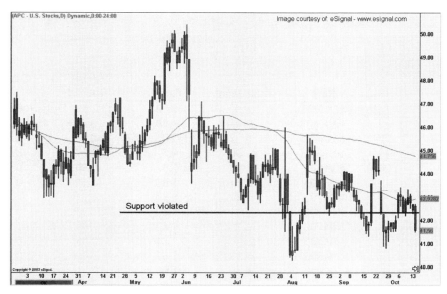

FIGURE 22.23 APC 10/15

			Total			Dollar	Percent
	Shares	Entry	Exposure		Close	Gain/Loss	Gain/Loss
Apache Oil (short)	1,000	70.5	$70,500.00		69.63	$870.00	
Anadarko Petroleum (long)	1,000	41.6	$41,600.00		41.56	($40.00)	
Differential		28.9			28.07		
Gain/Loss						$830.00	
Total Exposure			$112,100.00			$112,930.00	
Commissions: # of trades * $20 per trade				2		$790.00	
Total Gain/Loss including commissions			$112,060.00			$112,890.00	0.70%

FIGURE 22.24 Trade Summary 10/15

Thursday, October 16

Not much new here. The pair expanded a bit over the last day, with the differential now at 28.70; the trade is still positive, but is struggling to make any serious gains. The density curve is still hovering in the 0.995 area, which is positive for the overall picture. Figure 22.25 depicts the last few days of density curve data, where you can see that it has traded as low as 0.994, but could not fall lower. This is getting old, I'm ready to close the position for a huge winner.

The profit has fallen to $160, which is obviously not a ton of money. I would also like to point out that Apache reports earnings in five trading sessions on the 23rd. (See Figure 22.26.)

	A	B	C	D	E
				Close	Density
	Date	Differential	Ratio	Spread	Curve
1	Pair Data	5.19	9.07		
5	10/16/03	28.7	1.69	0.63	0.995
6	10/15/03	28.07	1.68	-0.45	0.994
7	10/14/03	28.52	1.67	-0.44	0.995
8	10/13/03	28.96	1.67	0.27	0.996
9	10/10/03	28.69	1.67	0.85	0.995
10	10/9/03	27.84	1.65	-1.58	0.994
11	10/8/03	29.42	1.69	-0.19	0.996
12	10/7/03	29.61	1.69	-0.17	0.996
13	10/6/03	29.78	1.69	0.08	0.997
14	10/3/03	29.7	1.71	0.95	0.997
15	10/2/03	28.75	1.69	0.46	0.995
16	10/1/03	28.29	1.68	0.71	0.995
17	9/30/03	27.58	1.66	0.47	0.993
18	9/29/03	27.11	1.65	0.39	0.992
19	9/26/03	26.72	1.64	0.41	0.991
20	9/25/03	26.31	1.62	1.38	0.990
21	9/24/03	24.93	1.56	0.94	0.985
22	9/23/03	23.99	1.54	1.20	0.981
23	9/22/03	22.79	1.51	-1.11	0.974
24	9/19/03	23.9	1.55	-1.01	0.980

FIGURE 22.25 Density Curve 10/16

Friday, October 17

The trade has slipped negative, with the differential now at 28.97, seven cents above the entry. Also, the density curve is once again headed higher and is now at 0.996. While this alone does not worry me, the fact that the ratio is at 1.70 is slightly unnerving. But, to ease my mind, the third standard deviation has ticked upward to 1.73. This is important to note, as all of the descriptive statistics are moving numbers that shift as each day provides more data. It is very important to keep this in mind, and keep a close eye on what is happening with not only the trade and individual stocks, but the statistical data as well. Figures 22.27 and 22.28 display the Main Page of the spreadsheet and the up tick in the ratio.

Monday, October 20

Back on track, today the differential made a large move down to 27.85, and our trade is yielding a profit of $1,010. Back in the black

	Shares	Entry	Total Exposure	Close	Dollar Gain/Loss	Percent Gain/Loss
Apache Oil (short)	1,000	70.5	$70,500.00	70.5	$0.00	
Anadarko Petroleum (long)	1,000	41.6	$41,600.00	41.8	$200.00	
Differential		28.9		28.7		
Gain/Loss					$200.00	
Total Exposure			$112,100.00		$112,300.00	
Commissions: # of trades * $20 per trade			2		$160.00	
Total Gain/Loss including commissions			$112,060.00		$112,260.00	0.14%

FIGURE 22.26 Trade Summary 10/16

APA-APC 10.17.03.xls

Main Spreadsheet

		Symbols
Close Correlation	0.53	APA
Change Correlation	0.31	APC

	Differential	Ratio	Closing Spread
Mean	5.21	1.13	0.03
Median	4.68	1.10	0.00
Mode	6.94	#N/A	-0.19
Average Deviation	7.54	0.17	0.62
Standard Deviation	9.10	0.20	0.84
Population Standard Deviation	9.09	0.20	0.84

Standard Deviations	Differential	Ratio	Closing Spread
3	32.50	1.73	2.55
2	23.40	1.53	1.71
1	14.31	1.33	0.87
Mean	5.21	1.13	0.03
-1	-3.89	0.93	-0.81
-2	-12.98	0.73	-1.66
-3	-22.08	0.53	-2.50

Current Data	Differential	Ratio	Closing Spread	Density Curve
	28.97	1.70	0.27	0.996

Fundamentals

Symbols	Current Price	Book Value	Beta	Earnings	Float	Price Book	Price Sales	PEG	P/E
APA	70.32	36.47	0.37	0.7	136	1.9	3.3	1.3	13
APC	41.35	30.61	0.48	0.17	150.3	1.4	2.3	0.6	8

	Dividend	Dividend Yield	Current Ratio
APA	0.48	0.68%	1.3
APC	0.4	0.93%	0.66

Main / Pair Data / Differential Data / Pairs Charts / Individual Charts / Stock 1 / Stock 2

FIGURE 22.27 Main Spreadsheet 10/17

again. Today is a huge day for our trade and what I think is the beginning of further convergence. The density curve has posted its lowest reading in seven sessions, while the ratio has fallen to 1.67. A breach of 1.64 would be extremely positive for our trade, as it would be the first time the ratio has been below 1.64 since September 26, when I first began looking at the trade. Statistically, it looks as if the pair has topped out and is now beginning to contract. Figure 22.29 shows the differential, ratio, and density curve, followed by the usual trade summary in Figure 22.30.

	Shares	Entry	Total Exposure	Close	Dollar Gain/Loss	Percent Gain/Loss
Apache Oil (short)	1,000	70.5	$70,500.00	70.32	$180.00	
Anadarko Petroleum (long)	1,000	41.6	$41,600.00	41.35	($250.00)	
Differential		28.9		28.97		
Gain/Loss					($70.00)	
Total Exposure			$112,100.00		$112,030.00	
Commissions: # of trades * $20 per trade				2	($110.00)	
Total Gain/Loss including commissions			$112,060.00		$111,990.00	-0.10%

FIGURE 22.28   Trade Summer 10/17

Tuesday, October 21

Another day, another pullback. The differential ascended to 28.15, though the trade is still positive. Despite the loss of profit, the trade is still in great shape and is acting exactly as it should. The density curve up ticked to 0.994, while the ratio is still holding steady under 1.70. Apache closed below $70 again, a good sign for our trade, especially right in front of earnings. Anadarko is hovering above $41, which is slightly relieving, but I would like to see the stock rally out of dangerous territory here and post some real gains.

The trade is now up $750—not exactly a huge winner, but positive nonetheless. (See Figure 22.31.)

Wednesday, October 22

Today, the trade went against us a little farther and is now up a mere $180. Today's trading action was to be expected, as stocks like Apache usually rally ahead of earnings. Then, if the company does not report blowout numbers, fickle investors will exit their positions into any strength remaining. As mentioned before, Apache stands a good chance of missing estimates due to charges related to currency fluctuations. Specifically, the weakening dollar should have some impact on the company's bottom line. If such occurs, we can expect Apache to decline some, and our pair will take another step forward toward profitability. The exhilarating part about today's action is that while the entire oil sector was up, so was Anadarko. And every bit that Anadarko moves away from $40, the better off the trade is. Figures 22.32 and 22.33 show Anadarko's trading action for the day. The stock has now paved the way for a possible retest of the $43 range. Tomorrow is going to be a very interesting day for our trade.

	A	B	C	D	E	F
	APA-APC 10.20.03.xls					
1	**Pair Data**	5.23	9.12			
2						
3				**Close**	**Density**	
4	**Date**	**Differential**	**Ratio**	**Spread**	**Curve**	
5	10/20/03	27.85	1.67	-1.00	0.993	
6	10/17/03	28.97	1.70	0.27	0.995	
7	10/16/03	28.7	1.69	0.63	0.995	
8	10/15/03	28.07	1.68	-0.45	0.994	
9	10/14/03	28.52	1.67	-0.44	0.995	
10	10/13/03	28.96	1.67	0.27	0.995	
11	10/10/03	28.69	1.67	0.85	0.995	
12	10/9/03	27.84	1.65	-1.58	0.993	
13	10/8/03	29.42	1.69	-0.19	0.996	
14	10/7/03	29.61	1.69	-0.17	0.996	
15	10/6/03	29.78	1.69	0.08	0.996	
16	10/3/03	29.7	1.71	0.95	0.996	
17	10/2/03	28.75	1.69	0.46	0.995	
18	10/1/03	28.29	1.68	0.71	0.994	
19	9/30/03	27.58	1.66	0.47	0.993	
20	9/29/03	27.11	1.65	0.39	0.992	
21	9/26/03	26.72	1.64	0.41	0.991	
22	9/25/03	26.31	1.62	1.38	0.990	
23	9/24/03	24.93	1.56	0.94	0.985	
24	9/23/03	23.99	1.54	1.20	0.980	
25	9/22/03	22.79	1.51	-1.11	0.973	
26	9/19/03	23.9	1.55	-1.01	0.980	

Main \ Pair Data \ Differential Data \ Pairs Charts \ Individual Charts \ Stock 1 \ Stock 2 /

FIGURE 22.29 Density Curve 10/20

	Shares	Entry	Total Exposure	Close	Dollar Gain/Loss	Percent Gain/Loss
Apache Oil (short)	1,000	70.5	$70,500.00	69.35	$1,150.00	
Anadarko Petroleum (long)	1,000	41.6	$41,600.00	41.5	($100.00)	
Differential		28.9		27.85		
Gain/Loss					$1,050.00	
Total Exposure			$112,100.00		$113,150.00	
Commissions: # of trades * $20 per trade			2		$1,010.00	
Total Gain/Loss including commissions			$112,060.00		$113,110.00	0.90%

FIGURE 22.30 Trade Summary 10/20

	Shares	Entry	Total Exposure	Close	Dollar Gain/Loss	Percent Gain/Loss
Apache Oil (short)	1,000	70.5	$70,500.00	69.73	$770.00	
Anadarko Petroleum (long)	1,000	41.6	$41,600.00	41.58	($20.00)	
Differential		28.9		28.15		
Gain/Loss					$750.00	
Total Exposure			$112,100.00		$112,850.00	
Commissions: # of trades * $20 per trade			2		$710.00	
Total Gain/Loss including commissions			$112,060.00		$112,810.00	0.63%

FIGURE 22.31 Trade Summary 10/21

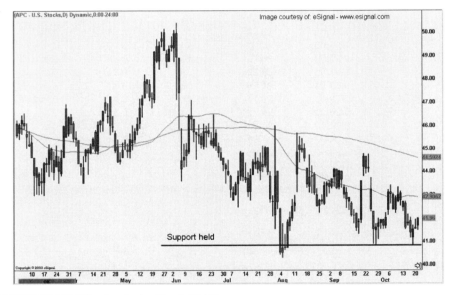

FIGURE 22.32 Anadarko Chart 10/22

Thursday, October 23

Apache reported third-quarter earnings today of $276 million, or $1.69 a share, up from $145 million, or 95 cents one year earlier. While this news is good for the most part, the company missed the consensus estimate of $1.77 a share. Of course, before charges it beat expectations; however, we look only at net numbers, and in this case the net number is a disappointment. The company had a 34 percent increase in oil-equivalent production for the quarter, which is remarkable. Regardless, because the stock has run up so much over the last two years, it would have taken some seriously whopping numbers to push the stock higher. In addition, the company said earnings would have been higher, except that it had to take charges for unfavorable currency

	Shares	Entry	Total Exposure	Close	Dollar Gain/Loss	Percent Gain/Loss
Apache Oil (short)	1,000	70.5	$70,500.00	70.64	($140.00)	
Anadarko Petroleum (long)	1,000	41.6	$41,600.00	41.96	$360.00	
Differential		28.9		28.68		
Gain/Loss					$220.00	
Total Exposure			$112,100.00		$112,320.00	
Commissions: # of trades * $20 per trade			2		$180.00	
Total Gain/Loss including commissions			$112,060.00		$112,280.00	0.16%

FIGURE 22.33 Trade Summary 10/22

exchange rates. I hate to bet against a company that doubled revenue year over year, but at this point the stock is a sloth. I have no doubt that Apache will come back in the near future to post another 52-week high, but for now, it will have to suffer while profit-hungry investors leg out of their positions. Figure 22.34 shows that Apache fell out of bed hard today, declining to the 50-SMA near $68 before rallying into the close. Now that the stock has tested the moving average support, it stands a good chance of breaching it in the next few sessions. This is *exactly* the kind of trading action that we like to see. Not only has the stock had a fundamental event that caused it to roll over, but on a technical level, it won't be long before momentum traders begin adding supplemental pressure as well. From here, it is very possible that the stock will fall into the $65 area, better known as longer-term ascending support. I don't want to completely count buyers out, as the overall trend is up, though for now, our short side looks pretty good.

Also encouraging, though Anadarko declined as well, the stock held up pretty well, indicating that sympathy selling—due to other oil companies—will not be much of a factor during this earnings season. For the time being, Anadarko is marching to the beat of its own drum.

Our trade is now up $890 with a differential of 27.97. This is the first time that the differential has been below 28 since October 9. The density curve is still hanging out at the 0.993 level, which we would like to see broken. For the time being though, the trade could not have more going for it, unless Anadarko makes a miracle merger announcement. (See Figure 22.35.)

Friday, October 24

Another day, another dollar. The Apache earnings news was definitely good for the position, as both stocks moved in the right direction today. Apache fell,

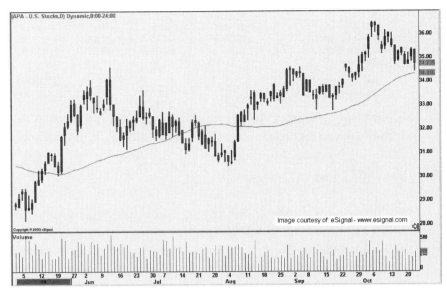

FIGURE 22.34 APA 10/23

	Shares	Entry	Total Exposure	Close	Dollar Gain/Loss	Percent Gain/Loss
Apache Oil (short)	1,000	70.5	$70,500.00	69.47	$1,030.00	
Anadarko Petroleum (long)	1,000	41.6	$41,600.00	41.5	($100.00)	
Differential		28.9		27.97		
Gain/Loss					$930.00	
Total Exposure			$112,100.00		$113,030.00	
Commissions: # of trades * $20 per trade			2		$890.00	
Total Gain/Loss including commissions			$112,060.00		$112,990.00	0.79%

FIGURE 22.35 Trade Summary 10/23

while Anadarko climbed, exactly the combination we are looking for. What's more, the density curve is at 0.992, the lowest point since September 30. The ratio has backed off of the 1.67 area, and the differential could soon be in the 26 region. Overall, the trade is working very well. We have been in the position for 16 trading days and we are up 1.27 percent. Not a bad take for less than a month of trading.

Apache continues to sit just above the 50-SMA and is the key to our trade's success right now. We need the stock to violate the major moving average in order to bring momentum sellers and—dare I say—day traders in off the fence to push the stock lower. (See Figure 22.36.)

	Shares	Entry	Total Exposure	Close	Dollar Gain/Loss	Percent Gain/Loss
Apache Oil (short)	1,000	70.5	$70,500.00	69.25	$1,250.00	
Anadarko Petroleum (long)	1,000	41.6	$41,600.00	41.81	$210.00	
Differential		28.9		27.44		
Gain/Loss					$1,460.00	
Total Exposure			$112,100.00		$113,560.00	
Commissions: # of trades * $20 per trade				2	$1,420.00	
Total Gain/Loss including commissions			$112,060.00		$113,520.00	1.27%

FIGURE 22.36 Trade Summary 10/24

Monday, October 27

The pair began the week on a positive note with the differential shrinking to 27.15 and the ratio falling back to 1.65. What's more, the density curve has fallen to 0.991, the lowest point since September 29. The trade is now yielding 1.53 percent, or in dollar terms $1,710. Not a bad profit for less than a month of trading. There was no significant news on either stock today; thus, I am left with the impression that the stocks are still digesting the recent earnings information from Apache. Figures 22.37 and 22.38 show that the stock has now fallen under the 50-SMA for the first time since August. In addition, the daily stochastics are now sitting on 20, and are indicating selling pressure. Should the indicator breach 20, the event would bring technical momentum sellers in off the fence. The MACD is approaching the 0 line, also signifying technical selling in the stock. The aforementioned events are a good sign for a continued pullback on the sell side of our pair.

Tuesday, October 28

The pair backtracked slightly, though the event is merely a technical blip with no significant news backing the move. In the previous entry for Monday, I mentioned that Apache was testing the 50-SMA. Generally, when a stock tests a major moving average, it does not go straight through but bounces for a few days, then pierces the moving average.

Another positive development in the pair, the differential and ratio have backed off of the third standard deviation and are now just about midway between the second and third standard deviations. Figures 22.39 and 22.40 display the statistical progress.

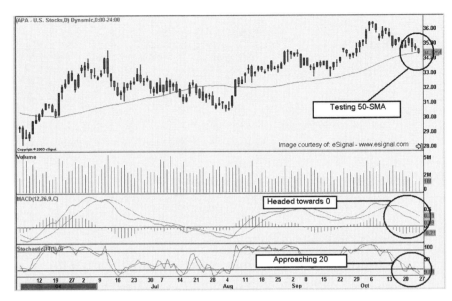

FIGURE 22.37 APA 10/27

	Shares	Entry	Total Exposure	Close	Dollar Gain/Loss	Percent Gain/Loss
Apache Oil (short)	1,000	70.5	$70,500.00	68.65	$1,850.00	
Anadarko Petroleum (long)	1,000	41.6	$41,600.00	41.5	($100.00)	
Differential		28.9		27.15		
Gain/Loss					$1,750.00	
Total Exposure			$112,100.00		$113,850.00	
Commissions: # of trades * $20 per trade				2	$1,710.00	
Total Gain/Loss including commissions			$112,060.00		$113,810.00	1.53%

FIGURE 22.38 Trade Summary 10/27

Wednesday, October 29

Apache bounced again today, causing our spread to open up slightly (see Figure 22.41). The event, however, is to be expected and gives the trade no cause for concern, as it is still firmly in the black. Anadarko had some good news, after the company (one of a few independent oil companies) was granted permission to explore the North Slope of Alaska. Public announcement of this news is great for the company (which was already exploring the slope anyway), as it sorely needs development projects. (EN 22.2)

APA-APC 10.28.03.xls

	A	B	C	D	E	F	G	H	I	J
1	**Main Spreadsheet**									
2			Symbols							
3	Close Correlation	0.50	**APA**							
4	Change Correlation	0.28	**APC**							
5										
6		Differential	Ratio	Closing			Standard Deviations		Closing	
7				Spread			Differential	Ratio	Spread	
8	Mean	5.34	1.13	0.03		3	33.18	1.75	2.54	
9	Median	4.68	1.10	0.00		2	23.90	1.54	1.70	
10	Mode	6.94	#N/A	-0.19		1	14.62	1.34	0.86	
11						Mean	5.34	1.13	0.03	
12	Average Deviation	7.67	0.17	0.62		-1	-3.94	0.93	-0.81	
13	Standard Deviation	9.28	0.20	0.84		-2	-13.23	0.72	-1.65	
14	Population Standard Deviation	9.28	0.20	0.84		-3	-22.51	0.52	-2.49	
15										
16										
17										
18	Current Data			Closing						
19		Differential	Ratio	Spread			Density Curve			
20		27.33	1.66	0.18			0.991			
21										

FIGURE 22.39 Main Spreadsheet 10/28

			Total		Dollar	Percent
	Shares	Entry	Exposure	Close	Gain/Loss	Gain/Loss
Apache Oil (short)	1,000	70.5	$70,500.00	69.04	$1,460.00	
Anadarko Petroleum (long)	1,000	41.6	$41,600.00	41.71	$110.00	
Differential		28.9		27.33		
Gain/Loss					$1,570.00	
Total Exposure			$112,100.00		$113,670.00	
Commissions: # of trades * $20 per trade			2		$1,530.00	
Total Gain/Loss including commissions			$112,060.00		$113,630.00	1.36%

FIGURE 22.40 Trade Summary 10/28

Thursday, October 30

Anadarko was upgraded from Neutral to Out Perform at CSFB, just one day before the company announces earnings. Investors are clearly expecting good news tomorrow, as the stock has gained a little over a point in the last two sessions. Apache is showing more weakness and may now be setting up to fall through the 50-SMA in the next few sessions. Both technical developments are extremely positive for our pair. The density curve has finally broken 0.990 and is now at 0.988. This is a very encouraging statistical development and shows that the pair is definitely in contraction mode. With the ratio at 1.61 and the differential sitting at 26.33, I am expecting additional gains over the next week or so. Anadarko's earnings announcement tomorrow should hopefully help the pair along. Because the publishing

	Shares	Entry	Total Exposure	Close	Dollar Gain/Loss	Percent Gain/Loss
Apache Oil (short)	1,000	70.5	$70,500.00	69.95	$550.00	
Anadarko Petroleum (long)	1,000	41.6	$41,600.00	42.34	$740.00	
Differential		28.9		27.61		
Gain/Loss					$1,290.00	
Total Exposure			$112,100.00		$113,390.00	
Commissions: # of trades * $20 per trade			2		$1,250.00	
Total Gain/Loss including commissions			$112,060.00		$113,350.00	1.12%

FIGURE 22.41   Trade Summary 10/29

	Shares	Entry	Total Exposure	Close	Dollar Gain/Loss	Percent Gain/Loss
Apache Oil (short)	1,000	70.5	$70,500.00	69.18	$1,320.00	
Anadarko Petroleum (long)	1,000	41.6	$41,600.00	42.85	$1,250.00	
Differential		28.9		26.33		
Gain/Loss					$2,570.00	
Total Exposure			$112,100.00		$114,670.00	
Commissions: # of trades * $20 per trade			2		$2,530.00	
Total Gain/Loss including commissions			$112,060.00		$114,630.00	2.26%

FIGURE 22.42   Trade Summary 10/30

deadline is coming up, I will now begin looking for an exit point, and will most likely scale out of the trade. I will look for a large up day, and then exit half of the position, and let the other half ride into the deadline.

As Figure 22.42 displays, the trade is now up 2.26 percent and has brought forward a profit of $2,530.

Friday, October 31

Anadarko reported third-quarter earnings of $374 million, or $1.09 versus $189 million, or 74 cents a year earlier. The earnings are a 45 percent increase year over year, and indicate that the company is slowly improving. What's more, the company announced that it was bumping up its quarterly dividend to 14 cents, a 40 percent increase. For the third quarter, revenue increased over 40 percent to $1.3 billion, with sales coming in at over 50 million barrels moved. Oil production for the quarter totaled 189,000 barrels, down slightly from 191,000 barrels. Looking forward, the company expects fourth-quarter earnings of $1.10 a share, almost in line with the consensus estimate. The company also expects full-year earnings to total $5 a share, versus the expected $5.05 a share. Great news came in the form of an announcement that the company plans on increasing its 2003 capital budget by $100 million to $2.8 billion, while also eliminating debt by roughly $300 million. With the exception of fourth-quarter and full-year guidance coming in under annual estimates, the report was very positive. The company's capex budget increase is a good sign for the development and upgrading of current equipment. Overall, this report should be received very positively, and indicates that the company is working hard to turn things around.

Looking at the daily chart of Anadarko, the stock is now testing descending resistance in the $44 region. A move above the resistance line will definitely gain the notice of technical momentum traders and will bring supplemental buying in off the fence. As Figure 22.43 displays, the stock has also just witnessed a bullish crossover of the MACD and is seeing strong momentum in daily stochastics.

The differential has now fallen to 26.10, the lowest point yet, while the ratio has also made a new relative low at 1.60. The trade is now yielding 2.46 percent with a $2,760 profit. Unless some sort of crazy news event transpires over the weekend, I will close half of the position on Monday morning. (See Figure 22.44.)

FIGURE 22.43 Anadarko 10/31

Monday, November 3

This morning, I exited half of my position, Apache at $69.75 and Anadarko at $43.50. The short half—Apache—earned $425, and the long side—Anadarko—brought forth $910. Both dollar figures are minus commissions. You will notice on the trade summary sheet (Figure 22.45) that I have already backed out the commissions; thus, they are zeroed out for the open positions. When I close the trade, I will then subtract the closing commissions as well.

The differential is now at 26.18, while the density curve is at 0.987. The trade is now on the home stretch, and I will close the remaining half of the positions (unless some major news event occurs) on Friday, November 14.

With earnings out of the way, the two stocks will now be left to third-quarter digestion and forward thoughts of the fourth quarter. There was no notable news today, and both charts seem to be acting in a normal fashion.

	Shares	Entry	Total Exposure	Close	Dollar Gain/Loss	Percent Gain/Loss
Apache Oil (short)	1,000	70.5	$70,500.00	69.72	$780.00	
Anadarko Petroleum (long)	1,000	41.6	$41,600.00	43.62	$2,020.00	
Differential		28.9		26.1		
Gain/Loss					$2,800.00	
Total Exposure			$112,100.00		$114,900.00	
Commissions: # of trades * $20 per trade			2		$2,760.00	
Total Gain/Loss including commissions			$112,060.00		$114,860.00	2.46%

FIGURE 22.44 Trade Summary 10/31

	Shares	Entry	Total Exposure	Close	Dollar Gain/Loss	Percent Gain/Loss
Apache Oil (short)	500	70.5	$35,250.00	69.57	$465.00	
Anadarko Petroleum (long)	500	41.6	$20,800.00	43.39	$895.00	
Differential		28.9		26.18		
Gain/Loss					$1,360.00	
Total Exposure			$56,050.00		$57,410.00	
Commissions: # of trades * $20 per trade			0		$1,360.00	
Total Gain/Loss including commissions			$56,050.00		$57,410.00	2.43%
Booked Gain/Loss	Price	Commissions		Shares	Gain/Loss	
Apache	69.75	40		500	425	
Anadarko	43.5	40		500	910	

FIGURE 22.45 Trade Summary 11/3

Tuesday, November 4

Another day, a missed dollar. The pair collapsed a little more today, the differential is now at 25 and the density curve has fallen to 0.981, the lowest point yet. Even more amazing, the ratio has declined to 1.58 and is now just 0.03 from the second standard deviation. The second half of the trade still open is yielding a total of 3.48 percent since the trade's inception almost exactly one month ago.

Though Anadarko tested—and failed—descending resistance, there was much more significant profit taking in Apache. The stock has now failed the 50-SMA and is headed toward ascending support. Technical momentum sellers will most likely push the stock into the $66 area, where the stock will face critical support. A failure of the ascending trend line will create a near-term reversal and could cause the stock to find significant selling pressure. Figures 22.46 and 22.47 also display that the MACD is crossing under the 0 line, and is indicating further selling pressure.

Wednesday, November 5

The pair bumped back up a little today, with the differential rising to 26.29, while the ratio is now at 1.61.

In an interesting development, Anadarko announced that its new platform Marco Polo is getting ready to pump oil out of a large find off the Gulf

FIGURE 22.46 APA 11/4

	Shares	Entry	Total Exposure	Close	Dollar Gain/Loss	Percent Gain/Loss
Apache Oil (short)	500	70.5	$35,250.00	68.1	$1,200.00	
Anadarko Petroleum (long)	500	41.6	$20,800.00	43.1	$750.00	
Differential		28.9		25		
Gain/Loss					$1,950.00	
Total Exposure			$56,050.00		$58,000.00	
Commissions: # of trades * $20 per trade				0	$1,950.00	
Total Gain/Loss including commissions			$56,050.00		$58,000.00	3.48%
Booked Gain/Loss	Price	Commissions			Shares	Gain/Loss
Apache	69.75	40			500	425
Anadarko	43.5	40			500	910

FIGURE 22.47   Trade Summary 11/4

of Mexico. However, the platform is not being used to pump Anadarko's well, but rather, that of the company GulfTerra Partners. This interesting twist could provide additional revenue in the future. Apache Oil is doing its best to hold the 50-SMA and has ascended back just above the important moving average. Buyers will have to pull out some big guns to keep the stock from breaching the moving average. (See Figure 22.48.)

Thursday, November 6

Today, the pair continued to expand; the differential is at 26.68 while the ratio is now at 1.62. Figure 22.49 shows the differential data for the last few weeks and indicates that the pair may be on its way back up. For the time being, I am glad that I booked half of the trade on the 3rd.

In an interesting bout of news, the CEO of Anadarko vowed that the company will begin more "focused" overseas efforts. (EN 22.3)

On a technical level, Apache has resumed its trend above the 50-SMA and may now be headed back higher. Because the stock could not fall below the 50-SMA with force, I am led to believe that the stock may soon retest highs. Anadarko, though, is still testing descending resistance, which may be the only real hope for further gains in this trade. I have stated that I will leave the position open until the 14th. However, normally, I would close another half of the position here, leaving only one quarter of the original trade open. Figure 22.50 displays Anadarko's attempt at breaking through descending resistance.

Friday, November 7

With only one week left, the trade is looking as if it will continue to open up. The differential is now at 26.37, while the ratio still above 1.6. There was no

	Shares	Entry	Total Exposure	Close	Dollar Gain/Loss	Percent Gain/Loss
Apache Oil (short)	500	70.5	$35,250.00	69.3	$600.00	
Anadarko Petroleum (long)	500	41.6	$20,800.00	43.01	$705.00	
Differential		28.9		26.29		
Gain/Loss					$1,305.00	
Total Exposure			$56,050.00		$57,355.00	
Commissions: # of trades * $20 per trade			0		$1,305.00	
Total Gain/Loss including commissions			$56,050.00		$57,355.00	2.33%

Booked Gain/Loss	Price	Commissions		Shares	Gain/Loss
Apache	69.75	40		500	425
Anadarko	43.5	40		500	910

FIGURE 22.48 Trade Summary 11/5

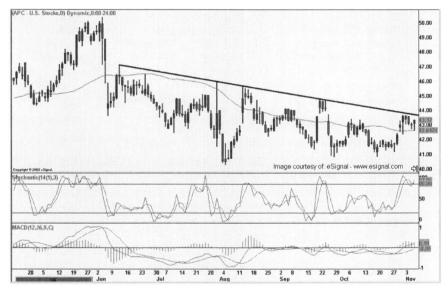

FIGURE 22.49 Anadarko 11/6

significant news today, though on a technical level, Anadarko looks to be headed up. The stock has built a base above the 50-SMA, and with any luck, buyers will attempt to push the stock higher. (See Figure 22.51.)

Monday, November 10

Today, the spread opened up a little more. This action is not boding well for the trade and my instincts tell me that the trade will most likely close nearly close to flat, given the little amount to time that is left. However, the trade is

	Shares	Entry	Total Exposure	Close	Dollar Gain/Loss	Percent Gain/Loss
Apache Oil (short)	500	70.5	$35,250.00	70	$250.00	
Anadarko Petroleum (long)	500	41.6	$20,800.00	43.32	$860.00	
Differential		28.9		26.68		
Gain/Loss					$1,110.00	
Total Exposure			$56,050.00		$57,160.00	
Commissions: # of trades * $20 per trade			0		$1,110.00	
Total Gain/Loss including commissions			$56,050.00		$57,160.00	1.98%

Booked Gain/Loss	Price	Commissions	Shares	Gain/Loss
Apache	69.75	40	500	425
Anadarko	43.5	40	500	910

FIGURE 22.50   Trade Summary 11/6

	Shares	Entry	Total Exposure	Close	Dollar Gain/Loss	Percent Gain/Loss
Apache Oil (short)	500	70.5	$35,250.00	69.9	$300.00	
Anadarko Petroleum (long)	500	41.6	$20,800.00	43.53	$965.00	
Differential		28.9		26.37		
Gain/Loss					$1,265.00	
Total Exposure			$56,050.00		$57,315.00	
Commissions: # of trades * $20 per trade			0		$1,265.00	
Total Gain/Loss including commissions			$56,050.00		$57,315.00	2.26%

Booked Gain/Loss	Price	Commissions	Shares	Gain/Loss
Apache	69.75	40	500	425
Anadarko	43.5	40	500	910

FIGURE 22.51   Trade Summary 11/7

still a winner, as Anadarko continues to pick up steam. The density curve is not at 0.987, while the differential is at 26.60. If I had not already made the previous commitment to close the entire position on the 14th, I would close another quarter of the pair tomorrow morning.

Apache has held the 50-SMA and appears to be keeping its footing. If the stock cannot punch through the major moving average in the next few sessions, it is most likely setting up for another leg higher. Anadarko, however, looks very promising, as the stock has moved above the descending resistance line and is setting up for a breakout. If I were simply directional trading at this point, I would purchase the stock long with a stop just under the near-term shelf and the 50-SMA. The actual stop would be just under $42, thus inferring a 3.4 percent loss if the trade were

FIGURE 22.52 APC 11/10

	Shares	Entry	Total Exposure	Close	Dollar Gain/Loss	Percent Gain/Loss
Apache Oil (short)	500	70.5	$35,250.00	70.05	$225.00	
Anadarko Petroleum (long)	500	41.6	$20,800.00	43.45	$925.00	
Differential		28.9		26.6		
Gain/Loss					$1,150.00	
Total Exposure			$56,050.00		$57,200.00	
Commissions: # of trades * $20 per trade			0		$1,150.00	
Total Gain/Loss including commissions			$56,050.00		$57,200.00	2.05%

Booked Gain/Loss	Price	Commissions	Shares	Gain/Loss
Apache	69.75	40	500	425
Anadarko	43.5	40	500	910

FIGURE 22.53 Trade Summary 11/10

to be stopped out. Figures 22.52 and 22.53 indicate the breach of the descending resistance line and illuminate the possible breakout pending.

Tuesday, November 11

The pair continued to open up today, and our profit has dwindled to $965, which translates to only a 1.72 percent gain on the second half of the position. The differential has moved up to 26.60, with no significant news affecting either stock. The density curve continues to expand as well, and is now at 0.987, indicating a potential retest of highs on the horizon. As a general rule of thumb, when the density curve falls below 0.990 and then begins to expand, it may be a good time to take profits off the table. No matter how you slice it, though, we are only "managing money" now—which means we are hanging onto profits. This is definitely a good position to be in. It's sort of like having a three touchdown lead going into the fourth quarter of a football game. We are just trying to run the clock out, and keep as much of our lead as possible. As mentioned before, if I had not already declared that I was closing the position in three sessions, I would have closed a quarter of it this morning. The problem is that while Anadarko looks great long, Apache also appears to be gaining momentum. And because Apache is the more expensive stock, if it really starts to ascend, it could move much quicker than Anadarko.

This is one scenario that you could scale back on your trade using a ratio strategy. By this I mean that you would trim your position to give each stock equal weighting in your portfolio. Our ratio is currently 1.61, which means that on a simple share valuation basis, we could either increase our Anadarko position, or sell some of the Apache. Since Anadarko looks outstanding at this point, our best course of action is to sell some Apache. Using the ratio of 1.61, some simple math would get us to where we need to be. We would simply subtract 0.61 from 1, which leaves us with 0.39. Then, we would multiply our outstanding position for Apache (500 shares) by 0.39 giving us 195 shares to sell. If we did this, the remaining position would be 500 shares of Anadarko and 305 shares of Apache. Also, because it is much easier to move 100 shares lots, I would most likely just sell out of 200 shares, giving the trade a 500 to 300 ratio. What's more, by taking this action, we would book additional profit on the Apache side, covering more of our costs, while removing some of the risk from the position. The important part to remember is that anytime you begin to shift the weighting of a position, you *must* put a tight stop on the other portion of the trade to ensure that you hang onto the profit, or simply to detour large losses.

If both stocks begin to fall south, we would lose out on profit opportunity from the short side, as we have eliminated some of our position. Our losses could quickly multiply, as the long portion of the trade has more exposure simply because it is larger.

Thus, looking at Figure 22.54 of Anadarko, we would utilize the same stop for the unbalanced portion of our trade—the extra 200 shares—at just under $42, or $41.99.

	Shares	Entry	Total Exposure	Close	Dollar Gain/Loss	Percent Gain/Loss
Apache Oil (short)	500	70.5	$35,250.00	70.07	$215.00	
Anadarko Petroleum (long)	500	41.6	$20,800.00	43.1	$750.00	
Differential		28.9		26.97		
Gain/Loss					$965.00	
Total Exposure			$56,050.00		$57,015.00	
Commissions: # of trades * $20 per trade				0	$965.00	
Total Gain/Loss including commissions			$56,050.00		$57,015.00	1.72%

Booked Gain/Loss	Price	Commissions	Shares	Gain/Loss
Apache	69.75	40	500	425
Anadarko	43.5	40	500	910

FIGURE 22.54 Trade Summary 11/11

Wednesday, November 12

The pair continues to open up, and the Apache side is now negative. If we had trimmed the short portion of the trade, our exposure would be limited, while we stand to gain on the long side. The trade is now presenting a $650 profit, not quite outstanding dollars, but not a loser either. The density curve is now at 0.990, a prudent place for conservative traders to exit the entire position. It is my impression that the second half of the trade will close flat at best.

Anadarko announced that the company drilled a successful well in Algeria, which will only help to keep the long side of the trade moving along. At this point, more adventurous traders could remove the entire portion of the short trade and put a tight trailing stop on the Anadarko long side of our position. This would be the *riskiest* thing to possibly do, as the position has naked exposure to the market, and defeats the entire purpose of the pairs hedge. However, in certain circumstances, if the trader understands the market and the pair, then additional risk can be taken on. I would only recommend instituting this strategy in situations where the pair is profitable. If you are in a losing trade, the best course of action is usually to just close the entire position and move on. Being able to cut losers short is just good money management. Taking on additional risk in winning positions is good trading. (See Figure 22.55.)

Thursday, November 13

Clearly, the long side of the trade is picking up momentum, while the short side is beginning to go sour. The differential is now at 27.73, while the density

	Shares	Entry	Total Exposure	Close	Dollar Gain/Loss	Percent Gain/Loss
Apache Oil (short)	500	70.5	$35,250.00	70.95	($225.00)	
Anadarko Petroleum (long)	500	41.6	$20,800.00	43.35	$875.00	
Differential		28.9		27.6		
Gain/Loss					$650.00	
Total Exposure			$56,050.00		$56,700.00	
Commissions: # of trades * $20 per trade				0	$650.00	
Total Gain/Loss including commissions			$56,050.00		$56,700.00	1.16%
Booked Gain/Loss	Price	Commissions			Shares	Gain/Loss
Apache	69.75	40			500	425
Anadarko	43.5	40			500	910

FIGURE 22.55 Trade Summary 11/12

	Shares	Entry	Total Exposure	Close	Dollar Gain/Loss	Percent Gain/Loss
Apache Oil (short)	500	70.5	$35,250.00	71.67	($585.00)	
Anadarko Petroleum (long)	500	41.6	$20,800.00	43.94	$1,170.00	
Differential		28.9		27.73		
Gain/Loss					$585.00	
Total Exposure			$56,050.00		$56,635.00	
Commissions: # of trades * $20 per trade				0	$585.00	
Total Gain/Loss including commissions			$56,050.00		$56,635.00	1.04%
Booked Gain/Loss	Price	Commissions			Shares	Gain/Loss
Apache	69.75	40			500	425
Anadarko	43.5	40			500	910

FIGURE 22.56 Trade Summary 11/13

curve is at 0.990. The second portion is yielding 1.04 percent, certainly off the larger percentage gain that we witnessed at the beginning of the month.

The chart of Apache indicates that the stock will soon retest highs. For the directional investor trading with the trend, this would area of the current move is known as the "sweet spot." The stock almost failed but held ground, and investors are still "buying the dip."

Our trade is now showing a profit of $585 and as tomorrow is the 14th, I will close the remaining 1,000 shares (500 on each side) in the morning. (See Figure 22.56.)

Friday, November 14

This morning I exited Apache at $71.50 and Anadarko at $44.25, the closing differential was 27.25. The original differential was 28.90, thus we yielded a profit of 1.65, or $461 (less $40 in commissions) on the second half of our trade. The total gain on the trade was $1796, or 1.6% on the original $112,100 invested. This is *good* money, and the trade was only open for 41 days, or 30 business days. Chances are that if we had left the trade open, it would have come in even more. Though Apache is on its way up, there are valuation concerns, while Anadarko has the possibility of ascending into range resistance at $50. The important part to remember here is that the trade was only negative for four days, and we had a "hedge" to boot. This trade was a very good example of what to expect from a properly set up pairs trade. Generally, pairs do not yield kazillions of dollars in profits, but instead can produce slow, consistent returns—better known as base hits. And as we all know, baseball games aren't always won by homeruns, but by players making consistent singles and doubles to round the bases all the way home.

CHAPTER 23

Correlating Stocks to Indices

*General Electric and
ExxonMobil
General Electric and
the DIAMONDS
ExxonMobil and the DIAMONDS
The Three Wise Men*

I n this chapter, we will go further into correlating stocks with indices to see if we can find some other tradable opportunities—or at least see if the additional information can help you to make more informed directional trading decisions. First things first, we must set up a spreadsheet with the proper information. For the sake of example, we will use the Dow Jones Industrial Average, ExxonMobil, and General Electric. Figure 23.1 shows the three together. Immediately, we can see a visual relationship, especially with ExxonMobil and the Dow.

GENERAL ELECTRIC AND EXXONMOBIL

What we will do is first look at the relationship between ExxonMobil and General Electric, and then cross-reference the two with the Dow. Figure 23.2 shows that the two stocks are 0.58 percent correlated. While this is not an outstanding relationship, what it does mean is that the two may provide a substantial amount of trading opportunities, as there is plenty of divergence and reconvergence.

It is very important to note that we made a change to the spreadsheet. On the Pair Data page, we changed the reference cells of the sheets Stock 1 and Stock 2 from cell E (closing data) to cell G, to reflect the adjusted closes.

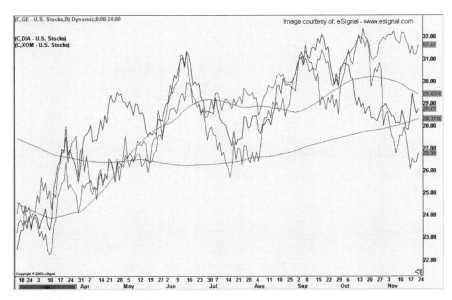

FIGURE 23.1   GE-XOM-DOW

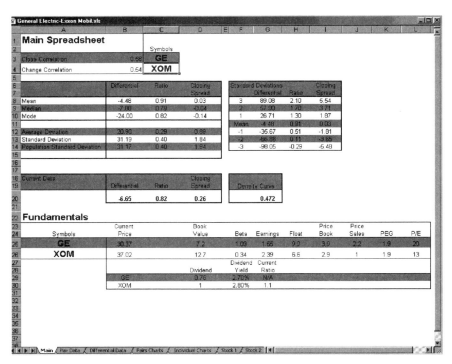

FIGURE 23.2   GE-XOM

When first glancing at the differential chart, we notice that the two stocks have had a fairly tight trading range between 0 and 10 over the last two years. Even though the two stocks are only 58 percent correlated, it shows that there was ample opportunity to trade. One area that would have not helped us was the density curve, which never traded close to 0 or 1. As mentioned earlier in the book, a trader would then want to move the density curve trade entry parameters to yield entry signals. However, by lowering the entry points above or below 0 and 1, the trade takes on additional risk.

GENERAL ELECTRIC AND THE DIAMONDS

The DIAMONDS (NYSE: DIA) are the Dow tracking stock. The purpose of the DIAMONDS is to let investors purchase the entire Dow in one stock, without having to purchase a mutual fund. The problem with mutual funds is that if you want to buy now, you have to wait until the end of the day before you get in, and then you will get the day's closing price. By purchasing an ETF (exchange-traded fund) like the DIAMONDS, you can instead, enter your position at any moment during the day. And, you can short-sell the DIA-MONDS also, if you believe that the Dow will go down. Even more exciting, the DIAMONDS and QQQ (NASDAQ composite ETF) do not require an up tick to go short. This means that in cases of rapidly descending trading you do not have to wait for a buyer to step in before shorting the stock. However, the liquidity (even though they trade millions of shares) can present prob-lems, and fills can be undesirable for the average investor. I have seen great traders try and pick apart the DIAMONDS and QQQs on an intraday basis in an effort to make money. However, the only outcome I have ever heard of is a lot of commissions and dwindled profits for the headache encountered.

The correlation between the DIAMONDS and General Electric is 0.58, much like General Electric and ExxonMobil. What this means is that GE and the DIA are not incredibly correlated but, much like GE and XOM, are volatile enough to provide some trading opportunity. (See Figure 23.3.)

EXXONMOBIL AND THE DIAMONDS

When looking at the spreadsheet of the DIAMONDS and ExxonMobil, we see a different picture unfold. The two have a high correlation of 0.80. We may presume that the reason for the higher correlation is that ExxonMobil is not as volatile as General Electric, and GE has had much turbulence over the last year.

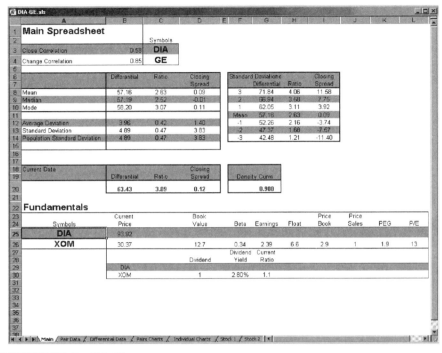

FIGURE 23.3   DIA-GE

In fact, if we look at the historical trading range of ExxonMobil and the Dow, we see that there is a very clear range from roughly 40 to 60 that would have provided some incredible trading opportunities over the last year. What's more, on a ratio basis, the pair had a significant range from 1.30 to 1.60. Figure 23.4 shows the pair's range over the last two years.

Now that we have seen the correlation possibilities, let's take our thinking one step further. Imagine that the DIAMONDS are a large bomber flying a straight course to a destination. GE and XOM are fighter planes that traverse the sky all around the DIAMONDS to protect it from other fighters. However, they stay on course with the bomber, regardless of conditions. When they are in battle, they can stray far away, but as their only purpose is to assist the bomber, they always come back to the original course.

Using this analogy, we can imagine that General Electric is a much more volatile fighter, while ExxonMobil stays closer to the DIAMONDS. Thus, when General Electric strays far off course, and ExxonMobil moves in the other direction, we have a divergence situation. What's more, instead of just buying and selling General Electric and ExxonMobil, we can also take a position in the DIAMONDS to further hedge the direction of our trade, while offsetting the capital used by decreasing our share size in the other two

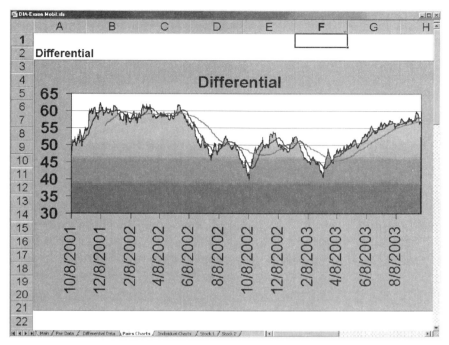

FIGURE 23.4 XOM-DIA

stocks. What we will have is a larger pairs trade consisting of three stocks. Let's look at our data and see how this translates to making money.

Looking at Figure 23.5, we see that on October 9, 2002, General Electric and the DIAMONDS were trading with a differential of 50.09, while Exxon-Mobil and the DIAMONDS had a differential of 39.76. Now, we know that ExxonMobil has a higher correlation to the Dow and is definitely trading on the lower portion of the historical range.

The problem is that we are thinking about buying ExxonMobil and shorting GE. However, further investigation points out that GE is trading barely above the mean, which is 57.16. Figure 23.6 displays GE's statistics.

On a simple pairs basis, we may be very worried about selling short General Electric, while the stock was also trading below the mean. And in reality, our instincts are well justified, as when we look at the General Electric–ExxonMobil pair, we see some *very* interesting developments. The pair is trading on the buy side of the mean and looks to be a notably promising trade if we were to buy General Electric and short ExxonMobil. However, ExxonMobil is trading below the mean in relationship to the Dow and looks as if it has the most potential in regard to a pairs trade with the index. The bottom line here is that even though the General Electric–ExxonMobil trade

DIA-GE.xls

	A	B	C	D	E
223	11/14/02	60.01	3.52	0.61	0.720
224	11/13/02	59.39	3.54	0.06	0.676
225	11/12/02	59.32	3.56	0.69	0.671
226	11/11/02	58.64	3.49	-0.40	0.619
227	11/8/02	59.07	3.42	0.26	0.652
228	11/7/02	58.84	3.32	-1.47	0.635
229	11/6/02	60.32	3.33	1.02	0.741
230	11/5/02	59.3	3.30	1.18	0.669
231	11/4/02	58.12	3.26	-0.11	0.578
232	11/1/02	58.21	3.30	0.77	0.585
233	10/31/02	57.42	3.34	-0.69	0.521
234	10/30/02	58.11	3.38	1.33	0.577
235	10/29/02	56.8	3.26	0.08	0.471
236	10/28/02	56.73	3.22	-0.59	0.465
237	10/25/02	57.32	3.25	1.32	0.513
238	10/24/02	55.99	3.21	-1.25	0.406
239	10/23/02	57.27	3.19	0.66	0.509
240	10/22/02	56.61	3.15	-0.60	0.455
241	10/21/02	57.21	3.17	1.77	0.504
242	10/18/02	55.43	3.14	0.60	0.362
243	10/17/02	54.84	3.10	0.70	0.318
244	10/16/02	54.1	3.17	-1.35	0.266
245	10/15/02	55.47	3.18	1.92	0.365
246	10/14/02	53.5	3.26	-0.19	0.227
247	10/11/02	53.68	3.28	1.88	0.239
248	10/10/02	51.76	3.36	1.65	0.135
249	10/9/02	50.09	3.34	-0.87	0.074
250	10/8/02	51	3.25	0.24	0.104
251	10/7/02	50.75	3.27	-0.13	0.095
252	10/4/02	50.91	3.18	-0.78	0.101
253	10/3/02	51.7	3.16	-0.35	0.132
254	10/2/02	52.06	3.16	-0.63	0.149
255	10/1/02	52.73	3.07	2.36	0.183
256	9/30/02	50.33	3.10	-1.01	0.081
257	9/27/02	51.33	3.16	-0.98	0.117
258	9/26/02	52.36	3.04	1.74	0.163
259	9/25/02	50.64	2.93	0.45	0.091
260	9/24/02	50.34	3.01	-1.19	0.082
261	9/23/02	51.54	3.02	-0.50	0.125
262	9/20/02	52.05	3.02	0.01	0.148
263	9/19/02	52.04	3.03	-0.93	0.148

Main / Pair Data / Differential Data / Pairs Charts / Individual Charts

DIA-Exxon Mobil.xls

	A	B	C	D	E
223	11/14/02	50.27	2.50	-0.08	0.134
224	11/13/02	50.32	2.55	0.94	0.136
225	11/12/02	49.4	2.49	0.16	0.109
226	11/11/02	49.24	2.49	-0.55	0.105
227	11/8/02	49.81	2.48	-0.88	0.121
228	11/7/02	50.68	2.51	-1.33	0.148
229	11/6/02	52.25	2.54	1.59	0.206
230	11/5/02	50.68	2.47	-0.14	0.148
231	11/4/02	50.77	2.53	0.79	0.151
232	11/1/02	50	2.49	0.52	0.126
233	10/31/02	49.44	2.52	-0.17	0.110
234	10/30/02	49.63	2.51	-0.22	0.115
235	10/29/02	49.82	2.55	1.09	0.121
236	10/28/02	48.78	2.46	-0.11	0.093
237	10/25/02	48.9	2.44	1.12	0.096
238	10/24/02	47.77	2.43	-1.69	0.071
239	10/23/02	49.47	2.46	0.54	0.111
240	10/22/02	48.94	2.44	0.14	0.097
241	10/21/02	48.82	2.40	2.27	0.094
242	10/18/02	46.55	2.34	0.66	0.050
243	10/17/02	45.9	2.31	1.22	0.041
244	10/16/02	44.66	2.30	-1.18	0.028
245	10/15/02	45.86	2.31	2.40	0.041
246	10/14/02	43.42	2.29	-0.44	0.018
247	10/11/02	43.84	2.31	2.74	0.021
248	10/10/02	41.08	2.26	1.29	0.008
249	10/9/02	39.76	2.25	-2.35	0.004
250	10/8/02	42.1	2.33	1.13	0.011
251	10/7/02	40.99	2.28	-1.32	0.007
252	10/4/02	42.3	2.32	-1.27	0.012
253	10/3/02	43.58	2.36	-1.06	0.019
254	10/2/02	44.62	2.41	-0.76	0.027
255	10/1/02	45.42	2.39	1.89	0.036
256	9/30/02	43.47	2.41	0.09	0.019
257	9/27/02	43.41	2.37	-1.57	0.018
258	9/26/02	45.02	2.36	-0.41	0.031
259	9/25/02	45.38	2.44	0.89	0.035
260	9/24/02	44.47	2.44	-0.92	0.026
261	9/23/02	45.41	2.44	-0.70	0.036
262	9/20/02	46.12	2.45	-0.30	0.044
263	9/19/02	46.4	2.48	-0.89	0.048

Main / Pair Data / Differential Data / Pairs Charts

FIGURE 23.5 XOM-GE

DIA-GE.xls

Main Spreadsheet

		Symbols
Close Correlation	0.58	DIA
Change Correlation	0.85	GE

	Differential	Ratio	Closing Spread
Mean	57.16	2.63	0.09
Median	57.19	2.52	-0.01
Mode	58.20	3.07	0.11
Average Deviation	3.96	0.42	1.40
Standard Deviation	4.89	0.47	3.83
Population Standard Deviation	4.89	0.47	3.83

Standard Deviations	Differential	Ratio	Closing Spread
3	71.84	4.06	11.58
2	66.94	3.58	7.75
1	62.05	3.11	3.92
Mean	57.16	2.63	0.09
-1	52.26	2.16	-3.74
-2	47.37	1.68	-7.57
-3	42.48	1.21	-11.40

Current Data	Differential	Ratio	Closing Spread
	63.43	3.09	0.12

Density Curve
0.900

Fundamentals

Symbols	Current Price	Book Value	Beta	Earnings	Float	Price Book	Price Sales	PEG	P/E
DIA	93.92								
XOM	30.37	12.7	0.34	2.39	6.6	2.9	1	1.9	13

	Dividend	Dividend Yield	Current Ratio
DIA			
XOM	1	2.80%	1.1

Main / Pair Data / Differential Data / Pairs Charts / Individual Charts / Stock 1 / Stock 2

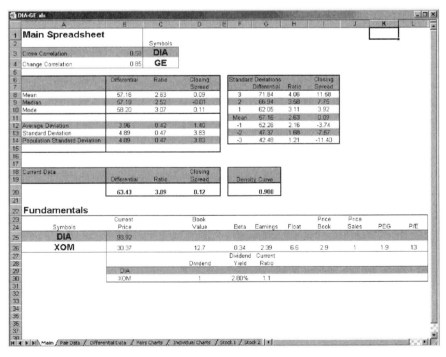

FIGURE 23.6 DIA-GE

presents a situation in which we should short ExxonMobil and buy General Electric, our data cross-referencing each stock to the Dow is not painting the same picture. Have you figured out where we're going? The solution is to do a three-part trade, wherein we buy General Electric and ExxonMobil, while shorting the DIAMONDS. Let's see how this works.

THE THREE WISE MEN

In essence, instead of buying and selling just General Electric and Exxon-Mobil, we would instead buy both stocks, while shorting the DIAMONDS. The fact that we are benchmarking two stocks against their respective indices completely pushes our paradigm to another level. What we are saying is that we believe that the two stocks we have chosen will perform better than the conglomerate 30 stocks within the Dow. The point here is that if you are long one stock like General Electric, what you can do to hedge your risk is look at your spreadsheet and figure out whether there are other statistical arbitrage opportunities to hedge your naked exposure. If you are long General Electric, you could then look at the other two stocks, Exxon-Mobil and the DIAMONDS, and institute a larger position. You would sell short a smaller position in the DIAMONDS, while implementing a long in ExxonMobil. The point here is not to make a ton of money but, rather, to ensure that you have some other type of hedge to protect your position. Thus, if the Dow continued to ascend, you would technically be market neutral, as your long position is hedged with ExxonMobil and short with the DIAMONDS. If the Dow falls, your position in General Electric will likely take a nosedive as well. However, your short in the DIAMONDS will (hopefully) help to pad any losses—or possibly earn additional money. What's important here is that you are actually trying to trade the convergence of the pair as well; thus, you stand a good chance of making money on the differential collapsing, as well as earning money in your GE position. Then, if the pair does work in your direction, when it nears the mean, you can unlock the ExxonMobil long and DIAMOND short, and resume your naked long position in GE. However, it is important to remember that you have increased your commissions significantly and must make sure that you do not overchurn your account. After all, it would be a treachery if the only people making money were the brokerage houses, while your account dwindled south.

CHAPTER 24

Option Basics

Scott P. Evans

O ptions are financial derivatives that give the owner the right, but not the obligation, to buy or sell the underlying financial instrument for a certain period of time, at a specified price. There are two types of options: call options and put options. It is important to note that the owner of an option never has an obligation, but the seller of the option does have an obligation to either sell the shares of the underlying instrument (in the case of a call) or to purchase the shares of the underlying instrument (in the case of a put). It is completely up to the owner of the option to decide whether to exercise the option or not. Once the seller has sold the contract he is at the mercy of the contract owner. The owner can always just let the option expire worthless—he or she would lose the money invested, but has no further risk.

On a more basic level, option contracts can be classified in one of two ways—as an American option or as a European option. With an American option, the contract owner can exercise the option at any point in time up until the contract expiration date. Contrastingly, European options can only be exercised on the expiration date. Because of the added flexibility with regard to the ability to exercise the option contract, an American option will always be worth more than a European option, except for on the expiration date. On the date of expiration, both the American option and the European option will have the same value. The contract owner has until the option expiration date to exercise the contract. That given amount of time is known as the time until expiration. Option contracts expire on the Saturday following the third Friday of each month (only for U.S. equity options).

There are many reasons and strategies for trading options. For many people the primary reason is that it increases the leverage you can get out of a limited amount of money. Since the premium paid to purchase the option is usually a fraction of the cost of the underlying instrument, you can control larger positions with a lot less money. Additionally, a single stock option (100 shares of stock) controls 100 shares of the underlying stock so you get even more leverage out of your money. Another reason that people trade options is to generate income. Options sellers receive a premium when they sell the options contracts; sometimes this can be a risky proposition, but in certain circumstances it can be a safe, income-producing strategy. One other reason people trade options is to hedge a portfolio. This strategy is most commonly used by institutional traders and people who want to protect large portfolios. The most widely used strategy to hedge a portfolio is to buy puts. If you own a large portfolio and believe that the market is going to decline, instead of selling out of all of your positions you can buy puts (usually on an index) and you will make up the money that you have lost on your portfolio during a market drop with the gains you will make on the put options. Figuring out the exact put ratio can be a difficult task because you have to calculate how highly correlated your portfolio is to the returns on the index that you are using to hedge. Once you have figured out the relationship of returns between your portfolio and the index, you purchase a proportionate amount of puts so that the value of your portfolio is protected. This sounds like a wonderful strategy, but it is actually difficult and expensive to execute. The relationship between the volatility of your portfolio and the index underlying the put options will change over time, and to remain completely hedged, put contracts must be bought or sold in order to keep the proportions in line. All of the buying and selling of put options generates large amount of transaction costs. Furthermore, when the put options expire they must be replaced with contracts that have later expirations. This too adds to the expense of the strategy. That is why the strategy is primarily used by institutions.

Options contracts can be traded on a variety of financial instruments. Foremost among these is the single stock option, an option written on one specific underlying stock. There are also index options written on a variety of financial indexes such as the Standard & Poor's (S&P) 500, the NASDAQ Composite, or the Dow Jones Industrial Index. Options contracts are also written on foreign currencies. The underlying financial instrument is a unit of the foreign currency such as a Canadian dollar or a German deutsche mark. If you believe that the value of the foreign currency is going to appreciate, you can buy a call on the currency, and if you are right you will make the difference between the strike price and the new price of the currency (less the premium paid). Finally, there are options on futures. In this case the underlying instrument is a futures contract. Futures contracts can be written on a large number of goods. Many futures contracts are written on agricultural goods, precious metals, financial indexes, and foreign currencies. Unlike equity all options contracts, the purchaser of the futures contract has an obligation to purchase the underlying instrument for a specified price for a specified length of time.

In an options transaction the buyer of the option contract pays the seller a premium for the right to call away (buy) the underlying shares of stock at a specified price for a certain length of time (in a call transaction) or to force the seller to purchase the underlying shares from the purchaser at a specified price for a certain length of time (in a put transaction). Subsequently, there is a greater risk of loss for the seller of the option contract than there is for the purchaser. The greatest amount of money that the buyer of the option contract can lose is limited to the premium that he or she pays for the contract. Conversely, the seller of the option can theoretically have unlimited losses in specific situations. When the seller of a call option does not own the underlying security, he or she is known to have sold (or "written") a naked call option. This position creates the single greatest potential for losses in options trading. For example, if a call was written on a stock with a strike price of $20 for a $3 premium and the price of the underlying stock climbs to $50, the writer of the call would lose $30 less the $3 premium that he or she was paid. In this transaction, the purchaser of the option contract would call away the underlying stock from the seller and pay him $20 per share for the stock. Remember, the seller of the option does not own the underlying security, so she must go out into the open market and purchase the shares for $50 apiece. It is important to note that each stock option contract controls 100 shares of the underlying security. Thus, it is easy to see how quickly the losses can add up when selling naked calls. If the seller had sold 10 contracts, the buyer would have the right to purchase 1,000 shares of the stock at $20 and the seller would have lost $27,000 ($50 minus the $3 premium, minus the $20 he or she received from the buyer, multiplied by 1,000 shares). This is obviously a very risky position to take because theoretically there is no ceiling for your losses—a stock's price could rise to an unlimited value. Similarly, the purchaser of a call option conceptually can experience unlimited gains. The easiest way to explain the overall strategy for options is that buying a call is much like going long the underlying security, and buying a put is similar to going short the underlying security. If you believe the price of the underlying stock is going to appreciate, you would want to buy a call option. If you believe that the price of the underlying stock is going to decrease, you would buy a put option. Meanwhile, an option seller is simply trying to generate the option premiums. It is much safer to be the buyer of any option than to be the seller, except for when you are writing covered calls, which will be discussed later in the chapter.

Writing put options is also a very risky proposition, but there is a limit to the losses that the seller can sustain. Since a stock's price cannot sink below $0, the most a put writer can lose is the exercise price of the option less the premium they received. If a put was sold with a strike price of $20 and the seller received a $3 premium, then the most they can lose would be $17 per share. This works the same way for the purchaser of the put option—his or her gains would be limited by the difference between the exercise price and zero, less the premium paid.

The price of the premium paid for an option contract varies according to several factors. First and foremost is whether the option is *in-the-money* or *out-of-the-money*. These terms relate to the current price of the underlying stock (or index, future's contract, etc.) in comparison to the strike price of the option. For a call option the contract will be in-the-money if the current price of the stock is above the strike price for the option. Referring to our previous example, a call option is written with a strike price of $20. If the price of the stock is above $20, the option contract is considered to be in-the-money. This is because the owner of the contract could exercise the contract at that time and would receive a gain of some magnitude. Of course, the contract owner had to pay a premium for the option contract, so in our example with a $3 premium having been paid, the stock would have to be trading above $23 for the contract owner to make a profit on the transaction, although if the stock were trading between $20 and $23, the option owner could still recoup some of the premium paid by exercising the option. For a put contract the relationship is reversed; if the price of the stock is below the strike price of the contract, the option is considered to be in-the-money. If a put contract has a strike price of $20 and the stock is trading at $15, the owner of the put could go out in the open market and purchase the underlying stock for $15, and the seller of the put would have to purchase the stock from the option owner for $20, thereby locking in a profit for the owner.

The opposite is true for an out-of-the-money option contract. A call option is out-of-the-money when the price of the underlying stock is below the exercise price of the option. This contract would not be exercised because the underlying stock could be purchased in the open market for less than the contract owner would have to pay if he or she exercised the option. Similarly, a put contract is out-of-the-money if the price of the stock is above the strike price of the option contract. It would not make sense to exercise this contract either, because the contract owner would be purchasing the stock in the open market at a higher price than he or she would receive from the contract seller. Buying high and selling lower is not a very good strategy to make money by trading options.

There are really two components to the premium price of an option: extrinsic value and in-the-money value. Extrinsic value is simply the concept that the farther away the contract expiration date, the more valuable the option. This is because the price of the underlying stock has the probability of moving to a much greater extent over a longer period of time. An option contract that has two weeks to expiration is much less valuable than one with two months to expiration (neglecting for a second in-the-money issue). The second component to option premium pricing is the in-the-money value. If an option is in-the-money, the option seller must be compensated for that value. Otherwise (in a vacuum, but not reality), traders would simply purchase in-the-money contracts, immediately exercise them, and take a profit on the transaction. Once again, we will use the prior example of an option contract with a strike price of $20. If the stock is trading at $25, the premium for the option will have to be at least $5 to make up for the guaranteed gain. Most likely, unless the option is at expiration, there will be an additional amount added to the in-the-money amount to account for the intrinsic-value aspect. There are a few other things that can affect the premium charged for an option. The volatility of the underlying stock has a lot to do with premium pricing. A high-volatility stock, say with a standard deviation of 30 percent, would have a much higher premium than a lower volatility stock with a standard deviation of 10 percent. The reason for this is similar to the time-value concept; the high-volatility stock has a much greater probability of experiencing dramatic price swings than the lower volatility stock, and consequently creates a greater risk of loss to the option seller. As with any situation in the investment world, risk must always be compensated. One final note on option premium pricing: Generally, the higher the price of the underlying stock, the higher the premium price for the option, all else being equal.

As previously mentioned, there is a safe income-producing strategy known as covered call writing. A *covered call* is the term given to the situation in which the call writer actually owns shares of the underlying security (in proportion to the number of call options they have sold). The call writer receives the premiums from the purchaser and if the stock gets called away from him he will also receive the exercise price of the call option. The risk in this transaction is purely the opportunity cost if the stock's price rises and it gets called away. The call writer will not actually lose any money because he can simply deliver the stock that he already owns, but he will miss out on the gains that would have been attained had he still owned the underlying stock. For that reason, most writers of covered calls hope that the stock's price remains around the exercise price of the calls so the option will expire worthless. That way, the covered call writer receives the premiums paid and still gets to keep the stock.

Another fairly basic options strategy is referred to as a straddle. A straddle occurs when a call and a put are bought with the same exercise price and the same expiration date. The purpose of a straddle is that the owner should make money if there is any price volatility, regardless of the direction of the movement. If both a call and a put are bought with a strike price of $20 and the stock price either gains or loses $5 in value, the owner of the straddle will face the same payoff profile whether the stock price moves up or down. If the stock price advances to $25 and the call option is exercised, the option owner will make $5 (disregarding the premiums paid) and the put option would expire worthless. If the stock price declines to $15, the put option would be in-the-money by $5 and the call option would expire worthless. Unfortunately, if the stock price remains relatively unchanged both the call and the put option will expire worthless. It is for this reason that the straddle strategy is most effective when used with high-volatility underlying stocks. The higher-volatility stocks by nature have a greater probability of price movement and this increases the probability that one side of the straddle will finish in the money. One application of this strategy is, using technical analysis, to buy a straddle with an exercise price that corresponds to a support or resistance level for a stock. That way, whether the stock breaks out or pulls back, as long as there is some price movement, your straddle will finish in-the-money.

Options trading has many applications in the investment world and is a useful tool to leverage your money, to hedge a portfolio, and for risk management purposes—usually used by financial institutions. The last major advantage of trading options is that options do not have symmetrical payoff profiles. You can limit your downside risk by purchasing options rather than the underlying stock because when buying options the maximum amount you can possibly lose is the price of the option premium. When purchasing stocks your maximum loss potential is the price of the stock, or all the money that you have invested. It is even worse if you are shorting stocks rather than buying puts because, as we discussed previously (when talking about selling calls), the potential loss is theoretically unlimited since stocks have no ceiling above which they cannot rise. Trading options can be a very lucrative investment strategy, but it should be approached with caution. If you are writing calls and puts, you can quickly get yourself into a dangerous loss position, and if you are buying options, you can end up paying a lot of money in premiums and have your options expire worthless. It is a good idea to educate yourself about the process as much as possible and then to practice by paper trading before you actually start working with real money.

CHAPTER 25

Understanding Volatility

*What Is Volatility?
Volatility Position Sizing
in Your Spreadsheet
Volatility and the
Individual Stock
Weighted Volatility*

WHAT IS VOLATILITY?

To begin, the definition of *volatility* is generally known as the speed of the market. (EN 25.1) By this, volatility is known as the speed at which your position moves up or down. Volatility is the percentage change of the stock over a given period of time. A stock that moves 2 points in two years has less volatility than a stock that moves 20. Though this concept is extremely simple, you will soon see that it has a wide variety of uses when trading pairs, stocks, and/or equities.

To further expand on our definition, volatility is known as the time it takes for a position to move. Volatility can also be incorporated in our statistics to provide a better indication of our position sizing, along with helping us decide what types of option strategies to implement.

VOLATILITY POSITION SIZING IN YOUR SPREADSHEET

Volatility can be a little confusing at first, as some can mistake the concept as an absolute percentage changes over a period of time. However, this is incorrect. Instead, volatility is a concept of speed that can have either a positive or negative impact. When we look at our KLAC/NVLS spreadsheet (titled KLAC-NVLS-Volatility on the CD-ROM), you will find the simple one-year volatility number located in each individual stock's worksheet and the

Volatility worksheet. In the Volatility worksheet you will find the actual numbers in cells F4 and G4. The volatility numbers in this case monitor the last year's percentage change, and will update itself with each new day of data added. Thus, the numbers encompass the past 256 days of trading, or one year of change.

While the numbers are a percentage change, we will instead view them as a standard deviation of movement of the stocks from the mean. In terms of speed, KLAC's volatility over the last year was 12.30 percent and has a mean price of $51.16. Thus, if we multiply 12.30 percent by $51.60, we come up with 6.34. Given the last year's trading range, we can anticipate that in the following year, the stock will trade at +/−6.34 points of $51.60. This would equate to one standard deviation, while two standard deviations would amount to the stock trading at +/−12.68 points of the mean. Now, looking at NVLS, we see that the stock has a one-year volatility of 5.79 percent, with a mean of $44.58. We can infer that over the next year (given the last year) the stock will have a one standard deviation trading range of +/−2.58 points of the mean. Figure 25.1 shows the Volatility worksheet with the data that we have uncovered thus far.

It is important to remember several things here. First, we are looking at percentage changes as a measure of volatility. This measurement is not incorporating past data of two, three, or even five years. Thus, we are really only looking at the volatility of the stock in the recent (one-year) trend. Why is this so important? Think about it—the volatility for KLAC is just

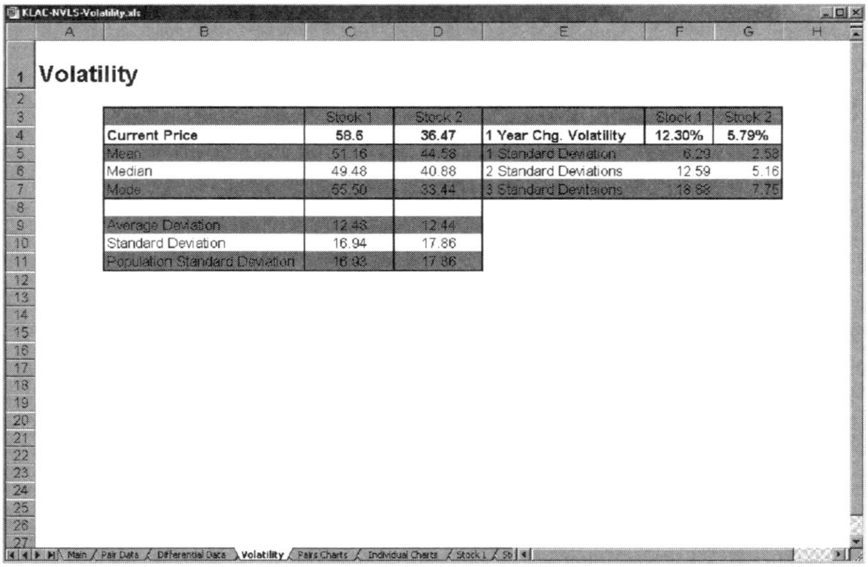
Volatility

	Stock 1	Stock 2		Stock 1	Stock 2
Current Price	58.6	36.47	1 Year Chg. Volatility	12.30%	5.79%
Mean	51.16	44.58	1 Standard Deviation	6.29	2.58
Median	49.48	40.88	2 Standard Deviations	12.59	5.16
Mode	55.50	33.44	3 Standard Devitsions	18.88	7.75
Average Deviation	12.48	12.44			
Standard Deviation	16.94	17.86			
Population Standard Deviation	16.93	17.86			

FIGURE 25.1 Volatility

over 12 percent; however, if we look all the way back to the top of the bull market and 2000, we see a different picture. The volatility dating to December 31, 1999, is −5.51 percent. When adding and subtracting the negative number to our mean, the volatility of the stock has been greater over the last year, than the last three years. *(However, please keep in mind that this is not accounting for adjusted prices, which include splits and dividends.)* What we can also surmise at this point is that the speed—or volatility—of KLAC is much faster than that of NVLS. This is important, as in our pair, we can assume that the stock with greater volatility—usually the more expensive stock—will move faster than the other. If our position is hedged on an even level, we can assume that the end result could leave us with one side of our trade overtaking the other on an uneven basis. This whole conversation is leading us to a ratio for our position on a volatility basis for position sizing. If we simply divide the volatility of the two stocks, we can find a simple measurement of position sizing to help guide our trade. In the case of KLAC and NVLS, we would divide 12.30 percent by 5.79 percent. Our conclusion is that we would take on 2.12 shares of NVLS for every one share of KLAC (shown in Figure 25.2). This is substantially different than our simple ratio of 1.61. However, given the speed of the trade, NVLS will move much slower than KLAC and thus deserves a larger position. This will mostly apply to options, which we will cover in the next chapter.

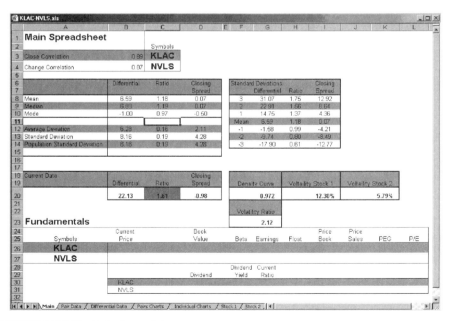

FIGURE 25.2 Main Spreadsheet

VOLATILITY AND THE INDIVIDUAL STOCK

To understand the daily volatility of each stock, we can use some simple math devised by Sheldon Natenburg. If we assume that the volatility of KLAC is roughly 12 percent, we can find an interesting result by dividing the square root of one year's worth of data by our aforementioned number. To do so, we would assume that there are 256 trading days in the year, of which the square root is 16. Then by dividing 12 percent by 16 we receive 0.75. What this means is that one standard deviation of each day's volatility—given the last year of trading activity—would equate to a +/−75 cent price change. Two standard deviations would equal $1.50, while three would come out to be $2.25. If at any given time, KLAC is trading up or down $2.25, we would surmise that the stock is trading at the outlying third standard deviation of its recent historical activity. On an intraday basis, if we scan our KLAC worksheet to find trading days when the stock closed above or below $2.50, in terms of intraday change, we only find 17 instances that it did so in the last 1,699 trading days! This means that if you either bought or sold KLAC when the stock was up/down $2.50 since January 2, 1996, you would have lost exactly 1 percent of the time. However, the losses on these days translate to just a few cents all the way to several dollars. The fundamental concept, though, is that by understanding the stock's volatility in terms of daily change, we have an opportunity to make money on an intraday basis. Where does this help the pairs trader? If you were to buy or sell KLAC when, on a volatility basis, the stock is trading at the third standard deviation of divergence, you have a good win/loss percentage basis to make money. What's more, if instead of taking a regular position, you had paired up with NVLS, you would have hedged your position for an intraday pairs trade. It is important to remember that we are looking at the volatility of the faster-moving stock, as we want to make sure our lagging—or hedged—position is merely a complement to the directional trade. Please keep in mind that on certain days when KLAC had *major* news moving the stock, it would not have been a good idea to trade. However, if there were no major news, taking a position based on the statistical volatility would have been a good move. The entire point of this chapter is that by understanding the volatility of an individual stock, we can find pairs divergences, without looking at the longer-term statistics of the "pair." If the pair has diverged on a long-term basis, however, and we wait for an intraday divergence in terms of volatility, we increase our chances of having succeeding by that much more. One last side note, the same sort of calculation can be applied to weekly volatility by using the square root 7.2 as a divisor.

WEIGHTED VOLATILITY

To forecast volatility we simply figure out what the historical volatility was for different time frames and then average the result. To do so, you will want to figure out what the volatility is for 30-, 60-, 120-, and 200-day periods. Once you know what the volatility is for different periods, you can then average the sum to gain a mean weighted volatility and then apply our normal statistics. The interesting part of volatility is that it always begins at zero for any given period and then moves either up or down. Thus, in terms of volatility, the concept is always mean reverting, as our foundation is always zero. To get a more accurate picture of volatility, you will want to actually weight the periods measured to gain a more accurate picture. As an example, we will use the same periods described above, along with the hypothetical return for each.

Stock 1

30 days	20%
60 days	15%
120 days	26%
200 days	30%

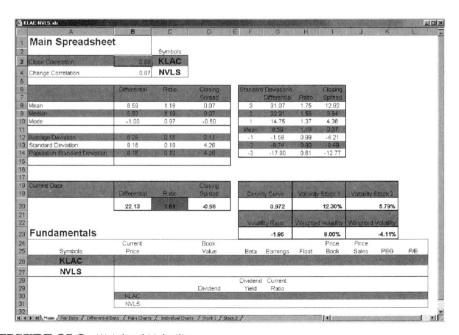

FIGURE 25.3 Weighted Volatility

The simple mean volatility is 22.75 percent for all periods covered.

Because we want to give more weight to the most recent numbers, we will actually divide them by a percentage to have a better understanding of where our pair is.

$$[(40\% * 20\%) + (30\% * 15\%) + (20\% * 26\%) + (10\% * 30\%)]$$

The weighted mean return for the periods covered is 20.7 percent, which is less than the simple average for the periods covered. To apply this to our pair, we can measure different periods, and then weight the pair's volatility to have a better understanding of where the pair is. On the Main worksheet, you will find each individual stock's weighted volatility in cells I23 and K23.

Looking at the KALC/NVLS spreadsheet (Figure 25.3), we now know that the weighted volatility for both stocks is lower than the simple volatility.

Though the volatility ratio in the worksheet is not configured for weighted volatility, the information is there and you can change the ratio from a simple ratio to weighted. However, this preference differs from trader to trader, with both numbers providing guidance for pairs trading.

CHAPTER 26

Understanding Volatility and Options

Speed and Option Premiums
Option Strategies for Pairs
Calls/Puts, Covered Calls/Puts

SPEED AND OPTION PREMIUMS

So why all this talk about volatility if it doesn't apply directly to your pair? Volatility does, and when taking option positions, if we understand the speed of the two stocks that we are using, we will be able to better determine what types of positions to take. When using options, we want to make sure that we have appropriate risk with the volatility of the position. If a stock is highly volatile, then we may want to use less risky strategies like butterflies and strangles, which have opposite price reaction to volatility. The point of volatility as we use it in relation to our pairs is to understand what types of positions we should take given the amount of time left to expiration. If there are only three weeks left to expiration for a contract and the 30-day volatility ranges from 0 to 5%, then we can assume that the risk for taking a pairs position based purely on buying puts and calls would be much more risky than a position that has much higher short-term volatility. In the case of KLAC/NVLS we can see that the 30-day volatility is −0.30 percent and −14.30 percent, respectively. We would infer from this data that buying a KLAC call and an NVLS put would have much more risk of expiration worthless for KLAC than NVLS. Why? NVLS is clearly showing much greater near-term volatility than KLAC. In other words, KLAC has been much more stable over the last 30 days than NVLS. What's more, this data coincides with taking a larger position in NVLS than KLAC, as it is more likely to actually move into the money than the latter stock. We are using our volatility data to understand how quickly each stock will move. There is conflicting data here, though, as historically KLAC is not only more expensive, but also almost twice as volatile. However, in the near term—what we are concerned with—the NVLS contract has a better chance of moving toward our strike price than KLAC. There is a contrary argument here that because NVLS has been moving faster than KLAC, it will begin to slow in the future, as KLAC actually begins to pick up more speed. However, I have generally found that taking a larger position based on the historical simple average, coupled with near-term speed, can benefit a position. What is critically important to remember is that the higher a stock's volatility, the more expensive an option is. The seller of an option knows that greater volatility means increased risk. If you are the buyer, that means a more expensive premium.

OPTION STRATEGIES FOR PAIRS

Pairs and options can quickly get very complicated and have many different combinations of positions. To keep it simple, we will use only a few position strategies for our pairs. For further reading, I highly recommend *Option Volatility and Pricing* by Sheldon Natenburg. (EN 26.1) Mr. Natenburg gives a much deeper understanding of volatility and more complicated strategies, such as Delta Neutral trading. As a brief side note, over the next chapter, as I speak of buying calls or puts, please assume that I am talking about buying at-the-money positions. At-the-money positions move more like the actual stock itself, and involve slightly—and I would like to reiterate *slightly*—less complicated decisions.

Calls/Puts

The simplest strategy for our pair is simply to buy calls and puts for each side of our pair. In the case of KLAC/NVLS, we would buy two NVLS puts for every one KLAC call in the position. However, we will begin to find the strategy complicated as we try and figure out what our premiums are and how far out of the money we should purchase each side. Thus, as mentioned earlier, our best bet may be to simply purchase at-the-money calls and puts. By doing so, the options will trade more like the actual stock. Our risk is that the options will not move far enough in-the-money to actually provide a profit; however, by purchasing options, we have limited our risk if the pair continues to expand.

Covered Calls/Puts

In a neutral market, a trader can implement a covered call to hedge risk. The strategy is simply to buy the actual stock, while selling call options against it. We would use this when we want to go long the stock and have immediate income. By executing a covered call on the long side of our pair, we would receive the immediate income from selling the call. What's more, if the stock rose, we would then also make money on the distance from where we bought the stock and the strike at which the call was sold. Once the stock rises above our call strike, on expiration we would be obligated to then hand over the shares to the call buyer if he or she decides to exercise the position. Conversely, we could also write covered puts on the opposite side of the pair, understanding that if the pair completely converged, we would have limited upside to the trade. However, if the pair continued to expand, we would be short and long both positions further at a higher differential. The reason this strategy is good for pairs trading is that it allows us take a "hedged" position, and raises (on the sell side) and lowers (on the buy side) our cost basis should the rubber band continue to grow. Let's actually see how this would work in terms of a pair. Suppose that our KLAC/NVLS position has expanded to a point where we believe that the rubber band has fully diverged. We would like to take a position, but are unsure whether the pair has reached a point where it will begin to reconverge. *Just to clarify, the following example is completely hypothetical and does not use real prices; it is just for the sake of explanation.*

Our KLAC/NVLS spreadsheet is updated through October 10, 2003. The differential is currently 22.13, while the ratio is 1.61. The pair (in differential and ratio) is trading just above two standard deviations. Normally, I would wait for the pair to expand much farther before taking a position. However, by implementing a covered call and put at this point, I would then leave

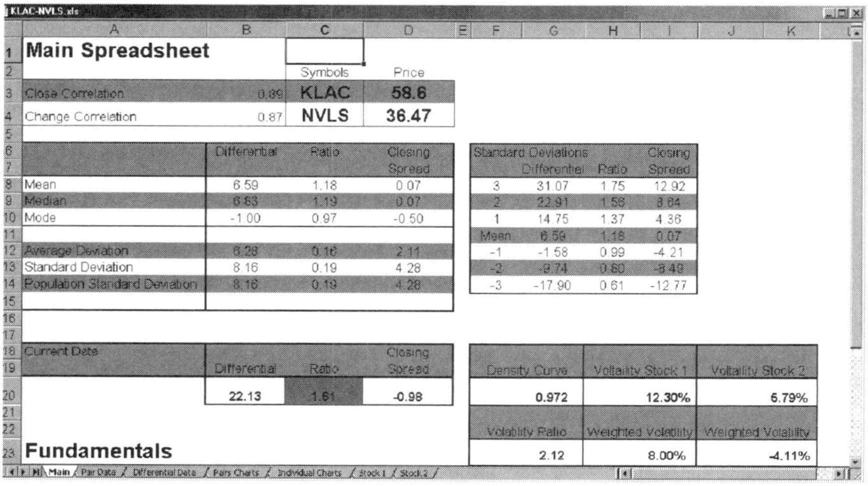

KLAC-NVLS.xls

Main Spreadsheet

		Symbols	Price
Close Correlation	0.89	KLAC	58.6
Change Correlation	0.87	NVLS	36.47

	Differential	Ratio	Closing Spread
Mean	6.59	1.18	0.07
Median	6.83	1.19	0.07
Mode	-1.00	0.97	-0.50
Average Deviation	6.28	0.16	2.11
Standard Deviation	8.16	0.19	4.28
Population Standard Deviation	8.16	0.19	4.28

Standard Deviations	Differential	Ratio	Closing Spread
3	31.07	1.75	12.92
2	22.91	1.56	8.64
1	14.75	1.37	4.36
Mean	6.59	1.18	0.07
-1	-1.58	0.99	-4.21
-2	-9.74	0.80	-8.49
-3	-17.90	0.61	-12.77

Current Date	Differential	Ratio	Closing Spread
	22.13	1.61	-0.98

Density Curve	Voltaility Stock 1	Voltaility Stock 2
0.972	12.30%	5.79%
Volatility Ratio	Weighted Volatility	Weighted Volatility
2.12	8.00%	-4.11%

Fundamentals

Main / Pair Data / Differential Data / Pairs Charts / Individual Charts / Stock 1 / Stock 2

FIGURE 26.1 KLAC/NVLS

myself extra room for divergence. KLAC is trading at $58.60, while NVLS is presently at $36.47. The pair is on the sell side of the mean, indicating that we would want to sell short KLAC and buy NVLS. Figure 26.1 brings us up to speed on where the pair is for the current scenario.

What we immediately notice is that in terms of regular standard deviations from the mean, if the pair were to open up to the third standard deviation, we could lose almost nine points by simply buying and selling the individual stocks. But by implementing a covered call and put and collecting premium, we would have the opportunity to engage the pairs position at almost 2.5 standard deviations, thus allowing us to actually take the position at better prices. Thus, we would buy the actual NVLS stock and write a call against it, potentially $1 to $5 out-of-the-money. On KLAC, we would sell short the stock, while writing a put against it, also $1 to $5 out-of-the-money. On both sides of this trade, we are hoping that the options will expire worthless and we will be left with the normal stock at better prices. It is extremely important to remember that this strategy has *much* higher transaction costs, which could quickly erode all premium and profits. Also, our risk is still just as high for the trade in the sense that we are left with naked stock in the end, where we are still left with substantial risk. If you can shoulder the transaction costs and understand the risks involved, covered calls and puts are definitely a very interesting strategy using pairs.

CHAPTER 27

Using Technical and Fundamental Analysis with Pairs

Technical Analysis
Moving Averages
Stochastics and Other
Indicators
Volume
Fundamentals
Price-to-Earnings (PE) Ratio
Price-to-Sales Ratio
KBH Homes and Tol Brothers
Moving Averages and Support
and Resistance as Stops

After many years of hard lessons, I would like to pass some of my knowledge on. I hope that what I am going to tell you will give you some insight into picking entry and exit points in your trades—outside of statistics. The problem with statistics is that even though they are amazing at helping us determine relationships, and assisting in finding entry/exit points, two standard deviations tell us nothing about when a company has accounting problems. Take Enron, for example. If you had been pairs or directional trading Enron a few years back, and you thought the stock had some sort of "correlation" that would bring it back to the mean when it began to nosedive, you most likely lost everything.

Thus, this chapter is to help us tie our pairs data into real decisions that are presented in everyday investing. While the foundation of pairs lies within descriptive statistics, we must use all other facets of knowledge to help us make our final decisions. In addition, descriptive statistics don't always give us exit signals or concise stop loss points. Thus, by using technical and fundamental analysis as a guiding tool of market direction, we can help define our trade targets and stops.

Along with technical analysis, we can also use fundamental analysis to help determine the valuation of the trade. While this may sound a little complicated, don't sweat it. What we're about to cover is actually very simple and requires little math. Fundamental analysis scares most people, who associate it with countless hours of reading and extensive research. And while for the analyst this is exactly the case, I will boil it down to some commonsense applications based on what we have already covered. This chapter will start with technical analysis, skip over to fundamentals, and then tie the two together.

TECHNICAL ANALYSIS

Moving Averages

As previously stated, one of the most important aspects of technical analysis is major moving averages, like the 50 and 200-DMAs. Why? The reason these two moving averages are so vital is that the bulk of the world's investors who keep an eye on technical analysis, watch the 50- and 200-DMAs. When a big part of the trading population may be making a decision based on two little lines on a chart, then the little lines become very important. In essence, they become self-fulfilling prophecies. At the same time though, I would be hard-pressed to say that tons of traders are making decisions based on the moving averages. In other words, it's hardly likely that many people buy a stock just because it bounces on the 50-DMA. However, it is very rational to say that many more people are watching the stock with a closer eye as it nears the moving average. Simply put, moving averages are like alert beacons in the night—something you want to pay close attention to when near.

We can even do statistical analysis on the two moving averages, to find out when the pair is spread apart on a 50-day historical basis. However, by doing so we are analyzing data that is already analyzing data. In short, we are applying statistics to something that is already lagging. If we were to do so (but we're not), then it would be much wiser for us to use an exponential moving average, rather than a simple moving average.

As previously stated, the 50- and 200-DMAs can cause a stock to ricochet off the average or plummet through. Why? As a trader, if you have 1 million shares to sell at the best possible price and you know the technical world will likely buy a stock as it hits a major moving average on a descending move, would you wait for a bounce to sell? Of course you would, as you would want to get the best possible price. Most traders handling order flow *never* look at a moving average as a "reason" for entering or exiting a trade, but they do take notice of the occurrence, and so should you—even when you are looking at statistics. Ok, so how does this help me with pairs? If you are about to buy a stock and it is trading *under* the 200-SMA, and your sole reason to buy it is because of statistics, maybe rethink the trade. Don't trade, you say? Yes, perhaps wait and see if the stock moves back above the 200-SMA before entering either side of the trade. Common sense tells us that regardless of statistics, the 200-SMA— that is hypothetically just above our imaginary stock—will pose substantial resistance. Thus, why take the chance on having one side of our trade fail? However, if we are aware of this commonsense scenario, and then wait for the stock to ascend above the moving average, we are much safer in the long run in both directional and pairs trading. So how do you put this into practice? Imagine that you are about to enter a pair that has been expanding for some time. The pair is close to three standard deviations, and the density curve is nearing a historical outlier. You are prepared to take the position, when you suddenly notice that the long side of your trade has a 200-SMA a half point above where you are thinking about entering the trade. The commonsense solution is to simply wait until the long side of the trade ascends above the moving average and builds a base. You may lose a little of your potential profit in doing so, but your risk has been minimized substantially. Think about it, taking the position ahead of the 200-SMA is similar to trying to speed across train tracks ahead of an oncoming locomotive. While you may make it, overall, you're taking a very stupid chance. Why not play it safe and let the train go by? And that would be the same for waiting for a major moving average to be on the correct side of your trade before taking a position. This is technical common sense when pairs trading.

Stochastics and Other Indicators

Other indicators like stochastics and moving average convergence divergence (MACD) are hardly ever reliable as a leading indicator for a position. They can be, however, a good confirmation tool when taking a directional position. In pairs, they can also help us decide whether the pair has room to open up more or whether it will begin to reconverge. Let's look at a few stocks, just to see how this could be used in our pairs strategy.

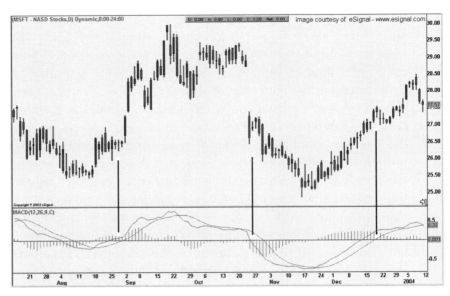

FIGURE 27.1 Microsoft

Figure 27.1 depicts Microsoft over 2003. As you can see, we have added a MACD and a slow stochastic. While we would never use either of these indicators to actually implement a position, we can use them as a confirmation of momentum within a stock. If you look at line 1, you will see that it coordinates with the MACD in the lower indicator window. When the MACD crosses above the 0 line, the stock clearly has more room to run up. If we were considering shorting the stock as a pair, this would clearly be the wrong time. However, if the statistics prompted us to buy Microsoft, then this would be a good time to do so. What's more, if you look at the stochastics at this time, they are clearly headed higher, while traveling in the upper portion of the indicator's range. This also would lead us to believe that the stock has more upside room left. Again, we would not use the MACD or the slow stochastic as an indicator to institute a position, but would look at it as a possible confirmation to the signal the descriptive statistics are giving us.

Volume

Volume is one of the most important indicators of a stock's direction. So how can we use volume as an indicator for entry into a pair? We will look for volume moves before entering a pair, and as a guide for further expansion or contraction. Looking at the following picture of ExxonMobil, we can see that volume gave us some pretty interesting ideas as to the direction of the stock. First, the volume spike labeled #1, came as the stock was in the middle of a pullback. Increased volume was a looking glass into institutional order flow, and indicated that many holders of the stock wanted out. If we were given a statistical signal to enter the stock long on this particular day, the increased volume would have been an indicator to stay out of the trade until further expansion occurred. Though the volume dump rebounded slightly in the following two days, overall, it was an indication that many traders wanted out of the stock, at least short-term. Conversely, if the descriptive statistics gave us a signal to sell ExxonMobil short, while taking a long position in another stock, we would have definitely been on the right side of the trade. If we actually look into the news of the stock on that particular day, I'm sure we would find some sort of event that triggered the sell-off. However, one thing that technical analysis does for us is to allow us to "infer" that something has transpired without actually having to sift through the news. As diligent traders, we would definitely want to find out what that event was; however, for the sake of example, it is enough for us to know that whatever instigated the sell-off, was enough to increase volume above the average daily volume. This mere inference is enough for us to assume that more selling will ensue. Further looking at the chart, we clearly see that our volume-driven instincts were right on, as the stock continued to decline several points in the following days. Though much of this seems like commonsense knowledge, many traders make the mistake of overlooking such obvious indicators of a stock's near-term direction.

Line 2 shows the exact same thing. The stock witnessed above average volume on an ascending day, when the stock was clearly in the process of a reversal. The increased volume indicated that the stock had many buyers trying to get in, potentially after whatever news drove the stock down in the first place dwindled. Many traders use volume as an indication of capitulation, when picking either a top or a bottom. While this is true in some cases, it can be a horrible mistake to always assume that increased volume indicates a reversal. As Figure 27.2 proves, increased volume in the middle of a move actually signifies that the spark has generated interest and is in the process of a continuation pattern in whatever the current trend may be. Never rule volume out, as it is one of the most important factors of investing. Volume is the empirical backing of a stock's direction.

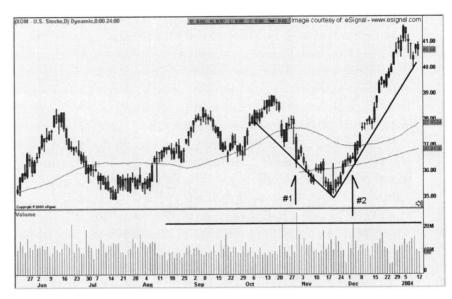

FIGURE 27.2 Increased Volume

FUNDAMENTALS

We have already covered what fundamentals are; now we will directly see
how we can use them to further validate or negate our statistical signals.
The fundamentals we will be using are a little looser than technical analysis, as fundamentals can always become overextended. However, it is
important to remember that institutional money *always* looks at fundamentals and can easily begin unloading positions when a stock becomes
overvalued. In essence (other than news), fundamentals are the catalyst
that controls the cyclical buying and selling of stocks. We will not dive into
complex math here; instead, we will attempt to find a few mainstream numbers that you can use to find a "rough" benchmark for your individual
stock's valuation.

Price-to-Earnings (PE) Ratio

As we all know, PE can be a good sign of investor dedication to a stock.
However, it is important to remember that PE is generally thrown out the
window when it comes to high-flying technology stocks like eBay and Ama-
zon.com. These stocks trade at incredibly high multiples in relation to earnings and, thus, do not give us an accurate picture of valuation when observed

in terms of PE. Some technology stocks don't even have PEs, as they have no earnings. Let's examine a few stocks just for the sake of argument.

When finding a stock's PE in relation to the historical average, Smartmoney.com has a great tool under the "Key Ratios" tab, once a stock is selected. We will look at Intel, to start our brief analysis. We can see in Figure 27.3 that Intel is currently trading with a PE of 48.70. While this is high for most standards, it is also far below the five-year high of 203.10. The industry average is 148.80. So what is our conclusion here? First, the stock is trading with a high PE in relation to traditional fundamental valuation. However, it is not completely exuberant given that the historical high and industry average are far above the current number. While I would personally be skeptical about taking a huge long-term position in the stock, it would not be completely out of reason to take a short-term pairs position, as the PE is not overextended. Let's look at another example.

FIGURE 27.3 Intel

Looking at Figure 27.4, we can see quite a different story for ExxonMobil than that of Intel. First, the historical PE range is substantially lower for the oil stock than for the chip maker. The five-year low for ExxonMobil is 13.70, while the high was 38.60. The stock is currently trading with a PE of 14.80, which is definitely on the low end of the historical range. At the time that this was written, oil was trading at close to $33 a barrel, a very high price for crude by any measure. However, the elevated price of oil also means that companies like ExxonMobil will report great earnings, at least for the current quarter. Given this knowledge, we would infer that Exxon-Mobil has upside room left in the stock. Thus, if our descriptive statistics gave us a buy signal on ExxonMobil and a sell short signal on another oil stock, on a fundamental PE basis, we would not have to be extremely worried about taking the long side of the trade. Of course, there are many other factors to consider, and we *never* take a position based purely on PE. But, at least in this scenario, the PE would give us some positive confirmation

FIGURE 27.4 ExxonMobil Corp.

to possibly institute the pairs trade, knowing that the fundamental PE for the long side is in our favor.

Price-to-Sales Ratio

Another important tool of five-minute fundamental valuation is the price-to-sales ratio. This number gives us some indication as to where a stock is trading in relation to revenue. The higher the value, the worse off a company is. In a nutshell, any number above 3.0 is very bad. Thus, if our statistics give us a sell short signal on a stock and it is trading at 6.0 times sales, we can feel fairly comfortable that some institutional money may be thinking that the stock is overvalued as well. While the price-to-sales number varies from sector to sector, we can be assured that we simply want the lowest number possible.

We will use Qualcomm as our example of price to sales. Figure 27.5 shows that the stock is presently trading at 11.98 times sales. Even though

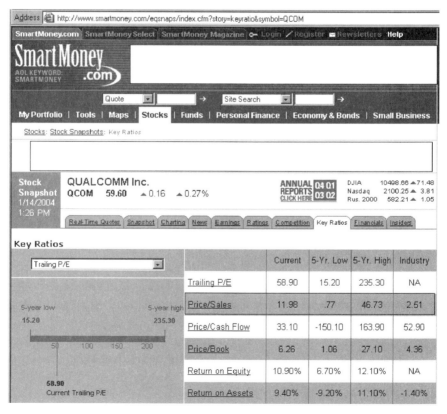

FIGURE 27.5 Qualcomm

the five-year high for the price-to-sales ratio is 46.73, 11.98 is very high. As a fundamental trader, I would not touch this stock on the long side with a 10-foot pole. The problem is that while trading at almost 12 times sales, the risk to reward is not in our favor. Using some of our previous knowledge, the PE is at 58.90. While this is a far cry from the high of 235.30, it is still exorbitantly high for any stock, even if it is in the technology sector. Thus, if our statistics gave us a buy signal for a pair between Qualcomm and another wireless stock, there better be a pretty darn good reason to take the position. Otherwise, I would let this opportunity go by, as missed money is better than lost money.

KBH HOMES AND TOL BROTHERS

Now that we have covered a few basics, let's put it into practice. We will use Tol Brothers Inc. and KBH Homes as an example. (That's Tol Brothers the home builder, by the way—not the cookies.) If we look at our descriptive statistics page, we see that the pair is trading just over -1 standard deviation from the mean. This would indicate that we would be thinking about buying Tol Brothers, while selling short KBH Homes. Keep in mind that as the pair is only trading just below -1 standard deviation, we would not actually consider the pair for convergence but, instead, for continued divergence. The pair is currently at -27.79, while one standard deviation is at -25.34. Looking through the pair data, we can see that the pair has recently traded as low as -39.66 on June 17, 2003 (Please reference the spreadsheet located on the CD-ROM.) And -39 is just one point from the second standard deviation of -40.88, which would have been a risky, but potentially good place to insititute a convergence trade. However, now that the pair has collapsed, we want to see if there will be any more divergence opportunities. We will start with technical analysis, and then look into each stock's fundamentals. (See Figure 27.6.)

As Figure 27.7 displays on KBH Homes, the stock has recently fallen out of bed, marked by a large-volume day—above the average daily volume. To me, this indicates that many larger players decided to exit the stock. It has since been building a base and is trying to hang in there. However, daily stochastics have since bounced and could now easily turn down for another leg south. The MACD has recently crossed beneath the 0 line and could (as historically shown) fall further negative should the stock break horizontal support. Thus, given that the statistics are indicating that we may want to sell short KBH Homes, the technical analysis side of the trade is confirming that

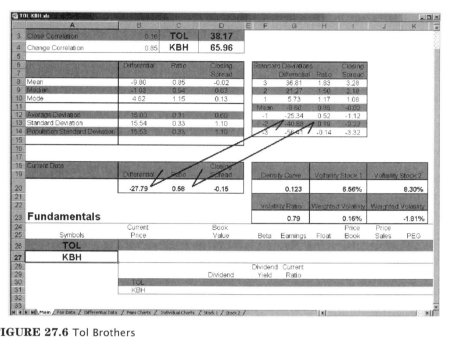

FIGURE 27.6 Tol Brothers

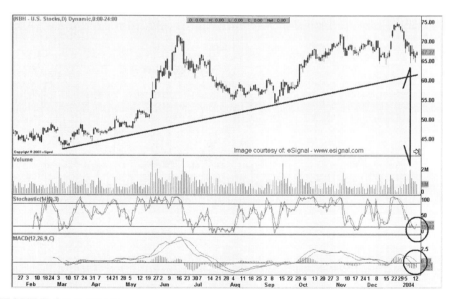

FIGURE 27.7 KBH Homes

there may be more downside left. What's the one thing we have going against us? The most important thing of all. Taking a short position in this trade would clearly be trading against the ascending trend. However, sometimes that's what pairs trading is all about.

Now, looking at the next chart of Tol Brothers in Figure 27.8, we see something else happening. First, the stock has sold off some, but has also built a base after the stock touched ascending support. In addition, the volume spike down day had a large recovery and did not close near the low of the day. This means that even though many players sold the stock that day, there were also many investors waiting on the sidelines to take on new positions. This was a good sign for bulls and shows how volume can show different things on different stocks. If the volume down day had closed near the low of the day, we would have inferred that buyers were nowhere to be seen. Therefore, taking a long position in Tol Brothers would have been much more risky.

On the same chart, we also see that the MACD fell much lower than that of KBH Homes and could now rebound more easily. This signal coupled with the daily stochastics, which are traveling the upper portion of the indicator window, would lead us to conclude that a short position would be much more risky. As the statistics are indicating, a long position would not be that bad of a decision, as long as a tight stop was instituted just below horizontal support, shown on the chart. Our conclusion thus far is

FIGURE 27.8 Tol Brothers

that though both stocks have recently pulled back, Tol Brothers looks like a better long than KBH Homes, which would bode well for convergence traders. However, there is considerable risk, and neither stock looks that enticing.

Moving to fundamentals, we see a different picture. KBH Homes is trading with a PE of 7.90, which is about in the middle of its historical five-year range. However, the stock is trading at 0.55 times sales, which is *very* close to the five-year high of 0.58. Immediately, this is a red flag to us that the stock is getting overvalued in relation to historical revenue, and, thus, we would infer that the descriptive statistics that are indicating a short position is right after all. And, if you remember earlier, the stock didn't look all that attractive on the long side anyway. (See Figure 27.9.)

Figure 27.10 displays the fundamentals for Tol Brothers. And here is where we see some very interesting things. First, the stock is trading with a PE of 11.10 and has a historical high of 11.00. Wow, is this another red flag or what? Technical analysis told us that the stock didn't look all that bad on the long side. However, the fundamental picture is *much* more dim. How can we justify buying a stock that is trading very close to its historical high in relation

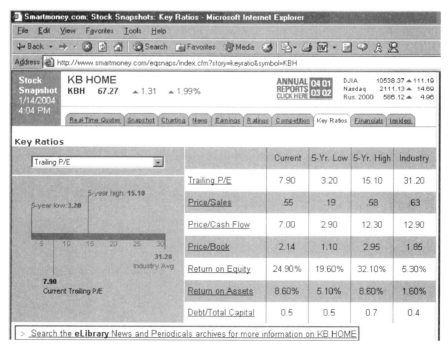

FIGURE 27.9 KBH Homes

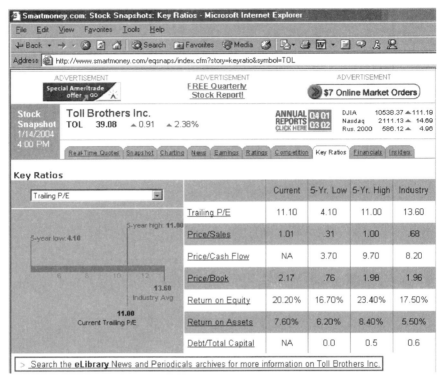

FIGURE 27.10 Tol Brothers

to earnings? If we take our research one step further, we will see that the stock is trading at 1.01 times sales, and has a five-year high of 1.00. Again, this is another *huge* warning beacon in the night. Clearly, the fundamental picture is telling us something completely different than the technical picture, and the aforementioned data indicates that the statistics may be misleading.

So what is our conclusion about this pair? First and foremost, both are overbought on the two fundamental indicators that we have examined. And even though the technical charts indicate that the statistics might be right, both stocks are set up to fall in the near future. One factor that we have not considered is interest rates, which are at 45-year lows at the time this was written. Historically, one of the last sectors to correct after a recession is residential real estate, which coincides with our thoughts that the endless run for homebuilders may be ending.

The most important thing to remember, though, is that all of the data is mixed, which is clearly *not* what we want when instituting a pairs trade. We want to see that the stock we are shorting is overbought on a technical and fundamental basis, while the stock we are buying is oversold—or, at least, undervalued.

If I had to guess, I would assume that if the pair reconverges, it will be mostly from KBH Homes falling more than Tol Brothers. However, both stocks are set up to decline in the future. While I know this goes against the current trend, it is common sense that the price charts are weakening, and the simple fundamentals are overbought.

I would like to point out that we have only covered a few technical and fundamental factors in relation to the pair. Thus, you *need* to make sure you also look at things like trend lines, support and resistance, price to book, PEG ratios, cash, price to cash flow, and forward PE.

It is vitally important to understand *why* a stock is doing what it is doing, before blindly trusting the statistics at hand. This is incredibly important, as trading purely off of statistics would be similar to never checking your oil and only depending on the gauges on your dashboard. The gauges can go bad, and are not errorproof; thus, you have to get under the hood and occasionally check for yourself.

MOVING AVERAGES AND SUPPORT AND RESISTANCE AS STOPS

Last but certainly not least, I would like to talk about the importance of support and resistance and trend lines as stop loss points for your statistical trades. This is very simple, but so vitally important. Statistics can always go against us, and thus it is critical that you have concise stop loss points for each side of your position. If one side breaks down, close the entire position. It's as simple as that. Moving averages and trend lines are major benchmarks of technical trading. Usually, when one or the other is broken, it signifies that some sort of news-related or fundamental event has occurred that is causing a paradigm shift in the stock. Simply put, if a major moving average or trend line is broken, something big is happening. Thus, in our pair, we can use moving averages and trend lines to assist us in making stop loss decisions. Let's go through a few examples.

Figure 27.11 displays eBay and the trading action over the last year when this was written. You can clearly see that the 200-SMA would have served as a significant stop loss point had we been long the stock in November. The stock was sitting just above $50, which was also *major* horizontal support at that time. If we were in a pairs trade and the stock had broken down—and we were long eBay—we would have wanted to close the entire position.

Major support of the
200-SMA and horizontal
support.

FIGURE 27.11 eBay

Horizontal support and the 200-SMA violated.

FIGURE 27.12 Marsh McLennan

However, when the stock sold off, it did *not* break either the 200-SMA or horizontal support. Clearly, we would have had a great stop loss point on the trade by using a breach of $50 as our exit signal.

Figure 27.12 is a chart of Marsh McLennan, which declined after the international mutual fund timing scandal hit close to home with the company's subsidiary Putnam Funds. The chart shows us that the stock had significant support of the 200-SMA and horizontal support just above $47. When news of the mutual fund scandals broke, the stock began to dump. If we had a stop just below the 200-SMA and a horizontal support at roughly $46.99, we would have saved ourselves much pain as the stock sold off. Though the stock eventually recovered, the chart shows that it was still trading below the 200-SMA at the time this was published. As this was a huge warning sign—I would have *not* wanted to be long this stock.

Overall, using moving averages and trend lines is an extremely simple concept, but should be readily used when trading pairs. After all, statistics are *not* always correct, and thus, we must make sure that each trade has some sort of stop outside of just standard deviations. I hope that this chapter has been helpful, and I would like to reiterate that though the concepts are very simple, they are extremely important. This is common sense, which is the most important factor of trading.

CHAPTER 28

Assorted Advice to Assist Trading

This is the last moment where I can tell you about some of my experiences trading pairs and what I have learned. First and foremost, never unlock a pair and close one side of the position, just because it is making more money than the other. There will be certain circumstances where you will want to maybe trim both sides or unlock a portion of one side if you have a plan. However, to just unlock a side merely to book profit is a bad, bad idea. Why? Simply put, if anything can go wrong, it always will. And if you unlock the winning side, the losing side will most likely move against you—at lease according to Murphy's Law. Thus, remember that if you are going to shuffle around your position, always have some sort of plan that justifies your actions, and even more importantly, have a predetermined stop loss to close the trade should it move against you.

• When trading intraday pairs, it is a good idea to generally take a break during earnings season. Why? From my experience, intraday pairs that are moving because of earnings-related news can very often close at the high of the day. This is because the outstanding earnings news has triggered a surge of order flow, wherein large funds are trying to get either in or out of a trade. Thus, during earnings season, there can actually be more opportunity trading divergence pairs than convergence. The best rule of thumb here, though, is: When in doubt, stay out.

• Always update your data once you are in a pair. While this seems like common sense, it's easy to get lazy and not update your data on a day-to-day basis. If you do not update the data, you will not be able to see the actual statistical numbers moving. And we have to remember that these numbers fluctuate on a daily basis—they never remain the same.

• As a trading idea, I have seen intraday traders trade mergers on a sort of pseudo risk arbitrage basis. What they do is find a pair of stocks that are merging. Usually, a merger pair is has a predetermined price at which both stocks have to close. Thus, intraday traders will set up a histogram that is a ratio or a differential of the two stocks. The histogram can be anywhere from 5 to 10 days, and gives visual representation of the pair's intraday trading range. Then, the trader will simply wait until the pair trades near one end or the other and then scalp the intraday trade for a few pennies or a dime. Does it work? In my opinion, not really. The problem is that the massive amounts of commissions on an intraday basis can put a serious dent in any profits. It is also my opinion that the institutional guys trading the stocks like to ramp them out of whack once in a while, just to railroad any day traders trying to actually trade the merger. Thus, my advice is set up a histogram of two stocks and watch the merger trade, but do not actually trade it yourself unless you really know what you are doing. After all, they're pros who have the single job of trading mergers, and if you are trying to compete with a few thousand dollars, well, the house usually wins.

• As another trading idea, I have also watched traders set up percentage graphs (you could say volatility) of three or more stocks benchmarked against an index. The idea is to wait for two- to three-day divergences of the stocks against the index, and then attempt to implement convergence swing trade or day trade positions. The idea is that on a percentage basis, stocks generally revert to the mean for the index they follow. As a good example of this, a trader would look at an index like the XOI.X, which is the AMEX Oil Index. Then, knowing that the stocks must trade relative to the index on a percentage basis, the trader will wait for individual stocks to move away from the index. Once the stocks have diverged (above the mean), the trader will short those farthest out, while buying those nearest to the index. This is actually an effective strategy and can provide hedging ideas for naked positions.

The faster the stocks, the tougher they are to trade. By this I mean that trading fast moving technology stocks can be more dangerous than trading slower utility stocks. Of course, there is always an exception to the rule. However, sometimes trading less sexy stocks like oil or truckers can provide better results than trading high flyers.

• My entire point here is: Don't rule out slower-moving stocks, as they may actually provide more opportunity than technology or Internet stocks.

If you are looking for stocks that will reconverge, remember that the correlation is the key. The stronger the correlation, the greater the chance that the two stocks will come back together. However, it is also important to remember that a strong correlation doesn't always mean the stocks have to come back together. Thus, never bank your account on the correlation alone. If the trade is opening up and moves past the third standard deviation, it may be a good idea to consider exiting your position.

• If you are in a swing-trading pair during earnings or warnings season, and one of your stocks warns or reports poorly in a direction that goes against your pair, close the entire position. This is important, as sometimes when in a pair, we can fool ourselves into thinking that because the position is a hedge, we will not lose money. However, this is wrong. If one half of the pair is working against you because of earnings-related news, you will most likely end up with a huge loser, as institutional money rotates in and out of the stocks. If you find yourself ever hoping a trade will come back, close it.

• Stay away from biotech stocks. This is my own personal opinion, but one that I find to be very accurate for the average trader. The problem with biotech stocks is that they are very dependant on Food and Drug Administration (FDA) approvals, clinical trials, research, and many other loose facets of drug research and manufacturing. Simply put, there is too much to be quantified, unless you have additional countless hours to do the proper research to understand what each company has in the works and where revenue will come from. All I am saying is that biotech companies can have huge surprises, like FDA approvals, which can pound a portfolio should you be on the wrong side of the trade. Thus, if you are willing to do the research to uncover each biotech company's entire repertoire of potential drugs, fine. If you're not, then, as mentioned earlier, slower-moving stocks with transparent business plans may be better to trade.

• Lastly, always put on the short side of the pair first! This is very important to remember, as you will find with some stocks you may not be able to get any shares short, or you may not be able to get an up tick to get into the short side. Please remember that it is vitally important to always make sure you first have the short side secured before entering your long order. I generally wait until I know that I actually have the short position, before even sending out the buy order. This is because sending both orders out at the same time can sometimes result in getting filled on the long side, then having your short order rejected for whatever reason.

CHAPTER 29

The Monitor Sheet

One of the last steps in our book is to use the spreadsheet that monitors many pairs at one time. The spreadsheet can be used as either an end-of-day tracking system or can also monitor pairs in real time if you use a quote vendor that interfaces with Excel. For the most part, Excel will pull in quotes from just about any vendor and can be a useful tool in monitoring intraday pairs. The one drawback is that the quotes are not recorded, and thus drop off moment by moment. Imagine a hollow pipe you are pushing dirt through. As soon as you push dirt in one end, it falls out of the other, and is only in the pipe so long as more dirt is not pushed in. I know this is a rough analogy, but it's exactly how Excel reacts to the quote dilemma. While you can record data in Excel, I will not cover it in this book. Just remember that if you are using a live quote vendor, your pair will show live data, but will not display historical intraday charts or movements.

The actual spreadsheet for tracking multiple pairs is located in the CD-ROM; thus, we will not actually build one from scratch, but it is important to understand what is going on in this sheet.

Figure 29.1 shows the sheet with only one line of data for KLAC/NVLS. However, the sheet in the CD-ROM has all of the actual data in it and includes just under 100 pairs. Figure 29.1 displays the left side of the Monitor sheet, with 48 pairs. The goal of the sheet is to enable the tracking of multiple pairs all at one time, without having to look at all of the individual sheets. When you open the Monitor sheet, it should then give you the option to open all of the corresponding sheets, and/or update itself automatically. It is important to note that this will take up sufficient memory and could slow

MONITOR PAGE.xls

PAIR		DIFFERENTIAL	RATIO	CLOSE	DENSITY CURVE	SIGNAL		90-DMA	160-DMA	250-DMA	STD DEV	COV
KLAC	NVLS	22.10	1.51	-0.980	0.97			1.93	2.27	2.42	8.16	0.89
TQNT	NVLS											
NVLS	SMH											
TER	MU											
AMAT	MU											
DIA	SPY											
AMAT	TER											
FCS	LSCC											
ALTR	LSCC											
LLTC	LSCC											
INTC	LSCC											
LLTC	QLGC											
MXIM	LLTC											
HWP	CPQ											
PALM	HAND											
MLNM	HGSI											
MLNM	PDLI											
MLNM	MEDX											
MEDX	PDLI											
IDPH	PDLI											
ABGX	PDLI											
MERQ	VRTS											
MERQ	BEAS											
AMGN	CHIR											
ELN	ICOS											
HOME BUILDERS/RETAIL SUPPLIERS												
HD	LOW											
HD	KSS											
KSS	LOW											
CTX	TOL											
KBH	LEN											
RYL	LEN											
PHM	TOL											
KBH	RYL											
OIL/GAS/OIL SERVICES												
APA	SGY											
APA	APC											
APC	SGY											
APA	MUR											
XOM	CVX											
CVX	BP											
RD	SC											
APA	NBL											
EOG	NBL											
EOG	BR											
APA	BR											
APA	EOG											

Mark Whistler

FIGURE 29.1 Monitor Sheet

your computer down considerably. Thus, if you are using a slower machine, you may wish to not open all of the sheets all of the time. However, you will have to open all of the sheets from time to time to update them.

The way the sheet is set up allows you to quickly scan the stocks to find one or two pairs that have either diverged or are in the process of. You will notice that on KLAC/NVLS that the differential and ratio are highlighted in pink and red. This is an automatic function of the sheet to notify you whenever the pair ascends or declines above/below +/– two standard deviations. This is a "heads up" function so you can then update the information for that particular pair on a daily basis. By doing this, you will improve your chances of finding a tradable pair that has diverged. What's more, the sheet also shows the correlation and mean, which will assist you in understanding the

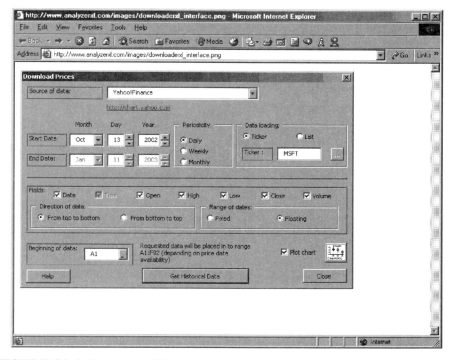

FIGURE 29.2 Downloader XL

reliability of the pair and where it has been trading. For fundamental traders, you may want to watch stocks trading close to the mean, and then using the fundamental analysis described earlier in the book, you may be able to unearth a prosperous divergence situation.

The sheet also contains the moving averages so that you may have a better idea of where the pair is trading. If you will remember from Chapter 16, the moving averages help us to identify entry points on a trade by making sure that all three moving averages are either on the upper or lower end of the respective ranges. In short, the Monitor sheet encompasses almost all of the data in your regular sheets to make finding your pairs much more easy. The only problem is that you do have to update all of the individual sheets manually, which can be an incredible pain in the derriere. If you do not wish to spend countless hours updating your sheets each day, I would recommend two things. First, I personally only open my sheets once every two weeks or so. Then I make a list of all the pairs that are nearing a possible entry signal. I then update those particular sheets daily but do not waste my time updating all of the sheets that are not even remotely within a possible trading point. You can also purchase software like Downloader XL (see Figure 29.2), which will help ease the process a bit.

CHAPTER 30

Conclusion

The Market Bubble
Words of Caution
Last Words of Advice

THE MARKET BUBBLE

Bottom line, there's always a bubble, and we have to constantly check to make sure we're not in it. While pairs trading is meant to hedge risk from possible extraneous circumstances, it is critically important to remember that even when you are hedged, your portfolio could still be devastated. Thus, when you hear of a "bubble," think more about your own money management skills than the actual market circumstances. If you have prepared yourself well, understand your stocks, and have tight stops, then any—and all—bubbles will simply be trading events that you either win big in, or get stopped out for small losers. As investors, we live in glass houses, and trading is like heaving huge stones of emotions. The true bubble is that of fear and greed, even if you are market neutral. Thus, pairs traders strive to break down the inevitable bubble paradigm by engaging in hedged trades. However, as previously mentioned, our risk increases with additional capital exposure, and more transaction fees. Our bubble is not one of market direction, but one of efficient trading action within our own account. So, the next time you hear someone speak of a bubble, ask them what they mean. After all, skydivers without parachutes are generally more fearful than those who do have them.

WORDS OF CAUTION

In my final words of caution, I would like to reiterate that the information presented in this book does not make up a "system" in which buy and sell

237

points are automatically produced. Rather, we have come up with a trading style, based on hedging risk. While we do use descriptive statistics to assist in our decision-making process, we do not isolate ourselves to this one path of trading indicators. Instead, we cross-reference our decisions with fundamental and technical analysis to make sure that the statistics alone will not provide false indicators. I would also like to add that trading on the density curve alone can be incredibly dangerous. On volatile pairs, the density curve can peg out at 0 or 1 for extended periods, while the pair continues to open up. If you do not have a tight stop loss for your trade, you can rest assured that you will lose money. What's more, density curve entry signals vary from stock to stock, so it is vitally important to make sure that you adjust the entry signal for *every* pair. Look through the historical data and see what works. Amazingly, a little common sense can save you countless hours of frustration, and may just be the savior of your entire account.

LAST WORDS OF ADVICE

Please remember that all of the information contained in this book is merely a basic guide to the pairs strategy. However, with a good understanding of pairs trading and a little research, you can become a very successful investor. All of the information in this book is meant to help you find a new market paradigm, with which to reshape the entire way you see investing. Lastly, please remember that the entry signals are the easy part of trading. Exiting trades successfully is what separates the novices from the pros. If you cannot emotionally distance yourself from your positions, you are almost guaranteed to hold on to losers when they move away from you. The best traders in the entire world are not stock pickers, but rather are money managers who *always* make sure that they have a trading plan in effect before a trade is ever entered. With this in mind, good luck in your trading ventures, and remember, please take life in strides. After all, it's only money—and family and friends are much, much more important.
Godspeed.

Economic Indicator Summary

This appendix is in place because as a pairs trader it is *crucial* that you understand the events surrounding your positions, including economic news. I cannot enforce strongly enough how vitally important it is to have a good understanding of the broader market. Thus, when an economic report is released, please reference this appendix to understand how the news will affect your position(s).

ABC NEWS/Money Magazine Consumer Confidence Index: Weekly

> Importance: 4
> Data lag factor: Several days

A rolling average with roughly 1,000 telephone interviews from American adults. The Index can range anywhere from −100 to +100, with participants rating the national economy, personal finances, and buying climate.

Bankruptcy Filings: Monthly

> Importance: 4
> Data lag factor: Two months

Measures chapter 7, 11, 12, and 13 bankruptcy filings for each quarter:

- *Chapter 7*: Business or personal liquidation, excluding some exempt property. Proceeds are given to creditors.

- *Chapter 11*: Businesses or individuals continue operations, but are temporarily protected from creditors while reforming finances.
- *Chapter 12*: Aids financially stressed or defunct farmers.
- *Chapter 13*: Creates three- to five-year payment plan for the repayment of creditors.

http://www.uscourts.gov/Press_Releases/index.html

Beige Book: **Published eight times per year**

Importance: 7
Data lag factor: Several days

Summarizes current economic conditions contributed by each Federal Reserve Bank, the data is then summarized by district. Analysts look for comments on construction and real estate, banking and finance, agriculture, energy and natural resources, regional labor market conditions, retail sales, consumer spending, and manufacturing activity. Does not include any hard data; thus, investors are left to sift through the Fed's chatter.

http://www.federalreserve.gov/policy.htm

Business Inventories: **Monthly**

Importance: 4
Data lag factor: Two months

Measures business inventories in terms of retail, wholesale, and manufacturing data. Analysts look at dollar value of merchant sales, along with end-of-month inventories. In addition, the inventory-to-sales ratio measures time versus inventory depletion or replenishment. A low ratio indicates that manufacturers must build more inventory.

http://www.census.gov/mtis/www/current.html

Chain Store Sales Snapshot: **Monthly**

Importance: 6
Data lag factor: One month

This index tracks consumer spending at larger chain stores, focusing on Department of General Merchandise locations. The index records data only from stores that have been in business for more than one year. Thus, in phases of rapid growth, the data may not accurately reflect actual market conditions. Reported as a percentage change, analysts like to see stable growth with stronger numbers during the holiday season.

http://www.btmny.com/reports/research/comment/Chain_Store_Sales.htm

Challenger Report: **Monthly**

Importance: 5
Data lag factor: Roughly one week

The private firm Challenger, Grey, and Christmas collects and compiles information about layoffs from press releases. This information is then categorized and summed in a report that attempts to give an accurate snapshot of labor market cutbacks, including layoffs from smaller firms. Report becomes much more important during bear markets.

Chicago Fed National Activity Index: **Monthly**

Importance: 3
Data lag factor: One month

Released by the Chicago Reserve Board, the Index is meant to uncover broader economic conditions and to forecast inflation. The Index fluctuates around zero, with a positive number indicating that the economy is expanding above its capability. Conversely, a number below zero potentially designates that the economy is not producing to its fullest potential.

http://www.chicagofed.org/economicresearchanddata/national/index.cfm

Chicago PMI: **Monthly**

Importance: 5
Data lag factor: Not much, end-of-month data

Survey compiles information from purchasing managers about the manufacturing industry. Any number above 50 indicates expansion, while a number below 50 alludes to manufacturing contraction. The Index can be seasonally weighted at different times.

Construction Spending: Monthly

> Importance: 4
> Data lag factor: One month

Attempts to report the total month-to-month amount of gains or losses (in dollar values) in construction spending. Report is broken down into public, residential, and nonresidential construction expenditures. Because of large revisions from month to month, analysts do not observe this report closely.

http://www.census.gov/const/www/c30index.html

Consumer Credit: Monthly

> Importance: 3
> Data lag factor: Five weeks

Measures household (consumers) loans (credit) used for purchasing goods and services, or refinancing other debt. Examines two categories, revolving and nonrevolving debt, but does not include any loans secured with real estate. The report is subject to huge revisions and, thus, does not have much market impact.

http://www.federalreserve.gov/releases/G19/

Consumer Price Index: Monthly

> Importance: 8
> Data lag factor: Two weeks

Regarded as one of the most closely watched indicators of inflation, the CPI measures changes of a fixed basket of goods and services. Most analysts only look at the "core rate" of inflation from the CPI, as food and energy can play havoc with the results. Thus, excluding food and energy gives economists more reliable results and helps to understand long-term inflation trends.

http://www.bls.gov/news.release/cpi.toc.htm

Durable Goods Orders: Monthly

Importance: 7
Data lag factor: Three weeks

Measures the total dollar volume of orders and shipments. The report is said to be a leading indicator of the factory orders report, which is usually released the following week. Durable goods are products with a life span of more than three years. Moreover, an increase in durable goods orders may allude to improving sentiment and demand from consumers who are willing to purchase larger-ticket items. Analysts recommend removing defense and aircraft orders to get a more accurate snapshot of durable goods' true picture.

http://www.census.gov/indicator/www/m3/adv/index.htm

ECRI Future Inflation Gauge: Monthly

Importance: 4
Data lag factor: One month

Measured by the future inflation gauge (FIG), which is a weighted average of eight separate sets of economic data. A rise in the FIG can precede an inflation increase.

http://www.businesscycle.com

ECRI Weekly Leading Index: Weekly

Importance: 5
Data lag factor: One week

The Index is theoretically intended to predict near-term economic conditions by weighting stock prices, bond yields, jobless claims, money supply, mortgage applications, and bond spreads. Much of the data is already known by the time this report is published; thus, it is not truly "leading." Perhaps it should be called "summary of leading indicators already published."

http://www.businesscycle.com/freedata.php

Employment Cost Index: Monthly

Importance: 7
Data lag factor: One month

This index is designed to record and measure the change in employers' costs for labor. Employment cost measures payrolls for the third month of the quarter and attempts to find changes in labor costs that potentially allude to growth in the broader economy. Gauged in quarter-over-quarter and year-over-year percentages.

http://www.bls.gov/news.release/eci.toc.htm

Employment Situation: Monthly

Importance: 6
Data lag factor: One month

This report is a breakdown of total payrolls by sector, average workweek, and average earnings. Report is summarized as total change in nonfarm employment for the month and year. This report is important to the Fed when gathering data for their decision on interest rates.

http://www.bls.gov/news.release/empsit.toc.htm

Existing Home Sales: Monthly

Importance: 5
Data lag factor: One month

Existing home sales measured in actual unit numbers for single-family homes. Report can vary from time to time with volatile weather conditions. Can precede retail sector moves, as consumers need either more or fewer items for new homes. For example, a massive rise in home sales can pave the way for a profitable quarter in home furnishing stocks.

http://realtor.org/Research.nsf/Pages/EHSPage?OpenDocument

Factory Orders: Monthly

Importance: 5
Data lag factor: One month

Simply, a more detailed release of monthly durable goods, which usually contains the same information. The durable goods report leads factory orders.

http://www.census.gov/indicator/www/m3/prel/index.htm

FOMC Meeting: Meets eight times per year

Importance: 10
Data lag factor: N/A

At FOMC meetings, the Fed makes decisions on monetary policy/interest rates and establishes its bias toward the economy. Minutes are released the following day.

http://www.federalreserve.gov/fomc/

GDP: Monthly

Importance: 7
Data lag factor: N/A

Gross domestic product (GDP) is a measurement of economic activity through the production and consumption of U.S. goods. The GDP is measured by income and expenditures for both production and consumption. The deflator is then used to define the cycles of GDP. GDP growth is expected to stay in the 2.0 to 2.5 range. Ideally, unemployment is not to exceed 6.0 percent. Growth above 2.7 percent indicates inflationary pressure.

http://www.bea.doc.gov/bea/dn1.htm.

Import and Export Prices: Monthly

Importance: 6
Data lag factor: One month

A large change in import prices can affect the way analysts view foreign manufacturers. In a nutshell, a weaker dollar means more exporting and less importing.

http://www.bls.gov/news.release/ximpim.toc.htm

Industrial Production: **Monthly**

>Importance: 6
>Data lag factor: One month

Weighted measurement of the output of mines, factories, and utilities. In addition, industrial production gives analysts insight into capacity utilization. Measured month-over-month on a percentage basis, economists like to see stable growth in capacity utilization.

http://www.federalreserve.gov/releases/G17/Current/default.htm

Internet Sales: **Quarterly**

>Importance: 5
>Data lag factor: One quarter

This report covers sales of goods and services over the Internet. Bullish analysts prefer to observe continued sales growth, thus supporting the continued expansion of e-commerce.

http://www.census.gov/mrts/www/current.html

ISM Index: **Monthly**

>Importance: 8
>Data lag factor: Several days

The *ISM Index* is comprised of data collected from purchasing managers about production, new orders, employment, deliveries, and inventories. The ISM usually precedes the employment report and is said to indicate economic expansion above 44 percent. The overall average break-even level for the broader report is 50 percent; however, production and employment break even at lower levels.

http://www.ism.ws/ISMReport/index.cfm

ISM Non-Manufacturing Index: **Monthly**

>Importance: 8
>Data lag factor: Several days

The ISM encompasses data collected from purchasing managers about business activity, new orders, inventories, and employment. All together, the data reflects 10 separate indexes, though we have listed only four here. A number above 50 percent indicates manufacturing expansion, while a number below 50 percent shows contraction.

http://www.ism.ws/ISMReport/index.cfm#nonmanufacturing

Jobless Claims: Weekly

> Importance: 6.5 in bear market, 3 in bull market
> Data lag factor: Several days

Self-explanatory, though analysts like to see both initial claims *and* the four-week moving average stay beneath 400,000.

http://www.dol.gov/opa/media/press/eta/ui/current.htm

Kansas City Fed Manufacturing: Monthly

> Importance: 5
> Data lag factor: Two weeks

This report surveys several facets of manufacturing plants to indicate expansion or contraction. A number above 100 is said to indicate growth, while a number below signals a reduction. Can help to affirm results form the ISM report.

http://www.kc.frb.org/mfgsurv/mfgmain.htm

MBA Mortgage Applications Survey: Weekly

> Importance: 5
> Data lag factor: One week

Counts mortgage and refinancing applications for personal real estate transactions. However, the survey is a leading indicator of conditions because applications are a proposed event to occur in the future.

http://www.mbaa.org/news/weekly_app.html

Monthly Mass Layoffs: Monthly

Importance: 4, with the exception of bear markets
Data lag factor: One month

This report consists of unemployment information collected from individual states. Increasing layoffs during tough times will not bode well for bulls.

http://www.bls.gov/news.release/mmls.toc.htm

NAHB Housing Market Index: Monthly

Importance: 4
Data lag factor: Very little

The NAHB Index is a builders' sentiment survey designed to rate current and future sales. However, current conditions and mood do not always accurately predict future trends.

http://www.nahb.org/

NAPM–NY Report: Monthly

Importance: 4
Data lag factor: Very little

National Association of Purchasing Managers, surveys purchasing managers to gain insight into the manufacturing sector. A reading above 50 is said to indicate expansion, while a reading below 50 alludes to contraction.

New Home Sales: Monthly

Importance: 5
Data lag factor: Very little

New Home Sales measures private homes that have either sold or are for sale. The report's inventory reading is an indicator into future trends of the housing markets.

http://www.census.gov/const/www/newressalesindex.html

New Residential Construction: Monthly

Importance: 6
Data lag factor: One month

Measures the number of houses planned, in process, authorized, started, and completed. All statistics are for private residential real estate. Measured in terms of total units, *New Residential Construction* is a looking glass into builders' inventories.

http://www.census.gov/const/www/newresconstindex.html

Oil and Gas Inventories: Weekly

Importance: 5
Data lag factor: One week

Measurements by the Energy Information Agency (EIA) and the American Petroleum Institute (API) are complied to get accurate readings on inventory levels of crude, distillates, and gasoline. Market mostly pays attention to whether the weekly numbers exceed or fail predictions.

http://www.eia.doe.gov/
http://api-ec.api.org/newsplashpage/index.cfm

Personal Income: Monthly

Importance: 5
Data lag factor: One week

Personal Income measures household income from all sources. Analysts seek constant growth to keep up with inflation and indicate healthy labor markets.

http://www.bea.doc.gov/bea/rels.htm

Philadelphia Fed Survey: Monthly

Importance: 7
Data lag factor: Very little

The Survey polls manufacturers on general business conditions. The outlook generated usually shows up in the NAPM report, but only behind the *Chicago Fed Survey*, which has slightly more weight.

http://www.phil.frb.org/econ/bos/index.html

PPI: **Monthly**

> Importance: 7
> Data lag factor: Very little

Basically, the *PPI* measures wholesale prices. Wholesale goods are lumped into three groups: crude, intermediate, and finished. Results are based on month-over-month and year-over-year results.

http://www.bls.gov/news.release/ppi.toc.htm

Productivity and Costs: **Quarterly**

> Importance: 5
> Data lag factor: One month

Measures productivity and costs associated with the production of nonfarm goods. GDP released before this report can foreshadow the expected results from productivity.

http://www.bls.gov/news.release/prod.toc.htm

Retail Sales (MARTS): **Monthly**

> Importance: 5
> Data lag factor: One month

Measures retail sales by total receipts of established companies in the United States. Many analysts take auto sales (ex-auto) out of the report in order to get a more accurate picture of consumers' spending habits.

http://www.census.gov/svsd/www/fullpub.html

Richmond Fed Manufacturing Survey: **Monthly**

Importance: 4.
Data lag factor: One week

Survey by the Richmond Fed, which polls manufacturers' purchasing managers, plant managers, and controllers about current conditions. The survey has a range of -100 to $+100$, with a value above 0 expressing expansion and a value below 0 indicating contraction.

http://www.rich.frb.org/research/surveys/mfg.html

SEMI Book-to-Bill Ratio: **Monthly**

Importance: 6.
Data lag factor: Two to three weeks

This survey compiles data on orders and shipments and then calculates the three-month moving average and the book-to-bill ratio. Basically, a ratio above 1.0 means expansion, while a value below 1.0 points toward contraction.

http://www.semi.org/web/wpress.nsf/url/booktobill

Semiconductor Billings: **Monthly**

Importance: 7 for semiconductors
Data lag factor: Six weeks

Report is a regional breakdown of circuit sales including almost all facets of chips. The report then creates a three-month moving average for the following regions: the Americas, Europe, Japan, and Asia-Pacific.

http://www.semichips.org/pressroom.cfm

The Conference Board Consumer Confidence: **Monthly**

Importance: 5
Data lag factor: One week

Measures consumer confidence by the direct mailing of 5,000 households. The survey initially began at 100 in 1985; thus, investors can use the 100 benchmark to gauge consumer trends.

http://www.conference-board.org/

The Conference Board Leading Indicators: Monthly

Importance: 5
Data lag factor: Three weeks

Takes 10 leading indicators and creates a weighted average that is supposed to lead turns in the economy. Look for trends of gains or losses lasting three or more months to indicate a potential economic reversal.

http://www.conference-board.org/

Treasury Budget: Monthly

Importance: 3
Data lag factor: Two weeks

Treasury budget data that attempts to unveil budget trends by uncovering monthly fluctuations in the national deficit. Watch analysts' estimates for market reaction.

http://www.fms.treas.gov/mts/

UBS Index of Investor Optimism: Monthly

Importance: 4
Data lag factor: One month

Telephone survey attempting to gauge consumer confidence, with data commencing in 1996. Has little market impact, but may be used to affirm other consumer confidence reports.

University of Michigan Consumer Sentiment Survey: Monthly

Importance: 7
Data lag factor: Not much

Telephone survey of 500 consumers. The Survey had a low of 70 in 1992 and a high of just over 110 in 2000.

http://www.sca.isr.umich.edu/

Vehicle Sales: **Monthly**

Importance: 4
Data lag factor: Two days

In a nutshell, this report measures vehicle sales broken down by types of automobiles. Simply look for ascending or descending trends that surprise or disappoint analysts.

Weekly Natural Gas Storage Report: **Weekly**

Importance: 4
Data lag factor: One week

Report gives total natural gas storage in the United States by Bcf (billion cubic feet). Analysts look for inventory fluctuations, along with where storage levels are relative to their five-year moving averages. Report is broken down into regional sections of the United States Producing (Alabama, Arkansas, Kansas, Louisiana, Mississippi, New Mexico, Oklahoma, and Texas), East, and West.

http://tonto.eia.doe.gov/oog/info/ngs/ngs.html

Wholesale Trade: **Monthly**

Importance: 4
Data lag factor: Two months

Measures the second stage of manufacturing by collecting information on sales and inventory. Most analysts look only at the inventory/sales ratio, which indicates whether manufactures will need to increase/decrease production.

http://www.census.gov/svsd/www/mwts.html

Websites, Books, and Software

Website References

Correlations—pay site
http://www.market-topology.com/

Hedge funds—general information
http://www.hedgeworld.com/

Hedge Fund Index
http://www.hedgefund-index.com/

News: Bloomberg.com
http://www.bloomberg.com/

News: CBS Marketwatch.com
http://cbs.marketwatch.com/news/default.asp?siteid=&avatar=seen

News and resources: Yahoo.com
http://finance.yahoo.com/?u

News and resources: Smartmoney.com
http://www.smartmoney.com/

News and resources—pay site: Briefing.com
http://www.briefing.com/

SEC link on hedge funds
http://www.sec.gov/answers/hedge.htm

Sectors: Barchart.com
http://www2.barchart.com/sectors.asp?base=industry

Books and Articles

Book: *The Complete Arbitrage Deskbook* by Stephane Reverre

Definitions: Investorwords.com
http://www.investorwords.com/cgi-bin/getword.cgi?5803

Paper: *Pairs Trading: Performance of a Relative Value Arbitrage Rule*
http://econpapers.hhs.se/paper/nbrnberwo/7032.htm

Stocks and commodities—article costs $3.95
Pairs Trading by Stephane Reverre
http://store.traders.com/traderscom/v19319pairtr.html

Time article on Hedge Funds
http://www.time.com/time/globalbusiness/article/0,9171,1101020701-265448,00.html

USA Today article on Hedge Funds
http://www.usatoday.com/money/perfi/funds/2003-02-10-hedge x.htm

Software

ACME Trader—pairs software
http://www.acmetrader.com/pages/576123/

Happy Trader—pairs software
http://www.happytrader.com/products/pairs.htm

ITG Pairs Software
http://www.itginc.com/products/quantex/qtx99-pairs.html

Linnsoft—pairs software
http://www.linnsoft.com/tutorials/pairsTrading.htm

Technical Analysis software
http://www.analyzerxl.com/

Tricom—pairs software
http://www.tricom.com.au/equities/articles/pairs.asp

Endnotes

Chapter 1

1.1. Source: *http://www.investopedia.com/terms/a/arbitrage.asp.*
1.2. Source: *http://www.investopedia.com/terms/s/statisticalarbitrage.asp\\.*

Chapter 2

2.1. Source: Tom Jacobs, "30-Baggers, Anyone?", *The Motley Fool*, *http://biz.yahoo.com/fool/030730/1059581940_3.html.*

Chapter 3

3.1. At the time this was written, there was legislation pending meant to recognize preferred stock as debt instead of equity. The result of this legislation would be that many companies will see their debt-to-equity ratios surge higher overnight, once they actually have to recognize the preferred stock on their books. Initially, the new laws will affect only trust preferred companies such as real estate investment trusts (REITs) and mortgage corporations.

Chapter 4

4.1. Slippage denotes the price received versus the price intended. If you enter a market order to buy XYZ at $20 and the stock is rapidly ascending, without a limit order, your actual fill price may be higher than the price you have anticipated. To best protect against slippage, it is a good idea to enter "limit orders" with all trades. An order to buy Stock XYZ at $20 with a limit of $20.25 ensures that investors will not receive a price higher than $20.25. The resulting downside is that if the stock is rapidly ascending and the price of the stock moves above $20.25, you may not get filled at all! However, perhaps it is better to miss a trade entirely than to get filled way above the desired level.

4.2. Steve Nison, *Beyond Candlesticks: New Japanese Charting Techniques.*
New York: John Wiley & Sons, Inc., 1994.

Chapter 11

11.1. As previously mentioned, a Gaussian curve is also known as a normal distribution, where the mean, median, and mode are all in the center of the upside down U, also known as a "bell curve." When we draw a normal distribution, our goal with standard deviations is to measure the data from the center of the curve to the outlying tails.

Chapter 16

16.1. Stephane Reverre, *The Complete Arbitrage Desk Book.* New York: McGraw-Hill, 2001.
16.2. The point of this equation is to divide a 90-day MA by the standard deviation of 90 days' worth of data.

Chapter 19

19.1. The CBOE Volatility Index (VIX) is a key measure of market expectations of near-term volatility conveyed by S&P 500 index options prices. Since its introduction in 1993, VIX has been considered by many to be the world's premier barometer of investor sentiment and market volatility. Source: *http://www.cboe.com/micro/vix/index.asp*

Chapter 20

20.1. Lisa Sanders, "Apache Posts Four-fold Rise in Profit."
CBS.MarketWatch.com. Last update: April 24, 2003.
20.2. Lisa Sanders, "Oil-drilling's Outspoken Captain: At 80, Apache's Plank Rides Hard, and He's Unapologetic," CBS.MarketWatch.com, November 22, 2002. *http://cbs.marketwatch.com/news/story.asp?siteid=mktw&guid=%7BFF334005%2DCB6C%2D40E8%2DBD1B%2DDB20D04CAC41%7D&.*
20.3. Lisa Sanders, "Apache Posts Four-fold Rise in Profit." CBS.MarketWatch.com, April 24, 2003. *http://cbs.marketwatch.com/news/story.asp?guid={78DF8265-EB81-49C1-8185-5E221E821517}&siteid=mktw&dist=&archive=true*

Chapter 21

21.1. Investopedia.com. http://www.investopedia.com/terms/b/bookvalue.asp.
21.2. Lisa Sanders, "Record Production Fuels Apache Q2. CBS.MarketWatch.com." 7-24-2003

Chapter 22

22.1. "Anadarko Petroleum Upped to 'mkt perform' at Wachovia." CBS MarketWatch.com, October 7, 2003. *http://cbs.marketwatch.com/tools/quotes/news.asp?siteid=mktw&docty*
22.2. Yereth Rosen, "Independents Win Rights to Explore Alaska N. Slope," October 29, 2003. *http://cbs.marketwatch.com/tools/quotes/newsArticle.asp?guid={6C8B7FD3-A8CC-4B2A-B5C5-3ADDED58A303}&siteid=mktw&archive= thirdtrue&dist=RegSignIn*
22.3. Joseph A. Giannone, "Anadarko CEO Vows More Focused Overseas Efforts," November 6, 2003. *http://cbs.marketwatch.com/tools/quotes/newsarticle.asp?siteid=mktw&sid=582&guid=%7B6A46A633%2D34B2%i2D4871%2DB927%2DD4192EB45881%7D.*

Chapter 26

26.1. Sheldon Natenber, "Option Pricing & Volatility," McGraw-Hill, 1994.

Glossary

Jonathan Crowell

Absolute return: A method of measuring investment results in terms of positive and negative, as opposed to comparing returns to a market index.

Active management: An investment process in which the fund or account attempts to outperform a benchmark. Active management is often referred to as the practice of market timing.

Active manager: A money manager who participates in several aspects of the investment process. An active manager may have a hand in risk management, investment selection, and asset allocation.

Accredited investor: An investor with a net worth in excess of $1 million or who has made $200,000 per year the previous two years, or a household that has made $300,000 per year the previous two years.

Alternative investments: Investments generally not available to the mass investing public. A common example is a hedge fund.

AMEX: The American Stock Exchange is the primary market for most exchange-traded funds.

Arbitrage: A low-risk strategy of simultaneously buying and selling securities on different markets to take advantage of price inefficiencies. An example would be to buy a security on one exchange and simultaneously sell it on another for a profit.

Bear market: A market condition wherein prices are heading lower. If an individual believes the market is going down, he/she would be considered "bearish on the market."

Blue-chip stocks: Large, well-known companies with long histories of dividends and earnings. Some examples are 3M, IBM, Disney, Alcoa, and Coca-Cola. The Dow Jones Industrial average is considered to be made up of blue-chip stocks. They are considered to be less risky or volatile than other classes of stocks.

Bond: A debt obligation of a corporation or a government. The bond is issued with a face amount and has a specific term. The issuer of the bond will pay interest during the term of the bond. When the term is expired, the bond is considered mature and the issuer is obligated to pay back the face amount of the bond. Bonds are similar to credit cards. When we use a credit card we pay interest on the amount borrowed and pay back the balance at a later date.

Market breadth: The measure of how many stocks on an exchange participated in a day's move. If the market goes up and three fourths of the stocks on that exchange go up as well, this would be considered good market breadth. It is used as an indicator to gain insight into potential future market movements.

Breakout: Term used in technical analysis. Refers to a stock price moving above a resistance level, important to technical analysts because it could be a precursor to a major price move. A breakout can be used as a buy or sell signal and also aid in choosing your exit point prior to entering an investment.

Bull market: A market condition wherein prices are moving higher. If an individual believes the market is poised to move higher, he/she would be considered "bullish on the market."

Correlation: A statistical measure of two numerical values. The market is full of correlations; for example, an increase in oil prices will increase an airline's fixed expenses, leading to airlines having lower profit margins or charging higher ticket prices. It could be said that the airline and oil sector are negatively correlated. An example of a positive correlation would be PC sales and microchip sales. If PC sales are strong, it would stand to reason that microchip sales would also be strong, since microchips power PCs.

Debt-to-asset ratio: A ratio used to measure the amount of debt a company has in relation to its assets. This is important when performing fundamental analysis of a company. This is also important when looking at a market sector because the level of debt may vary from sector to sector. The higher the debt level, the more vulnerable a sector could be to interest rates and credit problems.

Debt-to-equity ratio: This is a measure of a company's leverage. This is an important number when performing fundamental analysis of a company. This measures the amount of debt a company has in relation to equity. It is calculated by dividing a company's long-term debt by market capitalization.

Derivative: An asset whose value is derived from an underlying security. An example of a derivative would be a pork belly future. The current value of the future contract is derived from or contingent upon the current market price of pork bellies.

Discount rate: The interest rate the Federal Reserve charges member banks for loans. This is the base rate used when banks set their loan rates.

Diversification: The strategy of investing across many different asset classes. The logic is that different asset classes will perform differently, leveling out performance and reducing the volatility of a portfolio.

DIAMONDS: An exchange-traded fund designed to duplicate the performance of the Dow Jones Industrial Average.

Dow Jones Industrial Average: An index of 30 major companies, representing the majority of the U.S. economy. This is also known as "The Dow." This is the most widely quoted and followed index in the United States.

Enhanced indexing: This is a strategy used when simply trying to outperform an index.

Equity: Represents ownership in a corporation. Also known as stock or shares in a company.

Federal funds rate: This is a widely followed number because it is the best indicator of the direction interest rates are headed. This is the overnight rate at which financial institutions lend money to each other. This rate is set by the Federal Reserve.

Federal Reserve System: Created in 1931 to regulate credit. Also known as "The Fed."

Folio: A basket of diversified stocks, giving the investor the flexibility to manage the stocks on an individual basis. Folios are made up of 30 to 50 individual stocks and can be quite difficult to track. Folios are better suited to wealthy investors who can afford a professional to aid them in managing the individual securities making up the folio.

Fundamental analysis: An approach to investment selection focusing on a company's balance sheet, business environment, sales, and managements skills.

Hedge: A strategy used to offset risk. The most commonly used hedging techniques are short selling, options, and futures. Hedging can limit downside risk, making it critical to risk management.

Hedge fund: An investment product, similar to a mutual fund. Hedge funds are usually set up for accredited investors only; they have high fees and a limited number of investors. Generally, the manager of a hedge fund will invest his or her own personal money in the fund. Hedge funds, unlike mutual funds, try to hedge or limit the risk they take on every investment.

HOLDRs: A diversified basket of stocks, similar to an exchange-traded fund. HOLDRs have an underlying basket of stock from which they derive their value. The owner of a HOLDR has the ability to convert from the HOLDR share to the basket of underlying stock. The tax consequences of converting a HOLDR to the underlying basket can be quite complicated and should be done only under the guidance of an investment professional. The commissions charged on this strategy will make it cost prohibitive for most small investors.

How to Short a Stock:

Written by aspiring author, Aaron J. Long (12 Years Old)

Shorting a stock is like taking a loan. You borrow a stock, sell it, and at some point you pay it back. Although unlike a loan, there isn't always interest. Sometimes you have to pay back less than you borrowed because you don't pay it back in money, you pay it back in stock. So say Ed wants to sell short 100 shares, of MGM stock. He finds the stock from the firm's list of stocks; he borrows 100 hundred shares, then sells them. Now at some point he has to pay it back. So he buys the stock again and pays it back to the firm. Let's say that in between this time MGM stock drops $1.27 per share. That way Ed has to pay $127 less to buy the 100 shares back. So he makes $127. But if he had shorted 1,000 shares, he would have made $1,270. In the same way what if that stock's value goes up? Ed would have to pay more for the stock. And therefore he would lose money. Shorting a stock is just as risky as buying and selling stock the old fashioned way. But as they say: "No guts, no glory."

Index: A numerical value assigned to a representative group of stocks or bonds. The purpose of an index is to benchmark the market's movement.

Index fund: A fund designed to perform exactly as the underlying index performs. Many exchange-traded funds are designed to follow or track specific indexes.

Indexation: The practice of a fund's attempting to duplicate the performance of an index.

Institutional investors: A term used to describe banks, mutual funds, brokerage firms, pension funds, insurance companies, and so on. Basically, any large interest other than an individual could be classified as an institutional investor.

Investment banking: The practice of raising capital for entrepreneurs. The term is most often used on Wall Street when referring to initial public offerings or raising money by selling new issues in securities.

Investment Company Act of 1940: Legislation passed in 1940 to regulate funds and investment advisors. This act gave birth to the modern-day mutual fund industry.

Investment horizon: The length of time an investor plans to hold an investment.

Investment objective: When referring to a fund or manager, it is the expected result of the management. When referring to an investor, it is what the investor hopes to achieve by investing. Some examples would be growth or income. Investment objectives are important because different objectives require different investments. Growth investors hope to see the value of the stocks in their portfolio increase, while income investors need a regular income and would be better off owning an investment that paid regular dividends or interest.

Leverage: Anything multiplying the effect of a price change in an underlying security. The most common form of leverage is margin borrowing.

Limit order: An order in which you state a specific price you will be buying or selling a security.

Liquidity: The ease with which an investment can be bought or sold. Factors affecting liquidity are volume and the number of market participants.

Market capitalization: The total value of a company's outstanding stock. The number can be figured by multiplying the total number of shares outstanding by the stock price. This can also be referred to as capitalization or a company's capitalization.

Market order: An order to buy or sell a security in the open market at the first available price.

Mutual fund: A professionally managed account in which investors can pool their money to accomplish a common investment objective.

NASD: National Association of Securities Dealers, a self-regulatory agency, charged with maintaining high ethical standards and uniform practices among member firms.

NASDAQ: A real-time quotation and trading system set up by the NASD.

NYSE: New York Stock Exchange, the oldest and most prestigious market in the United States. The NYSE is a self-regulatory agency similar to the NASD.

Passive management: The opposite of active management. Passive management begins with a set portfolio that does not change. Indexation is a common form of passive management.

Pullback:

Written by future novelist, Andrew C. Long (16 Years Old)

A pullback occurs when the demand for a particular stock drops and with the demand goes the price. This is good if you are waiting to buy the stock, but if you are already "riding the train" and trying to get off . . . you're in trouble.

QQQ: Also known as the Qs. An exchange-traded fund designed to duplicate the performance of the NASDAQ 100 index.

REIT: Real estate investment trust. They trade on an exchange and are managed portfolios of real estate.

Risk/reward ratio: A basic concept used in determining the merits of an investment. It measures the expected return versus the maximum loss on an investment. If you make money on 50 percent of your investments, a minimum ratio for an investment should be 3 to 1. For every $3 you expect to earn in profits, you are willing to risk losing $1.

RIA: Registered investment advisor. A company registered with a state or the Securities and Exchange Commission. RIAs give investment advice on a fee-based basis.

Rule 12 (d)(1) Limit: Limits the amount of stock a mutual fund can hold in a particular issue.

SEC: Security Exchange Commission, created by congress in 1931 to oversee the investment industry.

Short sale: The practice of selling a security not currently owned in hopes of purchasing it at a lower price in the future.

Short sale rule: Requires that certain market conditions be met prior to entering an order to sell short.

Specialist: An exchange member responsible for keeping a fair and orderly market in a security during exchange hours. Specialists are located on the floor of the exchange.

SPDRs: Also known as the spiders. An exchange-traded fund designed to duplicate the performance of the S&P 500 index.

S&P 500 index: Standard and Poors 500 index. An index comprised of 500 industry-leading companies.

Stop order: A two-part order. The stop price, the first part of the order, is a price the security must trade at before the second part of the order may be activated. Once the stop price is triggered, the order converts into a market order. This order is difficult to understand, yet essential to your success. Be sure to ask your broker for assistance when you are first learning to use this order.

Stop limit order: This order works like a stop order, but when the second part is activated it turns into a limit order. This order is difficult to understand, yet essential to your success. Be sure to ask your broker for assistance when you are first learning to use this order.

Systematic investment plan: An investment strategy used to invest in open-ended mutual funds. This is a good strategy for low-dollar investors. It allows investors to invest a regular amount on a regular basis, as little as $25 and as often as twice a month. These plans are good for smaller investors because there is generally no additional fee for the service.

Technical analysis: The use of charts and graphs to identify trends and price patterns that may predict future price movements.

Ticker: The symbol used to buy and sell an investment.

Third market: Trading of an exchange-listed security on the over-the-counter (OTC) market.

Top-down investing: The practice of focusing first on major market trends, then narrowing the view to specific industries and finally to individual stocks.

Value investing: Focusing on stocks with a low price-to-book ratio with a good dividend yield.

Volatility: The price fluctuation of the market, a fund, or an individual stock.

Volume: Usually measured on a daily basis. It refers to the total number of shares traded on an exchange or an individual stock. This is an important factor in technical analysis. When compared over like periods, it is considered to give insight into the strength of a price movement.

Index

WILEY

About the CD-ROM

INTRODUCTION

Trading Pairs includes a CD-ROM with pairs spreadsheets/worksheets in Excel that aim to help investors track multiple pairs positions. The individual sheets are supported by market data that can be downloaded free from Yahoo.com. The worksheets aid investors in analyzing the descriptive statistics of their pairs. Each sheet is part of a larger network of sheets that funnel all data into one main sheet called the Monitor Page. By updating the data on a weekly—or daily—basis, pairs enthusiasts have a way to easily track where many pairs are at one time. Though the sheets are not intended to directly produce trading signals, they assist in keeping a close eye on where an investor's pairs' of interest are. The individual sheets include the historical statistics, standard deviations, the density curve, volatility measurements, data, and charts.

An Excel viewer has been provided on this CD-ROM for readers who do not own MS excel software. However, MS Excel is recommended for optimum usage of this ancillary product.

CD-ROM TABLE OF CONTENTS

Excel Viewer

MONITOR PAGE.xls - Main tracking page for all spreadsheets.
Individual sheets included on the Monitor Sheet (in alphabetical order):
AA-AL.xls - ALCOA Inc & Alcan Inc

ABGX-PDLI.xls - Abgenix, Inc & Protein Design Labs Inc

ABX-NEM.xls - Barrick Gold Corp & Placer Dome Inc

AEM-PDG.xls - Placer Dome Inc & Agnico-Eagle Mines Ltd

ALTR-LSCC.xls - Altera Corp & Lattice Semiconductor Corp

AMAT-MU.xls - Applied Materials Inc & Micron Technology Inc

AMAT-TER.xls - Applied Materials Inc & Teradyne Inc

AMGN-CHIR.xls - Amgen Inc & Chiron Corp

APA-APC.xls - Apache Corp & Stone Energy Corp

APA-EOG.xls - Apache Corp & EOG Resources Inc

APA-MUR.xls - Apache Corp & Murphy Oil Corp

APA-NBL.xls - Apache Corp & Noble Energy Inc

APA-SGY.xls - Apache Corp & Stone Energy Corp

APD-PX.xls - Air Products and Chemicals Inc & Praxair Inc

ATK-LLL.xls - Alliant Techsystems Inc & L-3 Communications Holdings, Inc

AU-PDG.xls - AngloGold Ltd & Placer Dome Inc

BBY-CC.xls - Best Buy Co Inc & Circuit City Stores Inc

BNI-CSX.xls - Burlington Northern Santa Fe Corp & CSX Corp

BNI-UNP.xls - Burlington Northern Santa Fe Corp & Union Pacific Corp

BP-CVX.xls - BP PLC & ChevronTexaco Corp

COST-WMT.xls - Costco Wholesale Corp & Wal-Mart Stores Inc

CTX-TOL.xls - Centex Corp & Toll Brothers Inc

CMI-CAT.xls - Cummins Inc & Caterpillar Inc

DD-PPG.xls - E.I. Du Pont De Nemours & Co & PPG Industries Inc

DF-KFT.xls - Dean Foods Co & Kraft Foods Inc

DIA-SPY.xls - DIAMONDS Trust, Series 1 & S&P SPDRs

ELN-ICOS.xls - Elan Corp PLC & Icos Corp

EMN-PPG.xls - Eastman Chemical Co & PPG Industries Inc

EOG-APA.xls - EOG Resources Inc & Apache Corp

EOG-BR.xls - EOG Resources Inc & Burlington Resources Inc

EOG-NBL.xls - EOG Resources Inc & Noble Energy Inc

FCS-LSCC.xls - Fairchild Semiconductor Corp & Lattice Semiconductor Corp

HD-KSS.xls - Home Depot Inc & Kohl's Corp

HD-LOW.xls - Home Depot Inc & Lowe's Cos Inc

HLYW-MOVI.xls - Hollywood Entertainment Corp & Movie Gallery Inc

INTC-LSCC.xls - Intel Corp & Lattice Semiconductor Corp

IP-BCC.xls - International Paper Co & Boise Cascade Corp

IR-PH.xls - Ingersoll-Rand Co Ltd & Parker Hannifin Corp

JBHT-HTLD.xls - JB Hunt Transport Services Inc & Heartland Express Inc

KBH-LEN.xls - KB Home & Lennar Corp

KBH-RYL.xls - KB Home & Ryland Group Inc

KLAC-NVLS.xls - KLA Tencor Corp & Novellus Systems Inc

KMX-SAH.xls - Carmax Inc & Sonic Automotive Inc

KSS-LOW.xls - Kohl's Corp & Lowe's Cos Inc

LEH-GS.xls - Lehman Brothers Holdings Inc & The Goldman Sachs Group Inc

LLTC-LSCC.xls - Linear Technology Corp & Lattice Semiconductor Corp

LLTC-MXIM.xls - Linear Technology Corp & Maxim Integrated Products Inc

LLTC-QLGC.xls - Linear Technology Corp & QLogic Corp

LMT-BA.xls - Lockheed Martin Corp & The Boeing Co

LMT-LLL.xls - Lockheed Martin Corp & L-3 Communications Holdings, Inc

MEDX-PDLI.xls - Medarex Inc & Protein Design Labs Inc

MER-GS.xls - MERRILL LYNCH & The Goldman Sachs Group Inc

MER-MWD.xls - MERRILL LYNCH & MORGAN STANLEY

MERQ-BEAS.xls - Mercury Interactive Corp & BEA Systems Inc

MERQ-VRTS.xls - Mercury Interactive Corp & Veritas Software Corp

MLNM-HGSI.xls - Millennium Pharmaceuticals Inc & Human Genome
Sciences Inc

MLNM-MEDX.xls - Millennium Pharmaceuticals Inc & Medarex Inc

MLNM-PDLI.xls - Millennium Pharmaceuticals Inc & Protein Design Labs Inc

MO-RJR.xls - Altria Group Inc & R.J. Reynolds Tobacco Holdings Inc

MWD-GS.xls - MORGAN STANLEY & The Goldman Sachs Group Inc

MYG-WHR.xls - Maytag Corp & Whirlpool Corp

NEM-AEM.xls - Newmont Mining Corp & Agnico-Eagle Mines Ltd

NEM-AU.xls - Newmont Mining Corp & AngloGold Ltd

NEM-PDG.xls - Newmont Mining Corp & Placer Dome Inc

PHM-TOL.xls - Pulte Homes & Toll Brothers Inc

PNC-KEY.xls - The PNC Financial Services Group & Keycorp

PNC-MEL.xls - The PNC Financial Services Group & Mellon Financial Corp

RCL-CCL.xls - Royal Caribbean Cruises Ltd ASA & Carnival Corp

RD-SC.xls - Royal Dutch Petroleum Co & Shell Transport & Trading Co PLC

RYL-LEN.xls - Ryland Group Inc & Lennar Corp

SGY-APC.xls - Stone Energy Corp & Anadarko Petroleum Corp

SMH-NVLS.xls - Semiconductor Holders Trust & Novellus Systems Inc

SPC-XL.xls - St. Paul Companies Inc & XL Capital Ltd

SSP-GCI.xls - EW Scripps Co & Gannett Co Inc

TER-MU.xls - Teradyne Inc & Micron Technology Inc

TGT-WMT.xls - Target Corp & Wal-Mart Stores Inc

TOL-KBH.xls - Toll Brothers Inc & KB Home

TQNT-NVLS.xls - Triquint Semiconductor Inc & Novellus Systems Inc

WERN-YELL.xls - Werner Enterprises Inc & Yellow Roadway Corporation

XOM-CVX.xls - Exxon Mobil Corp & ChevronTexaco Corp

All sheets represented as APA-APC 00.00.00.xls correspond with a date referenced in Chapter 22, Trading Diary.

Example_pairs_sheet1.xls—Sample spreadsheet referenced in Chapter 12

Example_pairs_sheet2.xls—Additional sample spreadsheet to assist readers in building their own sheets

General Electric-Exxon Mobil.xls—Spreadsheet referenced in Chapter 23

DIA-Exxon Mobil.xls—Spreadsheet referenced in Chapter 23

DIA-GE.xls—Spreadsheet referenced in Chapter 23

MINIMUM SYSTEM REQUIREMENTS

Make sure that your computer meets the minimum system requirements listed in this section. If your computer doesn't match up to most of these requirements, you may have a problem using the contents of the CD.

For Windows 98, or above:

- PC with a Pentium processor running at 120 Mhz or faster
- At least 32 MB of total RAM installed on your computer; for best performance, we recommend at least 64 MB
- A CD-ROM drive
- Microsoft Excel

For Macintosh:

- Mac OS computer with a 68040 or faster processor running OS 7.6 or later
- At least 32 MB of total RAM installed on your computer; for best performance, we recommend at least 64 MB
- A CD-ROM drive
- Microsoft Excel. (An Excel viewer has been provided on this CD-ROM for readers who do not own MS excel software. However, MS Excel is recommended for optimum usage of this ancillary product.)

USING THE CD WITH WINDOWS

To install the items from the CD to your hard drive, follow these steps:

1. Insert the CD into your computer's CD-ROM drive.

2. A window appears with the following options: Install, Explore, Links, and Exit.

   Install: Gives you the option to install the supplied software and/or the author-created samples on the CD-ROM.
   Explore: Enables you to view the contents of the CD-ROM in its directory structure.
   Exit: Closes the autorun window.

   If you do not have autorun enabled, or if the autorun window does not appear, follow these steps to access the CD:

1. Click Start @> Run.

2. In the dialog box that appears, type **d:\setup.exe**, where *d* is the letter of your CD-ROM drive. This brings up the autorun window described in the preceding set of steps.

3. Choose the Install, Explore, or Exit option from the menu. (See Step 2 in the preceding list for a description of these options.)

USING THE CD WITH THE MAC OS

To install the items from the CD to your hard drive, follow these steps:

1. Insert the CD into your CD-ROM drive.
2. Double-click the icon for the CD after it appears on the desktop.
3. Most programs come with installers; for those, simply open the program's folder on the CD and double-click the Install or Installer icon. *Note:* To install some programs, just drag the program's folder from the CD window and drop it on your hard drive icon.

TROUBLESHOOTING

If you have difficulty installing or using any of the materials on the companion CD, try the following solutions:

- **Turn off any antivirus software that you may have running.** Installers sometimes mimic virus activity and can make your computer incorrectly believe that it is being infected by a virus. (Be sure to turn the antivirus software back on later.)
- **Close all running programs.** The more programs you're running, the less memory is available to other programs. Installers also typically update files and programs; if you keep other programs running, installation may not work properly.
- **Reference the ReadMe:** Please refer to the ReadMe file located at the root of the CD-ROM for the latest product information at the time of publication.

If you still have trouble with the CD-ROM, please call the Wiley Product Technical Support phone number: (800) 762-2974. Outside the United States, call 1(317) 572-3994. You can also contact Wiley Product Technical Support at www.wiley.com/techsupport. Wiley Publishing will provide technical support only for installation and other general quality control items; for technical support on the applications themselves, consult the program's vendor or author.

To place additional orders or to request information about other Wiley products, please call (800) 225-5945.

USING THE SOFTWARE

Each file is a tracking Excel spreadsheet that can be used to better understand pairs trading. By updating the data on a weekly—or daily—basis, pairs enthusiasts have a way to easily track where many pairs are at one time.

USER ASSISTANCE

If you have questions about the software, please contact John Wiley and Sons.

If you need assistance or have a damaged disk, please contact Wiley Technical Support at:

Phone: (201) 748-6753

Fax: (201) 748-6800 (Attention: Wiley Technical Support)

Email: http://www.wiley.com/techsupport

To place additional orders or to request information about Wiley products, please call (800) 225-5945.

For information about the CD-ROM see the
About the CD-ROM section on page 273.

WILEY

John Wiley & Sons, Inc.